critique
influence
change

critique confronts the world. Without dogma, without new principles, it refuses to conform and instead demands insurrection of thought. It must be ruthless, unafraid of both its results and the powers it may come into conflict with. Critique takes the world, our world, as its object, so that we may develop new ways of making it.

influence is a step from critique towards the future, when effects begin to be felt, when the ground becomes unstable, when a movement ignites. These critiques of the state of our world have influenced a generation. They are crucial guides to change.

change is when the structures shift. The books in this series take critique as their starting point and as such have influenced both their respective disciplines and thought the world over. This series is born out of our conviction that change lies not in the novelty of the future but in the realization of the thoughts of the past.

These texts are not mere interpretations or reflections, but scientific, critical and impassioned analyses of our world. After all, the point is to change it.

GN00537365

TITLES IN THE CRITIQUE INFLUENCE CHANGE SERIES

Reclaiming Development
An Alternative Policy Manual
by Ha-Joon Chang and Ilene Grabel

Realizing Hope
Life Beyond Capitalism
by Michael Albert

Global Governance and the New Wars
*The Merging of Development and
Security*
by Mark Duffield

Capitalism in the Age of Globalization
*The Management of Contemporary
Society*
by Samir Amin

Ecofeminism
by Maria Mies and Vandana Shiva

**Patriarchy and Accumulation on a
World Scale**
*Women in the International Division
of Labour*
by Maria Mies

Grassroots Post-modernism
Remaking the Soil of Cultures
by Gustavo Esteva and
Madhu Suri Prakash

Debating Cultural Hybridity
*Multicultural Identities and the Politics
of Anti-Racism*
edited by Pnina Werbner and
Tariq Modood

A Fundamental Fear
*Eurocentrism and the Emergence
of Islamism*
by S. Sayyid

The Lords of Human Kind
*European Attitudes to Other Cultures
in the Imperial Age*
by Victor Kiernan

Male Daughters, Female Husbands
Gender and Sex in an African Society
by Ifi Amadiume

Marxism and the Muslim World
by Maxime Rodinson

Planet Dialectics
*Explorations in Environment and
Development*
by Wolfgang Sachs

Another World is Possible
*Popular Alternatives to Globalization
at the World Social Forum*
Edited by William Fisher and
Thomas Ponniah

ABOUT THE AUTHOR

Professor Maxime Rodinson was a French historian, sociologist and renowned specialist on Islam and the Arab world. Rodinson was a talented linguist and a committed Marxist, despite his dramatic split from the French Communist Party in 1958. He died in 2004 aged 89.

MARXISM AND THE MUSLIM WORLD

MAXIME RODINSON

WITH A FOREWORD BY

GILBERT ACHCAR

Zed Books
London

Marxism and the Muslim World was first published in French
by Editions du Seuil in 1972, and in English, with a new
preface by the author, by Zed Books, in 1979.

First published in paperback in 1981

This edition was published in 2015

www.zedbooks.co.uk

Cover designed by www.alice-marwick.co.uk

A catalogue record for this book is available from the British Library

ISBN 978-1-78360-336-7

MIX
Paper from
responsible sources
FSC® C013604

Printed and bound by CPI Group (UK) Ltd, Croydon, CR0 4YY

Contents

Foreword by Gilbert Achcar   ix

Acknowledgements   xii

Author's preface to the original English edition   1

1. Marxist Ideas and the Study of the Muslim World   5
2. The Nature and Function of Myths: Marxist Communism and Arab Nationalism Compared   19
3. Relationships between Islam and Communism   34
4. Problems Facing the Communist Parties in Syria and Egypt   60
5. Marxism and Arab Nationalism   76
6. The Bolsheviks and Colonized Muslims   125
7. A Forgotten Precursor   133
8. Islam and the Modern Economic Revolution   142
9. The Political Structure of Egypt under Nasser   163
10. Islam as a Political Factor in Egypt after Nasser   189
11. On the Contemporary Culture of the Muslim World   194
12. A Marxist Policy for the Arab Countries   204

Index   225

Bibliographical Information   229

Foreword

Maxime Rodinson (1915–2004) was the last survivor of an exceptional group of French Orientalists – in the pre-Saidian non-pejorative meaning of this term, i.e. scholars of Islam and the Arab world – who lived through most of the twentieth century and rose to fame in the 1960s, a decade that saw the emergence of an impressive contingent of French thinkers whose names loom large in the social sciences of our time. The group of brilliant Orientalists to which Rodinson belonged, and which included other luminaries such as Jacques Berque and Claude Cahen, reclaimed the field of Arab and Islamic studies with impeccable erudition, scientific rigour, and a critical solidarity with the peoples they studied that made their writings largely free from the deficiencies of the colonial 'Orientalism' of yesteryear and their own time.[1]

They all actually sympathized with the cause of Muslim peoples fighting Western domination, even when wielded by their own country.[2] Cahen and Rodinson did so from a Marxist-inspired anticolonial perspective, which led them both to adhere to the French Communist Party for several years until 'de-Stalinisation' opened their eyes to the flaws of that quite dogmatic atheistic Church whose Vatican was in Moscow. They did not, however, repudiate Marxism as a school of thought: Maxime Rodinson in particular, while remaining very much involved in political discussions as this collection attests, developed a critical open brand of Marxism, which he labelled 'independent'. His relationship to Marxism evolved into an effort to salvage Marx's method of enquiry along with key tenets of his thought, while engaging in provocative, iconoclastic debates with organised Marxists: from seeking at first to convince or influence them – the perspective that informs the essays gathered here – to an increasingly disenchanted and mordant attitude as the Communist movement went deeper into agony.

Marxism and the Muslim World is a collection of essays originally published between 1958 and 1972, the year when the original collection – from which this selection is taken – came out in French. The very fact that this book is republished today, forty-three years after its original publication and thirty-six years since its first publication in English translation, bears witness to the ongoing value of its analyses, with regard to their methodological and theoretical dimensions in particular. Along with Rodinson's key works, especially his biography of the Prophet Mohammad and his now classic *Islam and Capitalism*,[3] the essays collected in this book constitute outstanding contributions to a Marxist investigation and interpretation of Islamic and Arab history and societies, hardly matched in the extent of its knowledge by the best input of native Marxist or para-Marxist intellectuals and scholars writing in local or even European languages.

It is indeed for their methodological and theoretical value that these essays should be approached: the reader will learn a lot about how to analyse and interpret the kind of issues and phenomena that are discussed in the present book, and learn a lot as well about the history of the Muslim world – both what was past history at the time when these essays were written, and what was then an ongoing present that has become 'contemporary history' half a century later.

This is also to say that this is not a book about the Muslim world as present-day observers might perceive it. In fact, the reference to the 'Muslim world' in the book's title was a sociological characterisation as much as a religious one, in the sense that whereas a few of the book's essays do indeed deal with Islam as a religion, several of them are about nationalism and Communism in Arab and (non-Arab) Muslim countries. Thus, 'Muslim world' in such cases becomes merely an extension of what Rodinson called 'sociological Muslims' in his preface to the original edition, i.e. members of Muslim-majority societies irrespective of their views on Islam as a religion.

As a matter of fact, and despite Rodinson's perceptive assessment of the possible role of religious fundamentalism in the future (our present), the spirit of the time that this book deals with as present is very different from the *zeitgeist* that unfolded throughout the Muslim world in the 1970s at the expense of the left, both nationalist and Marxist – a *zeitgeist* which became dominant thereafter and remained so until our time of new and highly chaotic and uncertain transition. One interest of this book actually is that it testifies to an era when Marxism was 'in the air' in the Muslim world: in some of the essays collected in this book, Rodinson tries to explain the reason for what he described in the original preface as an 'enthusiasm for Marxism' among various circles in the Muslim world in the late 1950s and 1960s.

Present-day readers who are not familiar with the history of the region may find it difficult to conceive of, but this was an undisputed observation in its day. In 1956 indeed, a Walter Laqueur, with political views symmetrically opposed to those held by Maxime Rodinson, could lament the fact that,

> the Arab countries are now more likely than most others in the world
> to provide a favourable breeding-ground for Communism... Islam
> has gradually ceased to be a serious competitor of Communism in the
> struggle for the soul of the present and potential elites in the countries of
> the Middle East.[4]

This was a time when the use of Marxist and para-Marxist categories was so common among Arab intellectuals that Abdallah Laroui described it in 1967 as an 'objective Marxism' which many practised unwittingly in the same way that Molière's *Bourgeois gentilhomme* spoke prose 'without knowing it' – an assessment that Rodinson endorsed.[5]

Thus, this book provides nowadays a very welcome antidote to the currently prevailing perception of the Muslim world as one doomed to be dominated by religious fundamentalism, the reason for this lying in the ideological nature of Islam itself according to a widespread *idée reçue* – a typically Orientalist mode of explanation, the term being here taken in the pejorative sense of a Western-centric culturalist essentialization of the 'Orient'.

This objective refutation of the Orientalist misperception is, of course, powerfully complemented in Rodinson's writings by his constant emphasis on the historical materialist (or rather, as he would prefer to put it, the non-historical idealist) view that the history of the Muslim world, like any part of the world for that matter, is not primarily determined by ideologies, but by economic, sociological and political factors. It is this methodological approach that made of Maxime Rodinson's writings such powerful counterweights to essentialist views that he ranked prominently among the very few Western scholars of Islam whom Edward Said referred to as positive counter-examples in his own most famous 1978 critique of Orientalism.[6]

For all the above reasons, it is a very timely and fortunate decision indeed to republish *Marxism and the Muslim World* and thus make its rich analyses available to a new generation of students of the Arab countries and of other Muslim-majority parts of our world.[7]

Gilbert Achcar

1. See Rodinson's own assessment of the development of Arab and Islamic studies in the 1968 and 1976 essays assembled in *Europe and the Mystique of Islam*, trans. Roger Veinus, Seattle: University of Washington Press, 1987, and London: I.B.Tauris, 1988.
2. Algeria, it should be remembered, achieved its independence from French colonial subjugation only in 1962.
3. Maxime Rodinson's *Muhammad* was first published in French in 1961, with a second revised and augmented edition in 1968; latest English edition, trans. Anne Carter: London: Tauris Parker, 2002. Rodinson's *Islam and Capitalism* was first published in French in 1966; latest English edition, trans. Anne Carter, with a foreword by Roger Owen: London: Saqi, 2007.
4. Walter Laqueur, *Communism and Nationalism in the Middle East*, London: Routledge & Kegan Paul, 1956, p. 6.
5. Abdallah Laroui, *L'idéologie arabe contemporaine*, Préface de Maxime Rodinson, Paris : François Maspero, 1967.
6. Edward Said, *Orientalism*, 25th Anniversary Edition with a New Preface by the Author, New York: Vintage Books, 2003.
7. It is to be hoped that this reissue will prompt the publication in English translation of its French sequel, which focuses on Islamic fundamentalism: the collection of essays that Rodinson published twenty years after the present one under the title *L'Islam: politique et croyance*, Paris: Fayard, 1993.

Acknowledgements

So many people have helped me write these articles that I cannot possibly thank them all. I would have to mention all the friends in the Muslim world who have taught me something, and they are just too numerous. I include, of course, all those who have criticized me, or who would have criticized me had they lived. My own thoughts have certainly been developed through consideration of what I see as their mistakes.

Since space is limited, I will merely mention my friend the ex-secretary of the Lebanese Communist Party, Farajallah al-Helou, an honest and upright man, who died horribly, tortured to death by the secret police of the U.A.R., at the time of the union between Syria and Egypt (1958–61). He would probably have disapproved of the course I have followed, but I learnt a great deal from his example. Mutual respect can transcend disagreements and even conflicts, uniting all those who are not content merely to complain about humanity's woes, who have not reconciled themselves to suffering nor decided to profit from it, who have felt obliged to seek some remedy, sacrificing time, effort and legitimate pleasures even to the extremes of abnegation; and such respect can prevail even when the efforts and sacrifices have been in vain, illusory, indeed even when they have had harmful consequences.

Maxime Rodinson

Author's Preface to the English Edition

The articles and essays which make up the present volume were written between 1958 and 1972. With one exception this is the first time any of them have been translated into English. The selection is drawn from a larger work which I published in France, in 1972 (Editions du Seuil). In the original I added a commentary to each of the 28 texts, describing how it came to be written and how my views on the matter subsequently changed. In order to avoid repetition and to produce a more compact work, these commentaries, which were in any case often full of references to specifically French debates, have been deleted from the English edition.

The magazine and newspaper articles, the contributions to conferences, and the papers given at colloquiums and congresses assembled here were obviously influenced by the social and political situation prevailing at the time they were written. And of course my own ideas were constantly evolving over this period, a point to which I shall return. Each text must certainly be seen in the context of its period. I do not intend to go into autobiographical and other details at any great length here. However, the English reader should know that the oldest of these texts go back to the period of my exclusion from the French Communist Party in 1958. I had been a member since 1937, and in fact I was born into a communist family and grew up in a communist atmosphere. But I nonetheless hesitated considerably before actually deciding to join. This may seem strange to those to whom this period when I was a member is chiefly notable for the Moscow trials. But one should not forget that it was also an era in which it seemed that only the Soviet Union and the Communist International were making any firm and determined stand against the apparently irresistible rise of Nazism and Fascism.

For me, the years during which these texts were written were those of my gradual adaptation to a new ideological situation. I had to revise much of the general approach which I had evolved during the period when I supported Stalinism. This revision began with a slow and gradual re-examination of certain dogmas, as part of an opposition within the Party after Stalin's death in 1953. In the process, I was influenced by events in the Soviet Union, in Eastern Europe, and in the internal evolution within the French Communist Party. As the reader will see, this did not mean that I ever came to reject those ideas and choices which I still think of as Marxism's valid contributions. I tried to learn how to be an independent Marxist, by slowly and painfully separating these valid contributions from deviations produced, in my opinion, by the mechanicalism of ideological thought as well as by the dynamic of constituted ideological movements. This led me to formulate a deeper and wider general analysis of this mechanicalism and this dynamism, which was in no way limited to the consideration of ideological elements in Marxism and the Communist movement.

In particular, this experience has, I think, helped me to understand more or less analogous processes in the ideology of Arab nationalism and the nationalisms of the Muslim world. I was thus able to provide a much more rigorous analysis of processes I had been observing for a long time. The history, culture and languages of the Muslim East had been an object of study for me since 1932, and despite the fact that my work was often concerned with this area's distant past, I always retained an interest in its contemporary evolution. My involvement with the communist movement had, of course, been very useful to me in this investigation of contemporary events. A stay of seven years in Syria and Lebanon, from 1940 to 1947, frequent journeys, friendships established and on the whole maintained with prominent left-wingers in all these countries, obviously also contributed considerably to my understanding.

Many things have changed during the last six years, in the Muslim world as elsewhere. But I do not think my analyses are invalidated, however much they may have been conditioned by the circumstances prevailing when they were written, and by what now seem to me the limitations of the conceptions I held then.

Generally speaking, all this was written at a time when the process of de-colonization had just come to an end, or was not quite yet over. The newly independent states aroused high hopes, not only amongst the nationalist militants of the countries concerned, but also amongst the left in Europe and America. Marxism had prompted me to have some reservations about these hopes, and many of them did in fact prove illusory. But a conservative viewpoint had often inspired far more serious reservations; while, in contrast, my Marxist orientation meant that I was not about to take sides against an evolution which was inevitable, legitimate and on the whole beneficial.

For me, the main thing was always to bear in mind that revolutions are relative and do not put an end to struggles between classes, categories, sections of society, ethnic groups and nations. History continues. Marxist ideology treated the final revolution, which would eventually do away with all private ownership of the means of production, as an exception to this law. But Marxist sociology strongly indicated that this was inaccurate. In any case, it was quite out of the question for a struggle or a revolution conducted mainly or exclusively under the banner of national independence to put an end to such internal and external conflicts. And it seems to me that this judgement has been resoundingly confirmed by the way things have turned out over the last few years.

There were, however, good reasons to believe that many regimes which came to power after independence would aim to heighten the struggle against the structures which conditioned the oppression and exploitation of under-privileged classes and categories, both at home and abroad. And one could hope that they would succeed in galvanizing the energies and vast reservoir of support from the suffering masses towards this end. It is with this perspective that, despite my initial reservations, and urged on by many friends from the Muslim world, I wrote the text which concludes the English edition, concerning the political orientation suggested by a Marxist sociology and ideological viewpoint.

One should not minimize the achievement of the newly independent regimes. The colonialist yoke has been broken. True, other forms of domination have largely taken its place. For instance, there are the extremely strong but hidden, indirect and subtle constraints imposed by participation in a world capitalist market. The advanced industrial economies make the rules and the less developed economies have to abide by them. This is quite indisputable, whatever one's opinions about the causes of underdevelopment and the opportunities for certain countries to break out of it. Even more generally, there is the domination effect necessarily entailed by technological superiority, or by the power derived from large populations and great raw material wealth, even when such technologically developed and wealthy societies are organized under a regime which calls itself 'socialist' and which others may call 'state capitalist'. Nevertheless, despite the importance of these domination effects, despite the existence of equally oppressive internal structures, political independence still gives far more room for liberating actions or manoeuvres than was ever possible in the days of brutal subjugation to colonialism.

As I write these lines, in the summer of 1978, there are fewer grounds for hope in the Muslim world than six years ago: fewer regimes are committed to the struggle against the domination effect exercized, under American hegemony, by the world capitalist system. Conservative state bourgeoisies have developed. Oil money has enabled the most reactionary systems to take the lead. Ideologically, the masses' lack of any realistic programme geared towards improvement of their lot has left them preoccupied merely with individual survival or restricted by the most narrow, backward and brutally repressive variants of religious ideology. The authorities have, to say the least, strongly encouraged this evolution. Political leaders seem set on building their countries up into world powers and forming blocs linked to the world capitalist system; the idea is no longer to break this system's hold, but merely to make it pay dearly for their collaboration with it. At home, this financial power is mainly used to consolidate conservative — and often retrograde — structures of exploitation and oppression.

The competition, rivalry and conflicts which are beginning to emerge between these new centres of relative world power do nothing to help matters. Wars between Muslim countries, and between Arab countries, are quite likely and are already being waged in embryonic and indirect form. The

Palestinian question continues to play a role which makes for war, for oppressive conservatism, or both. Its dynamic has pushed the Arab left into internal competition and conflict, in which the least involved are by no means the least aggressive. Israeli intransigence gave the most extreme elements among the Arabs the advantage, but this irredentist extremism did not necessarily coincide with any progressiveness in internal policy. Those for whom peace was most necessary had to subject themselves to capitalist hegemony (not that this was particularly contrary to their own innermost tendencies) and to adopt reactionary or conservative internal policies. The terrible catastrophe which destroyed Lebanon did not result from a diabolical Machiavellian conspiracy, it was the outcome of this whole dynamic. Let others rejoice at the huge massacres which civil or international wars bring about. But we have to admit that there are far fewer chances today for relatively peaceful and gradual progress towards the destruction of the Islamic world's most oppressive structures. Many contradictory lessons can be drawn from the teachings of Marx and his disciples, even those lessons counselling a certain resignation. But, in another sense, Mao Tse-Tung was right, for a change, when he summed up Marxism in a single energetic phrase: Be rebels. One may justifiably have become somewhat sceptical about the aftermath of struggles for liberation, believing, as I do, that a completely harmonious and free society is only a dream. But one can still hope to impose new demands, which any future society will have to consider, even if it often scorns them in practice. That, too, is a considerable gain. Marxist thought does not deny that, over long periods, the most acceptable political solutions will be gradual reforms, with a gradual cumulative effect and ultimately profound change. But when it is patently obvious that unacceptable calamities are the direct result of fundamental oppressive and exploitative structures, then the remedy must be radical; it must, as Marx put it, go to the root of things. And in that case there is but one valid stand for those unable to resign themselves to accepting humanity's avoidable suffering: to be a rebel.

Maxime Rodinson
Paris
1978

1. Marxist Ideas and the Study of the Muslim World

What Is Marxism?

The way the average Marxist militant sees Marxism is really quite peculiar.
He conceives of it as some sort of complete science or scientific doctrine
and, without going into its relationship with the other recognized sciences
or with scientific method, he expects it to supply the one and only answer
to just about all the questions he can ask. It is almost as if the revolutionaries
of the First, Second and Third Worlds see Marxism rather like one of those
electronic boards in Paris Metro stations, which indicate the correct route
from one point to another. One presses a button next to the name of the
station one wants to go to and one's itinerary is mapped out in illuminated
dots, showing all the right lines and interchanges. Hopefully it will not dis-
appoint you that this naive conception will not be my starting point. For me
there is not just *one* Marxism, but *several* Marxisms, all with a common core,
it is true, but also with many divergences, each version being as legitimate as
any other.

To go further we must distinguish clearly between two meanings and two
conceptions of what Marxism is.

Let us first look at the most obvious idea of Marxism, the one which stems
from the conception I mentioned above. From this viewpoint Marxism is a
series of neo-Marxist totalitarian syntheses, each claiming to be the only
legitimate one. These ideological syntheses serve as the doctrines of what I
call 'a constituted ideological movement', which was once unified but is now
fragmented. The syntheses comprise a philosophy, a sociology, an aesthetic, a
politics; they are expressed by symbols and rites, and generate practical guidelines. In each case the whole is unified as a single complex of elements presented
as both necessary and rigidly interconnected.[1] The initiates of each synthesis
claim that one cannot isolate any particular element, to dispute it; for instance,
if one agrees with the basic principles, it is argued, one must logically accept
the conclusions which the given movement draws on the basis of its particular
synthesis. If one draws other conclusions, it is because one is, subjectively or
objectively, dishonest, and one becomes open to accusations of treason. Within

each of these vast wholes, very few variant readings are treated as admissible, and even then only concerning certain specific theses. The Soviet *Diamat* (an abbreviation of *Dialektitshesky Materializm,* Dialectical Materialism) is a perfect example. This total synthesis of the human and natural worlds supposedly provides answers to everything. Progress is only possible on points of detail. Any marginally important modification of the doctrine is only acceptable if launched by the Central Committee (in practice, by the Politburo) of the Communist Party of the Soviet Union. Any other innovation is stigmatized as 'revisionism' and denounced as treason and dishonesty. How close all this is to the *bid'a* of classical Islam. The followers of dissident Marxist movements, who ridicule the Soviet model, often fail to realize that they use exactly the same conception of things. True, there is less solemnity in their proclamations and in their doctrinal excommunications, but this is due to an external factor, namely the difference in size and power between their groups and the Communist Party of the Soviet Union.

The above are decidedly odd operational conditions for the pursuit of an endeavour which claims to be scientific. One expects scientists, in their own fields, to be relentlessly dedicated to the use of a system of verification, based on extremely strict hypotheses constantly open to revision. Yet it seems that some scientists can accept the bizarre methods we have mentioned quite without qualms, when it comes to sorting out political facts and hypotheses, which after all often have a far greater bearing on their life. Ideological blinkers are surely the only possible explanation for these double standards.

Unless, of course, one is a fanatical supporter of one of these syntheses, one may easily conclude from the divergences between them that none can really claim to be Marxism itself. One can say, however, that Marxism is the complex of ideas and attitudes which has contributed to the formation of these syntheses. To anybody with an open mind it is clear that one can judge each of these ideas and attitudes outside of the system or systems in which they feature. One can judge them on their own merit, accept them or reject them, without necessarily being obliged to accept the ideological complex in which they are integrated.

At the root of these various systems I see a largely valid common core, which is the descendant of Marx's thought. The first thing one finds in it is a sociology, or rather, fundamental sociological theses, which I have defined in other works.[2] Here I will simply point out that, as against some current ideas, we are dealing neither with a pure economism which reduces all social phenomena to mere by-products of the economy, nor with the view that ideas are absolutely conditioned by economic phenomena. It is true, however, that these core sociological theses insist on the importance of fundamental social necessities in the conditioning of the historical dynamic. They insist on the importance of the essential tasks which any conceivable human society must accomplish. They also insist on the important role of these social necessities in the formation of ideas, even when this role is not consciously felt.

These theses are the groundwork of an anthropology which was sketched, but not really developed, by Marx. Broadly speaking, one can say that we are dealing with a conception of Man as a social animal who joins groups with different aspirations and interests. The individuals who make up these groups defend them; the groups tend to maintain their identity and are necessarily in competition with one another. This competition can, at any moment, lead to real conflicts, except perhaps during prehistoric and posthistoric periods. The groups are also in constant evolution.

One can assent to such a set of scientific theses, irrespective of the particular one one follows. These theses can and must be developed. In particular, as I have already pointed out, their classical formulations have neglected the relatively autonomous areas of organization and ideology. In my opinion, each of these scientific theses and their possible developments can give rise to a contradiction with some elements of the Marxist ideology which I am going to describe, and with some elements or even the totality of the neo-Marxist ideological syntheses to which I have referred above.

The common core of Marxism also comprises an ideology, or rather ideological tendencies, elaborated round a given existential option. Every society, and every group, every 'class', even every individual, needs to find an answer to the truly important questions: What is Man in the Universe? How can he give meaning to his life? For which values must he tame and sacrifice his instinctive drives towards unbridled pleasure, towards unrestricted selfishness, towards what Freud called the *id*?

There are only a few possible answers. This world either is or is not susceptible to improvement by human action, and such action either can or cannot give meaning to life. One can undertake to tame one's instinctive drives in order to serve the interests of the group, or those of Man in general, or to obey God. The ideological options are limited, although each one can be given different tones, different accents. It is also important to remember that we are talking about proposed options, not constraining scientific answers. Somewhere along the line we have to make a jump, a choice. For instance, it is not Science which can tell us whether one should be optimistic or pessimistic about the future of mankind.

The Marxist option is the most complete of those choices which opts for man and for action within the framework of an active optimism. It implies the possibility of a harmonious society in which competition would be limited and would never lead to conflict. It also implies the possibility of Man becoming perfectly adapted to his society. Again, the validity of these conceptions cannot be guaranteed by any scientific demonstration. Perhaps this choice is based on too optimistic a vision of things, but one must remember that it is also a call for social action to improve the human condition.

In the hands of the founders of ideological movements, or of God according to the followers of religious ideologies, each answer, each option becomes the basis on which an ideology or an organization is built. A community then forms and evolves, shaped not only by the original option, but also by the tasks it must accomplish, the situations in which it operates, the specific dynamic of its organizations and ideological syntheses, and the social base of the organization, with all its cultural and historical characteristics. A whole evolutionary process is put in train which modifies, bends, re-interprets and revises the original ideology. In general, however, the basic options continue to be expressed, as an underlying, accessible and perceptible core, often in the form of a body of holy script, at the heart of the evolved ideological synthesis.

The basic options reappear when one looks afresh at the total ideology to which one has committed oneself. They reappear when new conditions, a new situation, the result of normal evolution and the weight of the factors mentioned above, have moved ideologies and organizations too far from their original principles. Finally, they reappear when the ideologies and organizations can no longer respond adequately to the new conditions created by the evolution of their milieu.

One can also find oneself modifying the original combination of values and ideological elements.

What the Theses of Marxist Sociology Can Contribute to the Study of the Muslim World

We are now dealing with issues which do come within the ambit of the sciences. One must emphasise that the theses of Marxist sociology have been widely broadcast and have strongly influenced all modern historical and sociological studies. This influence has extended far beyond the confines of Marxist organizations. In this way, Marxist theses have already made important contributions to these studies and have been integrated into many works which have advanced our understanding of the human universe. These developments are actually part of a general movement of scientific thought, to which Marx simply gave more conscious, more lucid and more systematic expression.

Nevertheless, the progress thus achieved in our historico-sociological conceptions was something of a revolution. Its central point was the rejection of the previously held fundamental conception of the historical dynamic. No one has expressed and justified this rejection better than Marx. The rejected conception claimed that men are shaped by ideas and act according to the ideas they adopt, without their practical circumstances having any influence on these ideas. It is this rejection which has been so inadequately labelled 'historical materialism'. One must realize that, above all, it is a rejection of historical idealism, and is therefore a negative basic principle which clears the way for many scientific options. I must emphasize that it is quite possible for a religious man to reject the archaic idealist conception, since, for him, God will remain the ultimate origin of national and social evolution. But he can easily admit that, in the natural world, God acts by means of what the philosophers used to call 'secondary causes'. The concept of laws of nature is accepted by religious thinkers, even in the Muslim world, where it once met with particular resistance, which I will not elaborate here. If God acts through the intermediary of natural laws, why should he not act in the human world through the intermediary of social laws?

Let us take a few examples from the history and study of Islam.

The Problem of Prophecy

The faithful obviously hold that Islam was founded by God, who, at a moment of His choosing, sent the Prophet to declare His will and to reveal to men the mysteries He intended them to know. Naturally, unbelievers account for the life and work of Mohammad in quite a different way. But these two interpretations can at least agree on the fact that social and human conditions also obtained at the time of the Prophet's appearance. The faithful can think in terms of God preparing Arab society and the personality of Mohammad for Islam. These would be the secondary causes I have mentioned and indeed Ibn Khaldoun explains the appearance and rise of the Prophet in this way, though no one would cast doubt on the strength of his Islamic faith. Marx was not without precursors. All that we are really rejecting here is the idea that the Prophet's mission was purely a miracle, that nothing in the evolution of the Arab society of the period had paved the way for it.

The Expansion of the Community

The traditionalist view is that this expansion was itself another miraculous event, a reign of Goodness and Truth brought about by impeccable men. If we look more closely, however, we see that even traditional historiography also speaks of non-religious motivations. For example, in Abou Yousouf Yacoub's *Kitab al-kharaj* we find the following significant reference to nationalist-type motivations: 'We Arabs were humiliated, the others trampled us underfoot and we could not answer in kind; then, from amongst our own people, Allah sent us a prophet, and one of his promises was that we would conquer this land and hold it for ourselves.'[3] Many attempts have been made to define these social and human motivations. In my opinion there is nothing to prevent the believer from collaborating in further, more systematic study of the causes of the Muslim conquests. Indeed nothing prevents him from again presupposing that the will of God was manifesting itself through laws He has laid down for the social world and for the dynamic of human thoughts and projects throughout history.

The Break-up of the Community

Traditional Muslim and non-Muslim views regard this break-up as the result of divergences in ideas, purely doctrinal/spiritual disagreements on theological doctrine. The image is of a thinker who, after studying the contents of the Law and the Faith, comes to conclusions in some way different from those of his predecessors, and therefore founds a school or a sect.

It must be said that, here too, Muslim historiography often speaks of other motivations than these purely ideological differences. One must remember the specific character of Islam, which distinguishes it from Christianity, say, or from Buddhism. Islam is a theologico-political religion, a means not only for each individual to seek his own salvation but for the creation of a society in keeping with divine law, with the *shari'a*. Thus, political and social motivations are implicit right from the start. Wahabism, for instance, now tends to be explained in terms of Arab nationalism rather than as some pure doctrinal divergence.

The Marxist contribution, in keeping with the direction of all contemporary historical thought, consists above all else in the search for the social and human factors behind the so-called 'sects.' This approach is already becoming more prevalent. There is also a secondary contribution which Marxism has made to the historical conception of things, and to the methods of historiography of the last two centuries. Inklings of this method can be found, in Muslim society for example, in the thought of a man like Ibn Khaldoun, although not in a systematically developed form. What I am referring to is the practice of basing oneself above all on those authors chronologically closest to the formation of the 'sects', a practice which is still not universal amongst researchers in the Muslim world. The formation of the 'sects' has too often been described by reference to later sources, whose analyses were based on a vision of the past conditioned by their own existing milieu. This elementary demand of historical method dramatically re-opens questions in every domain.[4]

The Reaction to Europe and Contemporary Nationalism

Here again an idealist conception of things is still widespread. For example, the history of Arab nationalism has often been presented as the history of an idea which came out of the blue, captured men's imagination, and galvanized them to work towards its realization.[5] But historians, in principle at least, believe that a serious study of the subject must concentrate on establishing the historical conditions under which such ideas were formed.

A diffuse Arab ethnic consciousness already existed in the days of pre-Islamic Arabia. At the time of the *sho'oubiyya*[6] there were many intellectual struggles between Arabs, Persians, Turks, and Blacks, at the heart of the Muslim Caliphate. But one must not make unwarranted assimilations between the conceptions of that period and the nationalist ones of today, though one can still look for the general factors of social life which may have been at work in both cases.

According to my conception of things, which I offer as a working hypothesis amongst others, the situation created during the 19th Century by the impact of Europe on the Muslim world provoked universal feelings of humiliation and revolt. Some sort of implicit ideology took root in the masses of the Muslim people, as a response to the social and political situation. It is on the basis of this implicit ideology that intellectuals such as Jamal ad-din, Mohammad 'Abdoh and Mustafa Kamil have formed their more or less divergent theories.

We must assume that each event has a complex history behind it. At each moment of history there is a struggle between contradictory tendencies, each expressing different social forces but all obliged to take into account the national aspirations which were, during the period in question, the foundation of the Muslim people's implicit ideology. There are and have been many contradictions, creating great tension, to say the least. For example, the ideal

of Muslim solidarity is to some extent at odds with ideals of Egyptian patriotism and Arab fraternity. The search for compromise has often been successful,
but even when the various points of view are based on the same situation and
the same diffuse general consciousness, clashes can occur. We must study the
precise conditions of this complex dynamic, bearing in mind the basic nature
of the various classes in Muslim society, but this does not mean we have to
adopt either a pure economism or a schematic conception of classes, as has
all too often been the case amongst institutional Marxists.[7]

A Marxist Answer to the Problem of Muslim Specificity

It would indeed seem that the problem of the specificity of the Arab world is
the fundamental problem for contemporary study of that world. 'Can Marxism
provide an answer?' is a familiar question. I will simply give my own opinions,
with the proviso of referring my readers to all the observations I have made
above concerning the use of the term Marxist.

On the one hand, it is quite impossible to give a definite, confident, answer,
at least not in the sense in which the illuminated board I referred to above
gives definite and confident answers to the problem of getting from one
underground station to another. To conceive of such a Marxist answer is to
draw a distinction between Marxism and normal science, which many Marxists
do indeed make in practice, although few willingly admit to this in their
theoretical writings.

On the other hand, we can propose a scientifically conducted investigation
and attempts at an answer based on the lines thrown up by this investigation.
Such an answer would be Marxist only in the sense that it would take into
account certain lines of research, certain indications suggested by the hypothetical and provisional conclusions of Marxist sociology. I would add that
the investigator will only come up with valid scientific results in this area if
he is conscious of the limits of Marxist ideology, that is to say, in practical
terms, if he has no axe to grind for one of the various ideological Marxist
movements.

The problem of the specificity of cultures was not understood by the
rationalist universalism of the 18th Century. Nor was it understood by classic
Marxism, which merely went further in the same direction. On the contrary,
the question of specificity owes its prominence first to the rather suspect
exoticism of romanticism, then to the nationalisms of the 19th and 20th
Centuries, and eventually to colonialism. Today, specificity is exalted and
highlighted by the anti-colonialist ideology, albeit with the reservations which
go with the need to base oneself on universalist principles. But the anti-
colonialist exaltation of specificity more often than not goes hand in glove
with a considerable misunderstanding of it.

The problem can be posed in rational terms open to scientific investigation
as follows. In the general evolution of the Muslim world is there an intangible
invariant core? If so, then what is this core? Various answers have been given.

More often than not the invariant core is given as a postulate and is sought in the Muslim religion. The contemporary nationalist ideology, however, has often looked for other answers; answers, moreover, which cannot apply to the entirety of the Muslim world, for instance Arabism and Egyptianity.

Since I do not intend to go into the question at any great length at this stage, I would merely like to indicate that we can at least reach certain negative conclusions. For instance, one cannot maintain that the Muslim religion is a total invariant. It has varied much over the centuries, and this is recognized by Muslim thought itself, since it currently uses such notions as *ihya* (revival), *tajdid* (renovation) and reform. If Islam needs to be periodically revivified, reformed or renovated, it is because it has fallen prey to torpor, archaism and various deviations which call for correction.

Religious Muslim thought proclaims that this variation is not total, and I think this is correct, given certain limits. At the foundations of Islam there is a core, an inspiration, an initial impetus, be it from Allah or from Mohammad; and this inspiration has been at least prepared, if not conditioned, by social, historical, political and cultural circumstances. Being conditioned in this way does not, of course, invalidate this core's claim to provide answers to eternal existential questions. The initial inspiration persists in latent form and underlies the various manifestations of the Muslim faith, as a source of reference.

However, it is also true that this spiritual impetus has manifested itself concretely in ideologies and active organizations, right from the start. The weight of ideology, of organization, of the continuously evolving social and national base constantly, if imperceptibly, gives rise to practical revision. Eventually one realizes that there is a considerable gap between Islam, as it has come to be, and the original inspiration. Were it not so, how could one explain these appeals to *ihya* and *tajdid* which recur throughout the history of Islam? This dynamic holds for all religions. Indeed it is also more or less valid for all ideologies and ideological movements, including Marxism!

It seems to me, therefore, that this is the direction in which we can seek a Marxist answer to the problems of this issue, with some hope of finding the elements of that answer. If we do this, we can move away from the idealist conception of religion as a set of ideas floating above earthly realities and constantly animating the spirit and actions of all its followers. We can assume, on the contrary, that religious ideologies, like all ideologies, have a concrete and real basis in the constantly competing human groups who share out the planet between themselves or form the different strata of a society. We can take into account the constant interaction of these groups and the fact that their primary consideration must be the demands of material and social life.

In my opinion this in no way prevents us from recognizing the fact that the existential problems which Man faces are perennial or that the fundamental answers to these questions are limited.

The Challenge of Marxist Ideology to Religions

The title of this section should not be misunderstood. The challenge in question is the one which confronts Mankind at the dawn of civilization and which conditions the formation of civilizations. According to Toynbee, the stringent conditions of survival which prevailed during the prehistoric period in the valleys of the Nile, the Tigris and the Euphrates, amongst others, forced those who sought to establish themselves there into considerable effort, into the search for more advanced technical solutions than those current in more favourable areas, and into a more developed social organization, in order to maintain group cohesion in the face of complex and arduous tasks. Therefore, when we talk of challenge we do not mean mockery or contempt, but something creative, a call to do better, to face up to the problems which Marxist ideology has itself met head on for over a century.

As you can see, my point of view is somewhat different from that of Roger Garaudy, who is also much preoccupied with the relationships between Marxist and religious movements. Garaudy is an organization man committed to militant movements. His primary concern is the alliance of two organized ideological movements, two organizations, two Churches. I will merely point out that an alliance of this type is necessarily burdened with the sociological load carried by the two organizations. The initial impetus of both organizations has a hard time surviving when it has to drag such a weight along with it.

I believe I see things differently since, in my view, the challenge of Marxist ideology to religious ideologies consists in pushing them towards integrating into their syntheses the necessary values of the modern world, values answering today's problems. Indeed I think that all religious people should ask themselves the following question: why do religions in their traditional forms no longer inspire the great movements of today? Why are these great movements formed round other ideologies?

The essential values which Marxism proposes today are basically the good of Mankind and action towards the improvement of his lot. The tendencies which correspond to it are universalism, humanism and a creative optimism.

I know that many contemporary struggles stem from nationalism. I willingly admit that this is a necessary stage when the issue is to defend the legitimate rights of an oppressed, humiliated or threatened nation. But today the world is linked in more ways than ever before. All perpetuation of nationalist ideology in its pure form, which accepts no alternative values to the good of the nation to which one belongs, is liable to lead to immense danger. The usual outcome is the consolidation of enemy nations, constantly struggling against each other, for there is no reason to believe in any pre-established harmony between the aspirations and interests of various peoples. This is so obvious that just about every nationalism seeks to give itself a universalist justification, attempting to demonstrate that the welfare of the nation coincides with the welfare of humanity. But this is often an apologetic and ideological superimposition without any real basis. Marxist ideology accepts

13

national values, recognizes their legitimacy and defends them when they are flouted, but integrates them and subordinates them to human values in general.

As to creative optimism, it is more necessary than ever in the context of the immense tasks which await us if we are to make the world a liveable place. The wealthy secure nations, as everybody can now see, face dramatic problems which they must solve quickly if they want to survive. Even more dramatic is the problem of 'underdevelopment', of the dynamic which seems to make the poor even poorer, and distributes the cultural resources produced by the labour of mankind more and more unequally, while the world population is kept growing faster and faster and without adequate resources to feed it. We need action but collective action is inconceivable without the idea that it is possible to improve the present situation. Hopefully, this idea would dispense with the usual utopian illusions, according to which the immediate, or at least rapid, outcome would be a perfectly harmonious society in which all conflicts would be resolved or worked out peacefully. I do not believe we can abandon the idea of utopia without damaging the quality and intensity of our action, but one can at least express certain reservations about this perennial utopianism, no doubt beneficial at some stages, but often subsequently disastrous.

One favourable condition for the integration of these elements into contemporary religious ideologies is the fact that they have often been thus integrated in the past, often out of simple vital necessity. And this is particularly true of Islam.

Islam is a universalist religion, appealing to all men in principle. Serious warnings against racism and the supposition of any inherent inequality between human groups form part of the *khotbat al-wada*, the Prophet's farewell speech which he is said to have delivered at the time of his last pilgrimage, shortly before his death. That these principles have not always been followed in the course of history is unfortunately more than obvious. The same is true of all religions and ideologies. There are very fine principles at the roots of Christianity, of Judaism and of the Marxist ideology. But one does not need to be a high priest to know that Christian, Jewish, Buddhist and Marxist states or societies have often disregarded them in practice. One cannot expect much more from human societies. But at least we can say that it is vital that these principles are always highlighted, that men of good faith should always be able to refer to them, to draw inspiration from them and at a favourable moment demand that they be put into practice. I would like to quote a *hadith*, a traditional prophecy, the interpretation of which can be debated both philosophically and historically, but which carries a universalist interpretation according to some: *Min al-acabiyya 'an yo ina r-rajol qaumaho 'ala zolm*. Can this not be read as: it is *'acabiyya*, ethnic fanaticism, for an individual to help his people commit an injustice?[8] At the very least we see here an indication that people were aware of the problem in the first days of Islam and that it was not automatically solved by calls to place loyalty to the group above all else. We know that this concept of *'acabiyya*, which was later presented in a sociological perspective by Ibn Khaldoun, and which has been considered as typical of Bedouin society before Islam, has been violently criticized by Muslim ideologists. In fact every man, every people is capable of *zolm* (oppression, injustice), no one is innocent by definition; there is no chosen people.

According to the ancient historians of Islam, Abou Dharr al Ghifari, the great companion of the Prophet, met with some difficulties because of his interpretation of a verse of the Koran which denounced the greed of Jewish and Christian priests. Abou Dharr claimed that this verse was equally applicable to the mighty of Islam. 'He spoke for us as well.' This seems to be an admirable example.[9] An ideology which has come to power always imagines that it is immune, thanks to its principles, to the failings it has so clearly pointed out in others. But it cannot escape the sociological weight of which I spoke earlier. There is a tendency for such an ideology to close its eyes to its own failings, to hide them, to exalt them, to organize a whole pretence according to which the realized society corresponds exactly to the one which had been dreamed of. A turning point is reached, a very important turning point, when a man gets up, alone at first, like Abou Dharr, and declares that principles have been violated and that they must nevertheless be invoked against the very members of the ideological organization of which one is a member. When somebody finally cries out 'This applies to us as well', it is an indication that history carries on, that the human conscience is not dead and still makes all its demands in spite of the impurities of reality; it is one of the rare signs in history from which we can draw some encouragement to have a little faith in human nature.

As for the idea of creative optimism, it has always existed in Islam. Right from the start we find the demand to realize a society without oppression by human action, albeit with divine assistance. Classical Islam lived with the idea that the *shari'a* could supply this guarantee against oppression. But I do not wish to be so indiscreet as to enter into this debate, which has long divided believing Muslims. I will simply ask the question: Is the *shari'a* sufficient in this respect?

These principles and values, therefore, are no strangers to Islam, although they must be reactivated whenever the weight of history has pulled them under.

In conclusion, I would say that, even if it is inevitable or necessary, or even beneficial, to entertain certain illusions, no concerted action can achieve its ends, unless it is carried out with a modicum of lucidity. The minimum condition of such lucidity today is to have assimilated what one can already consider as valid in the lessons of social science. In my opinion quite a few of these conclusions can be found in the theses advanced by Marxist sociology. I believe that the latter are scientifically based theses, even if the ideological opposition to their acceptance forces us to stamp them with the sectarian label 'Marxism'. There will perhaps come a day when one will be able to say, without ambiguity and without reticence, that they are simply valid theses of sociological science.

If there is a lesson to learn from history and from the analysis of society by following the guidelines of Marxist sociology, it is, for all the furious denials of Marxist ideology, that there is no earthly paradise, no society without conflicts, and therefore no definitive revolution, victorious once and for all. It is also that constant self-criticism is indispensable, that perpetual revision is and always will be necessary, that no revolution will put an end to the need to struggle against *zolm*, against that will to oppress which has long been struggled against and which has always recurred in other forms.

But no science can confer automatic understanding of what one must do. Even if Marx's demonstration of the internal contradictions which rack capitalist society and which one day will bring it down was even more forceful and penetrating than it already is, it would still be possible for capitalists, or groups of capitalists, to seek to profit as much as possible from the advantages conferred upon them by capitalist society, and even systematically to use Marx's observations on the countervailing tendencies which, he claimed, delay that evolution, in order to prolong the system's survival. Even if it was even more clearly demonstrated that this system results in inhumanity and cruelty, even if one demonstrated rigorously — and one may justifiably be sceptical about the rigour of those demonstrations advanced so far — that the proposed alternative would have only beneficial characteristics, the deduction that one must therefore fight against the system would still be moral and not scientific.

Nothing 'scientific' can be set against the man who decides to profit by the system or who simply does not suffer by it and refuses to fight it. Even if one is determined to go beyond selfish motives, the causes before us are sufficiently varied, each with its multiple and complex consequences, for the choice not to be an obvious one between Good and Evil. One must choose according to the values to which one gives priority. There is no mandatory 'scientific' ideology or 'scientific' choice, despite the fact that in the Soviet Union the prevailing doctrine has evolved such a self-contradictory concept. There are existential and eternal options which we must face up to. Science can provide elements to guide our choice, but the choice itself must come from elsewhere.

Men of all cultures, of all nations, of all religions can, I believe, agree on the following programme: to work, in constant communication with those who have made other ideological choices, towards the situation in which the greatest number of men have the maximum access to liberty, understanding, equality, progress and fraternity, towards the achievement by human effort of the maximum possible resistance to those blind and savage forces which move within each man, the essentially intrinsic selfishness which is perhaps indelible.

However, I am not sure that this struggle will achieve its ends, but at least it resists the terrifying weight of those blind social forces I have attempted to describe. Only this struggle for the best, with this ever-present vision of improvement can help to mobilize men towards their own better natures. What I am trying to express has been magnificently described by the greatest living Russian writer, Alexander Solzhenitsyn. It is the description of a painting which the artist, Kondrachev, is attempting to realize; it is to be the artist's greatest work and he will probably never paint it. It is the image of a moment, Parsifal's first sighting of the castle of the Grail.

The painting was twice as long as it was wide. There was a deep gorge between two cliffs. On each side, to right and to left, were dense and primitive forests. Bracken and hostile bramble bushes had invaded the sides of the gorge. On top, to the left, coming out of the forest, one could see a grey horse, mounted by a helmeted rider wearing a grey coat. The steed had no fear of the precipice and stood with hoof raised, quite ready to follow his rider's command to retreat or to leap across.

But the rider was not looking at the precipice. Astonished, he was looking into a distant light, all red and gold, perhaps from the sun or perhaps from some source purer than the sun, which shone from behind a castle. On that terraced mountain peak just visible through the trees and bracken, there rose, tower by tower towards the sky, like a building carved in the clouds, the vibrant, vague and yet resplendent perfection of the violet-haloed castle of the Holy Grail.[10]

References

1. For an enthusiastic and naive expression of this approach, one may turn to the work of the French communist philosopher, Lucien Seve, a very orthodox militant who tells us that 'the discovery of the real essence of humanity, the scientific basis of communist policy and the conscious adoption of the proletariat's point of view (i.e. the point of view of the French C.P.'s Political Bureau) are inseparably linked to one another.' Lucien Seve, *Marxisme et theorie de la personnalite*, Editions Sociales, (Paris, 1969), p. 477.
2. 'Sociologie marxiste et ideologie marxiste' in *Marx and the Contemporary Scientific Thought*, Mouton, (La Haye–Paris, 1969).
3. Abu Youssef Yacoub, *Kitab al-kharaj*, Cairo, 1347H., p. 39, 1.8ff.
4. Cf. Claude Cahen, 'La changeante portee sociale de quelques doctrines religieuses' in *l'Eaboration de l'Islam*, Colloque de Strasbourg. (12–14 June 1959), P.U.F., (Paris, 1961): *Travaux du centre d'etudes superieures specialise d'histoire des religions de Strasbourg*, pp. 5–22 and foreword; also W.M. Watt, 'The Great Community and the Sects', in *Theology and Law in Islam*, G.E. von Grunebaum, O. Harrassowitz (eds.), (Wiesbaden, 1971), pp. 25–36.
5. This point of view has been very clearly expressed in Fayez A. Sayegh, *Arab Unity, Hope and Fulfilment*, Devin-Adair, (New York, 1958); but it also features far more implicitly and insidiously in the work of many other authors, both Arab and European.
6. *Sho'oubiyya* is the name given to a set of tendencies which did not accept Arab superiority under the Abbassid Empire but which expressed themselves mainly through intellectual controversy. The Arab Nationalists of today have re-adopted the term to designate the tendencies of

non-Arab minorities. They apparently give it a pejorative connotation which the non-Arabs find it hard to endorse.

7. Cf. my article 'Economic History and the History of Social Classes in the Muslim World' in *Studies in the Economic History of the Middle East from the Rise of Islam to the Present Day*, M.A. Cook (ed.), O.U.P., (London, 1970), pp. 139–55.

8. Ibn Maja, Sunan XXXVI (Kitab al-fitan), bab 7; Ahman ibn Hanbal, Masnad, IV, p. 108.

9. The relevant verses of the Koran are in Sura 9:34s. See *Islam and Capitalism*, p. 258ff, Penguin, (London,1974) for references. Also J. Robson's short article 'Abu Dharr al Ghifari' in *Encyclopedie de l'Islam*, 2nd edn., Vol.I, M. Besson (Paris, 1960), p. 118.

10. A. Solzhenitsyn, *Le Premier Cercle*, R. Laffont, (Paris, 1968), p. 261.

2. The Nature and Function of Myths: Marxist Communism and Arab Nationalism Compared

Preliminary Definitions

I offer the following 'operational' definitions simply as guidelines for my own research. By socio-political movements I mean those which draw dissatisfied masses into a struggle. The dissatisfaction in question may be political, which in our example is essentially the result of domination exercised by one ethnic community over another; or social (the result of domination of one 'class' or horizontal stratum over another). By myths I mean certain central themes of an ideology[1] which describe past or future situations as realities. As theologians, a group of researchers not previously mentioned here despite their extensive treatment of myths, have clearly pointed out, such myths are functions of a *kerygma*,[2] a call to organize, maintain, defend or transform both the world in which men live, and, eventually, their personal lives, by means of symbolic (ritual) or pragmatic (magical, technical, and organizational) actions.

Marxist Communism

What follows is only a schematic exposé, highlighting those of this movement's characteristic features which distinguish it from the sort of movement represented by Arab Nationalism.

I believe that a Marxist approach to the communist movement, by which I mean an approach which is faithful to the fundamental aims of Marx's sociological theses, requires us to start from an original basic situation. The starting-point was the dissatisfied masses, a Western proletariat whose misery had been increased by the beginnings of industrialization, and an educated stratum whose frustration was particularly acute. There was generalized disappointment amongst all the underprivileged. The bourgeoisie had promised a classless society (a promise which had been and would be constantly reiterated throughout history).[3] In a sense, this promise had been kept, in that all were equal before the law and the specific statutes applying to the various 'orders' of society had been abolished. But, as usual, a horizontal social differentiation persisted, and was keenly felt by all except the victors, who dismissed it as irrelevant.

This basic situation provoked reactions both at the level of consciousness and action. Denunciations and vehement appeals were made, although not in the context of any particularly elaborated ideology. Small organizations set out to accomplish the more immediate political tasks. Amongst the intellectuals, who generally had ruling-class backgrounds, more complex ideologies developed, denouncing bourgeois society's breach of faith towards its own myth; bourgeois society had not abolished private property. Since classes had been revealed as functions of private property, and not of personal status, as had previously been thought, it was necessary to destroy private property. Then and only then would one achieve the *true* classless society. The central myth in such an ideology was thus still the classless society, a concept made more precise by the notion that in such a society private property would be restricted, so that it could no longer serve as the basis for the constitution of a privileged social stratum.

Early ideologies of this type did not catch on enough among the masses, not in fact because they were elaborated by intellectuals, although some colleagues have claimed, groundlessly in my opinion, that ideologies developed by intellectuals and ideologies influencing the masses are incompatible. No, these ideologies failed because they offered the masses no programme of action to which they could immediately commit themselves as a whole, in order to realize the central myth. Where there was a programme of action it was such that it could only affect small groups (Cabet, Owen, etc.). In short, such ideologies had little if any mobilizing force.

Furthermore, these ideologies had to struggle against old ideologies, which offer the masses identities other than that of oppressed proletarians, national or religious ones, for instance. Indeed, it is important to note that the fact that the radical ideologies had to struggle against the earlier identifications is one of the key features which distinguish them from ethno-national myths. The old identifications implied attitudes of a very different sort, which, for all their inadequacies in terms of the people's need for radical change and protest, nonetheless corresponded with deep-seated patterns of reaction learnt in childhood. The new ideologies also had to struggle against reformist ideologies, which claimed that bourgeois society could gradually be improved by such things as education and universal suffrage. Although these reformist ideologies were inadequate to the masses' suffering and indignation, they benefited from the immensely powerful backing of the bourgeois ideology — as Marx said, the ideas of society are those of its ruling class — which had dominated the previous period.

Marxist communism then arrived on the scene, an ideology which relied on very much the same myths as the other socialist ideologies — Marx himself insisted on his own lack of originality from this point of view. But this ideology called much more vigorously, much more convincingly, much more specifically, for a radical break with all the other identifications. This is the fundamental sense of the famous slogan, 'Proletarians of the World, Unite!' The call contained a much more vigorous and convincing denunciation of any reformist attempt to prolong the bourgeois myth. It placed far more stress on the spontaneous indignation and rebelliousness of the proletariat and of those members of the bourgeoisie whose situation pushed them to revolt, such as intellectuals and young innovators driven by a psychologically-based crisis of originality. This Marxist ideology was very complex and scientifically set out, a reflection, perhaps, of the immense prestige of contemporary science! All these factors combined to demonstrate the accessibility of a central myth. But above all the new ideology proposed immediate transition to action according to a programme through which the central myth could be realized. Vigorously, if implicitly, it proposed an ethic which offered each convert a high degree of moral satisfaction in his commitment: the proletariat *must* overthrow the unjust social system condemned by science; man in general, for reasons of universal morality, *must* support this overthrow; the individual can only be at peace with his conscience by contributing to this overthrow; any contribution not geared to this end can only be a form of complicity with evil. Once one is committed in this way, every action which tallies with the ideology, even in one's private life, is a step forward towards the realization of the myth. Just so, in the Zoroastrian religion, each good thought, each good deed contributed to Ahura Mazda's cosmic victory over the monstrous Angra Manyu.

This ideology certainly lent itself to the creation of a strong and adequate organization. The necessity for this is obvious, for the permanent mobilization of the masses has never been an easy task. Throughout, there has been a constant struggle against the tremendous grip of other identifications — the Second International was broken, in 1914, by the persistence of national identification — and against the power of reformism, strengthened by every improvement in bourgeois society, and against the power of the Christian *kerygma*. The latter is particularly strong the moment it frees itself, even superficially, partially or only apparently, from its complicity with the rulers of an oppressive society. It has a superior existential resonance, it appeals directly to man's unhappiness as man.

After various famous attempts, Marxist communism achieved its most adequate form of organization under Lenin, demanding a radical break with reformism and other identifications. Its structure was very coherent: having been modelled on the military, it required a high level of discipline and made much use of practices, rites and symbols which reinforced both the unity and separatism of the group. From one point of view the 'person-ality cult' was such a symbol. This separatism *vis-a-vis* the rest of society is one characteristic trait clearly recognized by General de Gaulle, who was no mean sociologist in his own way, albeit a little empirical in his approach. The idea was to set up a counter-state, as M. Janne puts it.[4] Hence the movement was marked by a growing totalitarianism, as its existential hold grew stronger and stronger, reaching a peak with Zhdanovism and such slogans as 'Be a Communist 24 Hours a Day', which fits in nicely with the demands of Islam, a religion which seeks to sanctify even the most trivial biological functions. It is also worth noting that this reinforcement of ideology and organization resulted from previous defeats. Each defeat had given momentum towards an even stronger organization, a better elaborated, more totalitarian ideology, in an effort to remedy the weaknesses brought out by defeat.

One must remember that this ideology is not a 'pure' one. In the beginning, when Marx and Engels were spreading their ideas without the benefit of an organization, then it was indeed a pure ideology. But it soon became the ideology of a movement, inseparably linked to that movement, thus acquiring characteristics which distinguish it from a 'pure' ideology. I have attempted elsewhere[5] to give a more precise definition of a category of movements which would include 'religions' such as early Christianity, early Islam, (also some forms occurring at various stages in the history of these movements) and Marxist communism. I have referred to such movements as militant ideological movements having secular socio-political programmes and totalitarian aims. I have attempted to list their common characteristics. But I believe that the essential point remains to define a category which transcends the opposition between secular and religious movements, between the sociology of knowledge and the sociology of groupings, and between the concept of ideology and the concepts of association or grouping.

Arab Nationalism: Foundations and Spontaneous Reactions

In the Arab East we also find dissatisfied and frustrated masses at the roots of a movement. This experience has been theirs since antiquity. The causes of this frustration have included not only the exploitation of one class by another, in the Marxist sense, but also national oppression and despotic political regimes. The two latter factors even affected the privileged classes, the bourgeoisie and the aristocracy, in some respects at least. However, an atmosphere of general resignation prevailed. The situation was considered natural, even sacred, justified by an 'ideological' way of thinking (in the Mannheimian sense). The only remedies available were thought to be personal ones, the individual quest for salvation or, at best, the preaching of just, humane and religious behaviour to the princes. The state promoted this quest for personal salvation as a safety-valve. It officered the mystic fraternities, for all that they were the remnants of mediaeval movements which had once had a temporal goal. Political power-struggles were not ideological. They remained struggles between clans, although one clan could occasionally draw support from a dissatisfied stratum by promising it certain advantages. But even this had no ideological implications. From time to time there were local movements to establish the ideal society, the 'classless society', based on justice and without privileges, laid down as the model by early Muslim society. And sometimes the aspirations of disadvantaged ethnic groups were channelled in this direction.

In the 19th Century a new situation emerged, although the background remained the same. The state which ruled over most of the countries of the Arab East, the Ottoman Empire, was weakened, as a result of military, political and economic pressure from Europe, whose power had been growing over the previous three centuries. This weakness manifested itself by revolts and separatist movements supported by Europe. There was also a heightened dislocation of the traditional structures. European trade flooded the Eastern markets (as it had done from very early on, going back to the 15th Century in places like Egypt), and little by little ruined the local artisans. Later, the capitalist economy itself penetrated these countries, and the dislocation became even more acute. The challenge of Europe made itself felt in every field. The Ottoman Empire was defeated and already Europe was seeking to realize colonialist aims, basing itself on indigenous minorities such as the Christians and the Jews, whose members came to enjoy exorbitant privileges.

But much-hated Europe also presented a model of the powerful political regime, a model which seemed a remedy for all the ills of the Muslim world. It was this model's presence which sounded the knell of the old resignation. The influence of the French Revolution was enormous, if sometimes slow in manifesting itself. It began to occur to people in the East that perhaps there was a form of parliamentary government different to the one which they knew from Venice, a new form which brought with it liberty (the liberty of the educated classes *vis-a-vis* the despot) and equality, (equality of ethnic groups).[6] It also seemed to include power, wealth and happiness. Indeed people were led to believe that here was the secret of Europe's strength, the secret which every cultured Oriental was attempting to decipher. This European model was more or less compromised by French secularism, which can seem repulsive to the religious. On the other hand this link with secularism made it more easily adaptable to Islam than if it had been obviously linked to Christianity.

In this situation, too, there were spontaneous and very marked reactions. All Orientals found themselves humiliated, from the lowly peasant to the despotic potentate.[7] This humiliation is typical of colonial situations, although I am mainly talking about independent countries, and it naturally went with a desire for revenge on the foreigner, on the European. Some imitated Europe. In any case, there was always a strong desire to use the Western model, to find out its secret in order to get one's own back. Governments were forced to react from day to day, which implied a rapidly elaborated series of 'little' ideologies, each linked to a development in the consciousness of the ruling classes, be they reactionary or reformist.

The Formation of Ideologies

It was on this basis that slower, but ultimately much more powerful reactions developed. Intellectuals who were aware of the situation, who understood these spontaneous reactions, began to construct ideologies, using the ideological models supplied by their own cultural tradition as well as those coming from Europe. I am using 'ideology' in the broad sense here, to mean a system of ideas.

1. Ideologies Linked to the Liberal-Humanitarian Ideology
These were local adaptations of the liberal humanitarian ideology, to use Mannheim's terminology, which was dominant during the 19th Century in

Europe. In general, they fitted either into the traditional framework of the Muslim religion, the latter being suitably reinterpreted, or into existing political frameworks. The central myth of these ideologies was that of bourgeois progress. The independent nation, enlightened by education, the sciences and arts, politically based on the equality of all before the law, thus implying a 'classless' society free of discrimination on grounds of social status or ethnic origin, and based on liberty, as guaranteed by parliamentarianism and the separation of legislative and executive power, was to achieve indefinite progress in its culture, its power and its prosperity. The local ideologies cast in this mould were not greatly elaborated and had little internal coherence. Generally speaking, they played on several concurrent identifications. They tended to be linked, to a greater or lesser extent, with rather unstructured organizations (cadres' parties) or had only a few supporters grouped in secret societies. They nonetheless succeeded in arousing significant numbers of people for demonstrations, rallies and strikes, which were the current forms of struggle at the time. This mobilization was achieved thanks to strong, simple slogans which corresponded to the aspirations and spontaneous identifications of the masses. The central myth took various forms according to the particular accent given to the proposed progressive liberal nation.

(a) Muslim Religious Nationalism: This ideology embraced the whole Muslim world; its minimum demand was that each constituent country should create a Muslim nation. It was in fact an effort to maintain the validity of the traditional ideological formal framework, namely Islam, which was made to agree with the myth of bourgeois progress by a series of bold exegeses and reinterpretations.[8] Notwithstanding the occasional absurdities of such a conciliation, the goal was a very serious one. The point was to show that Islam is not essentially opposed to progress, that on the contrary a return to primitive Islam could further progress. Islam was even presented as the most rational religion, corresponding most closely with the modern ideal; this conception was incidentally quite common during the 18th Century in Europe. But this fundamental tendency, Muslim religious nationalism, could also manifest itself in different political projects. Jamal ad-din al Afghani's revolutionary liberal pan-Islam (1839–97), for example was based on secret and exclusive conspiratorial organizations, in addition to freemasonry. His friend and disciple, Mohammad 'Abdoh (1848–1905), however, very soon rejected a revolutionary attitude in favour of a reformist one. His ideology aimed at a gradual transformation of Egyptian society by means of an education programme geared to slowly changing the people it reached through a variety of organizations, such as free universities, benevolent societies and the organs of the Egyptian state, still controlled by the British. One can see that such a programme places little emphasis on political cadres; it even relies on the British colonialists to come up with a long-term decolonization policy.

I will not elaborate on those movements in Muslim India which fit into this category. A more relevant case is the movement of the Algerian 'Ulemas', which flourished in the 1930s, long after Mohammad 'Abdoh's period. This movement parallels those mentioned above in that Algeria was a marginal Arab country and backward compared to other Arab countries for various reasons, notably because colonization of Algeria had started early and was very complete. The Ulemas' movement had a reformist ideology, although they did not exclude the use of revolutionary means in principle. There was an underlying political programme, namely the struggle against French colonization. But, significantly enough, the Ulemas' conception of a reformed Islam did not stress modernism, tolerance and opposition to conservatism as other movements in the East had done in the period 1870–1910. On the contrary, the stress was on an Islamic fundamentalism, in opposition to the secularized Algerians of the period, who were assimilationist at the time, as is strikingly exemplified by Ferhat Abbas. The organizations created by the Ulemas were on the whole not very developed.[10]

Generally speaking, in movements of this sort one finds an appeal to that Muslim identification which has remained basic and vital amongst the masses – and this appeal is often exploited by conservatives who denounce the innovators and the imitators of the West as ungodly. One side appeals to an attachment to Islam, the religion of progress and reason, in order to move things forward, while the other side appeals to the same attachment to denounce the former. There is always somebody to whom one appears ungodly.

(b) Ottoman Political Nationalism: Any study of Arab Nationalism must at least mention it. It began with the poet, Shinasi (1826–71), of whom an unauthenticated but very widespread Turkish anecdote would have us believe that he had manned the barricades in Paris in 1848. One can see how the movement tied itself in with the political myths of Western Europe. After Shinasi came another great poet, Namik Kemal (1840–88). There were two waves: first, that of the Young Ottomans (1865), continued by the Young Turkey Committee, which led to Midhat Pasha's constitution in 1876, and the ensuing reaction under Abd ul-hamid; then there was the reorganization of the Young-Turk movement towards 1894–95, which led to the victorious revolution of 1908.

For the Young Turks, it was the Ottoman Empire itself which was to become the liberal, progressive and independent nation. Their ideology was basically positivist, rationalist and secular.[11] But the movement ran into the problem of eliciting positive reactions to the Ottoman identification *per se*, for the Empire was a political framework which evoked more resignation than enthusiasm among non-Turks. Hence there were from time to time appeals both to Muslim feeling and to a purely Turkish identification. A myth was being born, the myth of the Turkish nation as the origin of all values. This naturally repelled non-Turks. The movement had organized itself into small secret societies. After its victory in 1908, Ottomanism's practice, dominated as it was by a centralism derived from the Jacobin model, tended to alienate both the dominated Arab ethnic group and the Christian ethnic groups. The latter were not very 'loyal' in any case and tended to look to the West. Following the same dialectic which has recently been repeating itself amongst the Jews of Algeria for instance, the dominant element's suspicion accentuated the 'disloyalty' of the minority, which in its turn reinforced the grounds for suspicion.[12] Once the Ottoman movement had won, it was impelled to rely on Turkish cadres, mainly landowners, which accentuated its reactionary character. Little by little all the minorities, including the Arabs, were repelled. The Turks stayed amongst themselves and the Turkish myth increasingly assumed a dominant role.

(c) Egyptian Nationalism: Its ideology was more or less created by a very gifted orator, Moctafa Kamil (1874—1908), who had very close links with France. He appealed to several identifications at once: Egyptian, Ottoman and Muslim identifications were all invoked in an attempt to mobilize the masses against British imperialism. But he energetically opposed the Arab identification which seemed to him to divide the forces struggling against British imperialism. In other words, he pinned his standard to the mast of Muslim Egypt, as part of an Ottoman Empire which supposedly incarnated Islam. This did not prevent him calling on Christians to join in the battle. Such a set-up was evidently incoherent. However, although his party was a cadres' party, it nonetheless succeeded in triggering off extremely virulent and efficacious mass demonstrations.

(d) Arab Nationalism: This developed in the Arabic-speaking part of Ottoman Asia from 1900 onwards. It was created mainly by Christians impatient to throw off the Turkish yoke and only gradually reached the Muslim masses who were still attached to the Ottoman Empire by their Muslim identification. But anti-Turkish sentiment was eventually reinforced, as mentioned above, by the centralizing policies of the preponderantly Turkish Young Turks after the 1908 revolution. These anti-Turkish Muslim sentiments were given a further boost by the secularism of the Young Turks, who mainly came from minority backgrounds and adopted a positivist freemasonry. But above all it was the repression of autonomist and decentralizing Arabs, Christians and Muslims ordered in 1916 by Jemal, the Young Turk governor of Syria, which finally influenced significant elements to break their attachment to the Ottoman Empire and to rally around the idea of an Arab nation.[13]

In this new nationalism, the appeal to a Muslim identification compensated for the originally weak resonance of the appeal to an Arab identification. People did still feel more Muslim than anything else. On the other hand the Arab identification allowed for the Christians to be brought into the movement. This Arab nationalism was both anti-Turkish and anti-European. But to use Mao Tse-Tung's terminology, the principal contradiction for most Arab nationalists of the period was the contradiction with Europe. Even during the struggle against the Turks, there was still a significant degree of solidarity with them as fellow Muslims and fellow victims of European encroachment.[14]

The movement's myths were a mixture of Muslim values and themes evoking past Arab greatness. This made it possible to operate both on the religious and national levels. The movement expressed itself in secret organizations, and later in cadres' parties. At first it attracted mainly the Arab aristocrats and 'haute bourgeoisie', but later it reached the new urban classes. The allied victory over the Turks in 1918, the breaking of promises made to the Arabs and the division of the Arabic-speaking areas into French and British mandates, turned the movement almost completely from an anti-Turkish position to an anti-European one. The strength of anti-European feeling compensated for the structural weaknesses of the organizations and the commutability of the central myths.

2. Ideologies Related to the Fascistic Ideology of the Strong Authoritarian State

These ideologies, which set themselves the task of forcibly annihilating any opposition to their role as servants of the nation, appeared about 1934 to 1936. This flowering was obviously linked with the popularity of fascism in Europe, which then seemed to be the most modern and efficient 20th Century ideology. Also the enemies of Arab national aspirations were also the enemies of fascism: Great Britain, France and the Jews. Other relevant factors contributing were the failure and disgrace of the nationalist liberals, the fear of communism, and, perhaps most significantly, the participation in the struggle for the first time of less cultured masses, whose respect for efficacity was greater than their concern for freedom of thought. These fascistic movements made great efforts to elaborate more coherent ideologies, although they continued to make appeals to several different identifications. There was, however, a temporary eclipse of the Muslim myth. The latter would have implied the unity of very disparate and disconnected movements, from Indonesia to Morocco.

(a) Arab Nationalism: The myth of the Arab nation, with all its more or less liberal and more or less authoritarian connotations, remained the core of the ideology of several movements. Born in Ottoman Asia, as we have seen, it then reached Egypt. Both in the East and in Egypt the enemies and the problems were the same. There was a profound reaction against all the efforts at divide and rule made by imperialist governments reliant on corrupt and disgraced local cliques. An objective solidarity between all Arab struggles emerged. The Arab myth was no longer a divisive myth, as it had been under the Ottoman Empire; it had become a unifying myth. No regional national feeling was strong enough to stand in its path. The Arab myth in no way detracted from the anti-colonial struggle in each country. It was the myth common to a multiplicity of particular movements and cadres' parties in various Arab countries. Furthermore, these movements did not hesitate also to appeal to a local identification. Their militants struggled against Britain as Egyptians *and* as Arabs, against France as Syrians *and* as Arabs. Often the struggle was seen on two levels. One could fight for the unity and independence of Arab Syria and, beyond that, for every Arab country's independence from France and Britain. The organizations involved did not need to be highly structured as it was very easy to reach the masses. The people were extremely receptive to the slogans proposed.

New theoretical attempts were made to give Arab nationalism a rational

foundation. Suffice it to say here that there was increasing stress on unconditional devotion to the nation, and to the idea of a nation as something
transcending the sum of the individuals which make it up. The inheritance of
Fichte's romanticism displaced the positivist utilitarianism of the 19th
Century. But in any case all these debates had little influence on practical
politics or on the strategy and tactics of the existing organizations.

(b) Syrian Nationalism: This was an original creation, and is interesting as
such, although it was not very successful. It took form in a party founded in
1933 by Antun Sa'ad, a Lebanese Christian. This party, the Syrian People's
Party (P.P.S.) was publicly active from 1936 onwards. Its last spasm of conspiratorial activity ended in disastrous failure a few months ago. However, it
was the only movement of this kind to elaborate a highly coherent fascist-
type ideology. Its central myth was that of the Syrian nation, geographically
defined but with considerable racial undertones. The nation in question was a
'Greater Syria', which included the western part of the Fertile Crescent:
Syria, Lebanon, Palestine, Transjordan. In this case there was a clear break
between the two concurrent Arab and Muslim myths. The ideology was
linked with a strong and, generally speaking, clandestine organization, a
party organized on military lines and using terrorist tactics. But it aroused
little enthusiasm, for it went against the dominant trends and ran into the
strength of Muslim and Arab identification.[15]

(c) Fascistic Muslim Nationalism: One sees this in its clearest form in the
movement of the Muslim Brotherhood, founded around 1927–28 but only
really developed after the Second World War, allegedly with British support.
It revived the old myth of a return to primitive Islam, modernized it and
made it more coherent, which in 1935 and 1943 meant more fascist. This
time primitive Islam was reinterpreted not as the model for a liberal state but
as the model for an authoritarian state with socialist implications, in the sense
in which Hitler could call himself a National Socialist. The movement proposed
a struggle for the Islamicization of the state in both Egypt and Syria as a pre-
lude to the extension of this Islamicization to the whole Muslim world and
the reconstitution of Muslim unity. It was a well-structured centralized mass
movement, with tendencies towards totalitarianism and no qualms about the
occasional use of terrorism. A strong organization was necessary in this case,
because of the strength of the identifications the movement set out to shatter.
Indeed the struggle proposed was not even mainly against the foreigners. It
was against the cadres of an Arab and apparently Muslim state, against Arab
and Muslim militants who themselves seemed to be honestly committed to
the struggle for Arab nationalist ideology and against the foreign powers. The
Brotherhood was thus often cast as a divisive movement, and there were
insinuations, as already mentioned, that it was financed by the British. The
conditions under which the often clandestine struggle was carried out also
contributed to the necessity for a strong organization. Direct appeals to the
masses through the press were impossible. Although the movement's supporters were fanatical, it could nonetheless be quite easily suppressed by any
government which offered proof of the sincerity of its nationalism.

3. Socialistic Ideologies Linked to the Myth of the Proletarian-led State and the Move towards a Classless Society

The definition of class used in this case was the Marxist one. Classes were defined in terms of the ownership or non-ownership of the means of production. I will not deal with the nationalist socialist Ba'ath movement here, since I do not have access to adequate documentation as to the structure of its ideology. The two other clearly defined movements of this type are as follows:

(a) Arab Communism: The central myth was that of the advance towards one or several socialist Arab nations. There were various approaches to this myth, and many significant strategic debates concerning it. Would the Revolution be made by the proletariat alone or in alliance with the national bourgeoisie? Would it be the proletariat or the bourgeoisie which would lead the Revolution? Naturally the direction taken by such debates depended on the global strategic decisions taken in Moscow by the General Staff of the Revolution.[16] The ideology was a complex one; since it soon became obvious that the myth could only be realized in the distant future, a set of more accessible myths sprang up as staging-posts. The myth which was actually proposed, for immediate realization, could be formulated as follows: the Arab nation, or independent Arab nations, was to move slowly towards socialism in the framework provided by parliamentary states allied to the Soviet Union, in which the Communist Party would enjoy the right to act and disseminate propaganda quite freely.[17] Indeed this was the general myth put out by the communist parties throughout the world as from the great turning point of 1933–34, except during the period 1939–41. The choice between a united Arab nation and individual but more-or-less linked Arab nations proved to be a difficult one, fluctuating according to changes in tactics.

The structure was obviously that of all the communist parties. They were 'militant movements' in the sense in which I have been using the term, but they had few supporters. It proved to be rather difficult to apply to these countries the organizational norms in force elsewhere, mainly because of the vagueness which characterized the Arab idea of a party. It was always difficult to bring in a regular flow of subscription income, and without subscriptions, as Lenin well knew, there cannot be a clear dividing line between those within the party and those outside it. In short, there were very coherent core-groups which had access to the tools of propaganda thanks to which they could influence a proportion of the unattached masses and make some rather feeble attempts at ideological totalitarianism. In Egypt there was a slightly different situation from about 1941, because of the lack of any organic link with the international General Staff. The Egyptian communist movement amounted to a small group of intellectuals who from time to time enjoyed a considerable degree of influence but who were faced with practically insurmountable organizational difficulties.

(b) Algerian Proletarian Nationalism: It was launched by Messali Hadj, with the North African Star group which he led from 1925. It then evolved into the Algerian Popular Party (P.P.A.), and eventually into the Movement for the Triumph of Democratic Rights, from 1947, which gave rise to the F.L.N.

on the one hand, the M.N.A. on the other. The basic starting-point was obviously a proletarian one, since the organization depended for a long time on the support of Algerian workers working in France. Its central myth was that of an independent and proletarian Algerian Republic. The proletarian aspect of the goal was at some times implicit, at others explicit; in fact the ideology was not very developed. Relations with Arabism, with Islam and with communism were far from consistent. The organization on the other hand was very coherent and disciplined. A certain totalitarianism predominated, justified more in terms of discipline than of ideology. The reasons for the existence of such a highly structured organization are clear: the exceptional difficulties of the struggle, the bitter fight against the other identifications, especially against an extremely deep-rooted assimilationism. As I said, this movement gave rise to the F.L.N., whose social base was broader and included just about every Algerian class. Its efforts to build an ideology were limited, because it never became anything more than a 'front' in which allies and rival groups co-existed, united only by a minimum common programme. Hence relationships with concurrent ideologies were far from being clearly defined. But a very coherent organization was necessary given the very difficult conditions under which the war was waged. In this case, too, the totalitarian approach was justified far more by the necessary level of discipline than by reference to an ideology.

Conclusions

These are, I believe, the main conclusions that one can draw from the premises set out above, in the context of a comparison between the two types of militant ideological movements in question.
1. In both cases one finds that the basis of the movement lies in the existence of dissatisfied masses, who, during a given period particularly favourable to such a process, see their needs and aspirations sublimated into ideologies, or systems of myths, in the name of which organizations mobilize them into action. But a clear contrast emerges: the universalist movement's myths are complex and elaborate, and its organizations are strong, solid and durable. By contrast, the nationalist movement's myths are simple, unstable, variable, commutable and incoherent, and their organizations, with a few exceptions, notably the F.L.N., are weak, ephemeral and lack structure.
2. Despite this weakness of the nationalist ideologies and organizations, they can be extremely effective, albeit for only a short period, in mobilizing the masses. However, their efforts towards totalitarianism, in the sense of taking over the whole of an individual's life, are both limited and very short-lived.[19]
3. Such a contrast can probably be explained primarily by the fact that the nationalist movements often meet with a quasi-unanimous and very ready response, because their usual appeal is to undisputed primary identifications very close to people's hearts. It is only when the struggle becomes particularly hard that the organization is significantly reinforced, and even then the

ideology rarely undergoes any degree of elaboration. The strongest primary identification may be a negative one, aimed against an outside body. In this case any myth will be acceptable, as long as it proposes a mobilization against that body. Only exceptionally, when the proposed identification is aberrant, new, or not particularly dear to the masses, does one witness a definite strengthening of both the organization and the ideology. In contrast, the universalist movements are always, in some sense, separatist. To mobilize the masses steadily, they have to develop complex ideologies and organizations which are capable of putting up a tough fight against the primary identifications to which they are opposed.

4. Myths and an ideology take root in a situation. They are the conceptual answer, formulated by intellectuals, to the needs, aspirations and primary reactions of the masses. There is often a struggle between concurrent ideologies which seek to provide answers to the same problem, but there can also be convergences and coalescence, especially in the case of nationalist movements. The myths and ideologies must meet certain requirements if they are to be successful, their content must reach out to popular needs, aspirations and reactions. But these myths are not just epiphenomena; they also have their own importance and efficacy, in that they condition the formation of organizations, and the elaboration of more-or-less efficacious, well-adapted and mobilizatory slogans.

5. The universalist myths can have an extremely long-lasting, perhaps even a permanent, validity, since what they propose is essentially a transformation of personal life, sometimes accompanied by an ideal which is timeless or which envisages the end of history, an ideal which can always be made to refer to the future. Their successes are only the starting-point for a new phase. They can always be reinterpreted or particularized, which ensures a perpetual rejuvenation. The nationalist myths, on the other hand, usually die out with the achievement of independence. True, their validity can be more or less artificially prolonged by irredentism, expansionism, bellicosity, or the denunciation of real or imaginary threats. But the applicability of such themes depends on conditions which lie beyond the control of the ideologists.

6. One of the most efficient ways of prolonging a nationalist myth is doubtless to graft it onto a universalist myth, hence the particular interest of the hybrid forms which are now appearing, such as Marxist nationalism. There is very often a passage from the one to the other. Primitive Islam is a universalist myth which soon became nationalist, then moved back into a universalist phase. Marxist communism, which is eminently universalist, has from time to time taken on the appearance of a nationalist myth, as in the Soviet Union, Yugoslavia and in France, for example. Even Christianity itself has often taken strangely nationalist forms, much to the horror of Christians faithful to the movement's primitive spirit. Even the nationalist myths of the independent countries have been forced to take on universalist aspects: thus, the victory of France or Germany in an international conflict has often been presented as the universal victory of Justice, Civilization, Christianity, Righteousness and Western values.

References

1. Broadly speaking 'a set of ideas, beliefs, and ways of thinking characteristic of a group, such as a nation, a class, a caste, a profession, a sect, or a political party.' M.Parmelee, in H.P. Fairchild, *Dictionary of Sociology*, Philosophical Library, (New York, 1944), p. 149.

2. Cf. especially the work of Rudolf Bultman, *Kerygma and Mythos*, H.W. Bartsch (ed.), 1948–55. Also James M. Robinson, *The Church's Kerygma and the Historical Jesus*, which contains a full bibliography.

3. During the Abbassid revolution in Islam, for instance: cf. H.A.R. Gibb, 'Government and Islam under the Early Abbassids, the Political Collapse of Islam' in *l'Elaboration de l'Islam*, P.U.F., (Paris, 1961), pp. 115–27.

4. Cf. H. Janne, 'Les mythes politiques du socialisme democratique', (*Cahiers Internationaux de Sociologie*, 33, 1962,pp. 19–37), p. 30ff.

5. See 'Relationships between Islam and Communism' in this volume. I have tried to treat primitive Islam from this point of view in my biography *Mohammad*, Penguin, (London, 1974).

6. Cf. B. Lewis's fine article 'The Impact of the French Revolution on Turkey. Some Notes on the Transmission of Ideas', *Cahiers d'Histoire Mondiale*, Vol.I, No.1 (July 1953), pp. 105–25.

7. Tawfiq, the Khedive of Egypt (1879–92) once said to one of his ministers: 'I tell you I never see an English sentry marching in my streets without feeling an urge to jump out of my car and strangle him with my bare hands.' C.S. Cooper, *The Modernizing of the Orient*, McBride, Nast and Co., (New York, 1914), quoted in L. Stoddard, *The New World of Islam*, Chapman and Hall, (London, 1921).

8. For instance, there were claims that primitive Islam preached modern democracy, women's liberation, and so forth.

9. Cf. J.M. Ahmed, *The Intellectual Origins of Egyptian Nationalism*, O.U.P., (London, 1960).

10. See Ali Merad's important work *Le Reformisme Musulman en Algerie de 1925 a 1940, essai d'histoire religieuse et sociale*, Mouton, (Paris– La Haye, 1967), (Recherches Mediterraneennes, Etudes, VII).

11. The ideology was given a strong theoretical basis by Ziya Gokalp, a disciple of Durkheim. See the excellent *Turkish Nationalism and Western Civilization, Selected Essays of Ziya Gokalp*, N. Berkes (ed.), Columbia University Press, (New York, 1959). For the complete evolution of the Turkish nationalist movements, see N. Berkes's fine book, *The Development of Secularism in Turkey*, McGill University Press, (Montreal, 1964).

12. The term 'disloyalty' carries no value judgement here. I simply mean that these communities refused to grant their allegiance to the 'Nation' which was the goal of the nationalist revolutionaries.

13. Cf. Z.M. Zeine, *Arab-Turkish Relations and the Emergence of Arab Nationalism*, Khayat's, (Beirut, 1958). The author probably underestimates the strength of Arab national feeling prior to 1914, but this is a useful counterweight to those who go to the opposite extreme.

14. Cf. the resolution passed by the *al-Fatat* secret society, which prepared for the Arab revolt but decided to support Turkey 'if the European projects begin to materialise' (late 1914 or early 1915) in G. Antonius.

The Arab Awakening, H. Hamilton, (London, 1938), p. 153. Feisal's own attitude was not dissimilar: cf. T.E. Lawrence, *Seven Pillars of Wisdom*.

15. For details of the Syrian People's Party see Labib Z. Yamak, *The Syrian Social National Party, an ideological analysis,* Harvard University Press *(Harvard Middle Eastern Monographs, 14),* (Cambridge, Mass., 1966).

16. See 'Marxism and Arab Nationalism' in this volume.

17. Hence the Syrian C.P.'s approval of the denationalization of Syrian industries and its apologia for the Syrian industrialists after the break-up of the U.A.R. cf. J. Couland, *Democratie Nouvelle*, (Nov. 1961), p. 75.

18. See 'Problems of the Syrian and Egyptian Communist Parties' in this volume.

19. The extreme totalitarianism of Nazism, for example, proves that the characteristics we have detected in ethno-national movements are in fact only typical of those which are still at the stage of their primordial demand, namely the demand for independence. Once this stage has been left behind, other characteristics appear within movements of the sort.

3. Relationships between Islam and Communism

The Problem Today

The problem which I am going to attempt to deal with here is a very tricky one, as you are well aware. Furthermore, one can hardly call it an original problem. As you know, there has long been a constant flow of books, articles, pamphlets and broadcasts on the subject. But even a brief and superficial examination of the literature – which I make no claim to have read in its entirety, far from it – reveals a number of very serious defects. These writings are, of course, of very uneven quality, and it would be quite unfair to tar the better works with the same brush as the more popular and more directly propagandist ones. Nonetheless one usually notices that the authors dealing with this issue know either very little about Islam or very little about communism. Often enough, they know very little about either. But there is commonly also a deeper failing which goes beyond inadequacies of information: Islam and communism are treated as fixed premises, as two immutable sets of doctrine, the implications of which are grasped by all the faithful.

This naive intellectualist attitude is clearly at odds with the evolution of scientific thought about this sort of problem. As an extreme case of this sort of misapprehension, I will cite an example which verges on caricature. In a recent work of vulgarization on contemporary Islam, a young specialist (who shall remain nameless) in one particular area of Islam, sets out in a table factors which he refers to as the ideological principles of Islam, communism and capitalism. Three vertical columns are given over to each of the three 'doctrines'. These are correlated with such headings as faith, the family, property, the economy, society, the nation. The various intersections give the attitude of each 'doctrine' on each issue. For example, we are shown that Islam and capitalism agree in their attitude to the family because both respect it, whilst communism, the author claims, favours the disintegration of the family. The same case is made out for property: upheld by Islam and capitalism, condemned by communism. In the 'economy' column, the entry for capitalism (pro-capital) is, for once, at odds with those under Islam and communism (anti-capital).

Obviously such a table hardly stands up to closer examination. For example, it is quite true that there were a few tendencies in the Soviet Union of 1920–24 which proposed and even attempted experiments towards transcendence of the Western family framework. However, apart from these tendencies, which remained marginal and barely tolerated, Marxist and communist theories of the family have usually evinced a positively Victorian conservatism on the subject. Similarly, the thesis that Islam is anti-capitalist can indeed be upheld since, as you well know, one of our most eminent masters does, from time to time, uphold it. There are several necessary qualifications and nuances, however. For we have seen very good Muslims participate in the launching and management of capitalist enterprises, and certain Muslim countries moving as a whole towards an economic structure dominated by capitalism. As for property, what sort of property are we talking about? In principle, communism only attacks the private ownership of the means of production. We could carry on expounding the specific inadequacies of this table at great length. It is the implicit problematic which inspires it, however, which calls for the sternest criticism.

Fortunately, certain authors have reacted against this approach to the matter, notably Bernard Lewis with his intelligent and sensible suggested solution to these problems.[1] Since the question is always formulated as: 'Is Communism compatible with Islam or not?', he has pointed out that doctrinal incompatibility has never prevented many individuals of Jewish or Christian faith from becoming communists. And he adds, very rightly:

> Of course the pious and fundamentalist Muslim theologian who has studied and understood the implications of dialectical materialism will reject it; but such a combination of circumstances is hardly common and is unlikely to acquire any great significance. The question we are faced with should rather be posed in the following terms: given the current competition between the Western democracies and Soviet communism for the support of the Muslim world, which factors or characteristics of the Islamic tradition and of contemporary Islamic society make it possible for intellectually and politically active groups to adopt the methods and principles of communist governments? Also, which factors make it possible for other members of society to accept these methods and principles?

This seems to me to be an excellent way of approaching the problem. I would however, like to point out that we are dealing here with the essentially practical, political aspect of the question. I believe one can widen and deepen the issue. My own approach tends more towards the following formulation of the question, which times does not permit me to justify in detail here. When communism and the Muslim religion come into contact with each other, be it through meetings between organizations which profess these ideologies, or through the encounters of individuals and social groups imbued with the spirit of these ideologies, or even through the clash of ideas in a single mind, what results are we to expect from such contacts, what changes will be wrought in the consciousness and activities of the organizations, social groups and individuals concerned?

This is the historico-sociological problem which I shall attempt to deal with in terms somewhat removed from those of practical political activity. Nonetheless the text will probably enable both the reader and myself to draw eventual practical political conclusions.

The Sociological Basis of the Problem

Any fruitful approach to the problem must first of all free itself from that naive intellectualist conception of chosen opinions and beliefs which has so far inspired most of the judgements on the issue. This conception is, amongst other things, individualist. For if it is only after a genuinely scientific weighing up of the intrinsic worth of various ideas that men embrace a party, a creed or a set of ideas, and if that choice implies that they will reject any principles, ideas, conceptions or commitments which stand in contradiction to those they have opted for, then the choice is indeed an individual one. It then depends not only on the intrinsic value of the adopted ideas, but also on the knowledge, level of culture and temperament of each individual person.

The invalidity of any conception which presents the choice of opinions and beliefs as a lucid, thought-out and logical decision has long ago been demonstrated by modern psychology and sociology. Psychology has revealed the important role of non-rational elements in the making of such a choice. As for sociology, it has shown that the said choice is dependent, to a considerable degree, on each individual's social situation, taking social in the widest possible sense here. This second point was already implicit in the romantic and Hegelian theories of the *Volksgeist*, and in the pre-sociological ideas of Vico and the French sensualist 'ideologues'. Marx and Engels were the first to put it forward clearly and systematically. It was then developed in a different way by sociologists such as Durkheim and Max Scheler. Eventually, it was elaborated in its most systematic form, notably in Karl Mannheim's typology of sets of ideas having a social origin; Mannheim was probably the main architect of a sociology of knowledge. Finally, W. Stak has provided us with a thorough examination of the subject as a whole.

Our first approach to the problem could thus be based on a psychological inquiry. We could ask which character and other traits lead certain individuals, of Muslim faith for instance, to accept communist ideas. This would make an interesting study, which would have to be based on a number of individual cases. However, the huge number of individual cases which would have to be taken into account makes it quite clear that there are also social factors at work, that it is the impact of these social factors on thousands of individual consciousnesses which is the key factor, and that this impact itself on the whole tends to produce similar effects on different people. Without seeking to deny the importance of the psychological approach to the problem, we will concentrate on the sociological aspects, whose importance is, as has just been pointed out, so great that they have considerable repercussions even for psychological studies.

Our sociological study must surely begin by determining the nature of the two entities we are talking about: communism and Islam. If our attempt to understand the way these two entities react upon one another is to be carried out scientifically, then this determination must be effected in terms which allow us to refer to the constants already discovered by sociology. And since, as we have already mentioned, we are dealing with dynamic rather than immutable entities, we will also have to determine the stage which these constantly evolving entities have reached.

If we turn to the existing sociological disciplines or sub-disciplines, in our search for appropriate frameworks, our first point of reference is the sociology of knowledge, supplying us with a fundamental category which seems eminently well-suited to our enquiry, namely the category of ideology. A dictionary of sociology will tell us that, broadly speaking, an ideology is 'the set of ideas, beliefs, and ways of thought characteristic of a group such as a nation, a class, a caste, a profession, a sect, a political party'.[2] This widely accepted broad sense of the word co-exists, in the work of various authors, with a narrower sense. For Marx and the Marxists, for instance, an ideology is often a system of ideas which distorts, 'alienates', or 'mystifies' reality. Most Marxists, however, believe that there can be a system of ideas — an ideology in the broader sense — which does not have these distorting characteristics. Karl Mannheim has established another distinction in his more detailed analysis of the modes of this 'mystification' pointed out by Marx. In Mannheim's terminology, ideology in the narrow sense is that set of ideas, beliefs and ways of thinking characteristic of a group which transcends the real situation of that group, but which the group does not seek to realize in practice. Ideology is thus the set of beliefs and ways of thinking which in effect expresses a desire to preserve the *status quo* by presenting it in an embellished, mythical and mystified manner. Mannheim then draws the distinction between ideology in this narrow sense, on the one hand, and, on the other hand, utopia. Utopian ways of thought are thus also ideologies in the broader sense, in that they transcend the real situation of the groups which adopt them. The difference is that a group which adopts a utopia orients its activity in terms of that utopia, in order to transform an existing historical reality.[3]

In a very recent book, W. Montgomery Watt has applied Mannheim's categories to Muslim history.[4] Mannheim's ideas do in fact provide a very useful framework for the study of the subject. It immediately becomes apparent that Muslim ideology, in the broad sense, has mainly been ideological, in the narrow Mannheimian sense, throughout its history and up to the present day. There are certain problems, however. Islamic ideology was originally utopian (partly so, at least), has continued to be so amongst various sects at various periods, and still is so in a state such as Pakistan, or in movements such as the Muslim Brotherhood.

Also, whilst communist ideology in the broad sense was incontestably utopian in the past, and still is so to a considerable extent, this is not the whole picture. In the communist countries and sometimes elsewhere, we are witnessing the transformation of communist thought into an ideology, in the narrow sense, a transformation which is close to completion.

Thus, Mannheim's concepts of utopia and of ideology in the narrow sense cannot be applied without reservation to the two entities in question. But can they be defined in terms of the wider sense of ideology? Islam, like communism, was an ideology in this sense at its earliest stage. The founders of these faiths diffused the ideologies to those around them by whatever means were available to them in their societies, without calling on those who heard them formally to join a group of people who were already more or less convinced. But, very quickly, during the lifetime of the founders, groups were formed which people could belong to in a formal sense, groups whose members committed themselves to common action and to a common attitude towards various issues. There developed the embryo at least of an organizational structure and people were able to share in the use of common symbols.[5] These characteristics are now essential to any definition of the entities in question, which are groups as much as ideologies. We must therefore go beyond the concepts supplied by the sociology of knowledge.

Must we then turn to the sociology of religion? Islam is obviously a religion, even though the typology of religious groups as evolved by the sociologists of religion is not quite adequate to the realities of the situation. Furthermore, it has often been said that communism is rather similar to a Church, with its credo, its councils, its excommunications, and the blind faith of its followers. However, the sociologists insist that one of the main distinctive characteristics of a Church is the content of its doctrine, which must come under a category such as the 'mystico-ecstatic', evolved by G. Gurvitch. The content of communist doctrine can of course in no way be classified as mystico-ecstatic. Even if we went no further, we would have to conclude that Islam and communism were irreconcilably heterogenous. There can, of course, be contacts and clashes between heterogenous phenomena. However there are many facts which do suggest that we are dealing with two entities which, on one level at least, are of the same nature. To understand this, we must go beyond the concepts supplied by the sociology of religion.

We can then refer to the sociology of groups for the sociologists have constructed several typologies of groups and classification systems which distinguish groups according to their size, duration and function. Some of the categories established by Max Weber, for example, enable us to make useful comparisons and bring us closer to some understanding of the phenomena in question. Originally, the Muslim *umma* and the Communist International were 'associations' (*Vereinen*), voluntary and open groupings, as G. Gurvitch would say. The Muslim community, of which there were several, each considering itself *the* rightful Muslim community, soon became an *Anstalt* (establishment), membership of which was determined not in terms of personal commitment but as the automatic effect of certain criteria such as birth.[6] This establishment was thus, in the religious field, a Church in the Weberian sense. The communist parties have, in principle, remained *Vereinen*. In the communist countries, however, the formation of a collective consciousness through monopolized control of information and education is a factor which highlights a certain similarity between these social formations and the Islamic ones; even the type of open community formed by the citizens conforms to the predetermined collective norm. This would be the Weberian translation of the formula used during Soviet elections, which talks of 'the communist and non-party bloc.'

But there is obviously a far deeper kinship between our two entities than the one suggested by these formal resemblances.[7] This is a matter both of the type of groupings they are, and of the content they have. To explain it, we need to do two things. On the level of content, we must set the religious function within the larger ideological framework. However, we must also establish a category which covers the form and dynamic of Islamic and communist groupings as well as their ideological content.

Definition of a Category

I would say that Islam, like communism, belongs to a kind of grouping, other examples of which can be found in more or less pure forms. I would prefer to call them 'movements' rather than groupings, to bring out their dynamic character. One might then refer to them as militant ideological movements having a temporal socio-political programme and a totalitarian purpose. Their main features could be defined as follows:

The first characteristic of these movements is a 'utopian' (in the Mannheimian sense) ideology (in the broad sense) to which members of the movement are explicitly committed. This ideology gives answers to a certain number of fundamental questions about man's situation and role in the world, about the nature of the world and of society. These 'ideological principles' form the basis for recommended or prescriptive directives concerning the individual's public or private behaviour. The principles are not 'pure' forms – as they sometimes are in other cases – but are appreciated as part of a dynamic system which brings a variety of elements into play, (hence the important contribution of such principles to social integration, as has been pointed out by W. Montgomery Watt). The ideology itself is a totalitarian one, that is to say that its directives and judgements tend to extend into all areas of private and social life. Another feature is that it is often expressed in a body of sacred or semi-sacred texts, sometimes open, sometimes closed. Finally, should the movement succeed completely, the ideology moves totally or partially from being utopian to being ideological (in the Mannheimian sense).

The second main characteristic is the existence of a temporal programme, which is designed to ensure that the ideological principles are put into practice. This is to be done by imposing, on as large a territory as possible, the rules of social life recommended or demanded by the principles and thus involves the setting-up of a state controlled by the movement. The implications include a strategy and a set of tactics which serve to attain this end, or, if the movement is successful, to defend, stabilize and if possible extend the said state. Within such a state, there is a constant effort to overcome forces hostile to the movement and to apply the various principles as fully as possible.

Thirdly, there is a structured organization which usually consists of a General Staff (often led by a single charismatic figure), a stratum of hierarchised functionaries and a stratum of ideologists.

Fourthly, there are usually practices, rites and symbols expressing commitment to the movement and its unity.

From a certain period onwards, the constitution of a movement of this sort, with some potentially important variants, seems to have been the necessary precondition for any large-scale organization of the vast masses to bring about a utopian transformation of various social, ideological and political traditions. Such a movement needs a social base supplied by dissatisfied masses, whose demands can be voiced. This mass protest can be on the social level, as it was to some extent for early Christianity and as is certainly true of communism; it can also operate on the national level, as in the case of Islam at the time of the conquests, during the first century of the Hegira. As you can see, the definition of this type of movement does not contradict the fundamental theses of Marxism, which we consider to be durable acquisitions for sociology. Indeed, the fundamental core of our argument is, despite some partially contradictory definitions, that historical primacy must be attributed to the history of the struggle between social strata and ethnic groups – here we do depart from the classical formulations – in their competition for the maximum degree of control over persons and goods. Our point is simply that the success of such struggles often involves the formation of a movement of the type defined above. Such a movement succeeds only to the extent that it attracts convinced and dedicated mass support. And it can only attract such support by answering and expressing the aspirations of relevant masses, social 'classes' or ethnic groups; these aspirations must therefore be incorporated into the programmes and principles of such movements.[8] There is one important point here, however, which Leninist thought, for example, has ignored for obvious tactical reasons; namely, that this incorporation is in fact a translation of the relevant aspirations, and can therefore never be completely accurate. The relationships between the masses and their aspirations on the one hand and the movement, as a structural organization and its ideology, on the other, can never be as unilaterally simple as Lenin envisaged. These relationships are in fact dialectical, with all the tensions and conflicts which that implies. Both the organization (with its various layers) and the ideology have a relative but definite autonomy.

A variety of 'religions' could be classified within movements of this type. Historically, the worship of Yahveh was possibly the first of these; although the organization was no doubt very weak when the movement started, it was clearly already established in the time of the Rekabites and the prophetic fraternities led by Elija and Elisha. The Catholic Church, during its first centuries at least, also seems to have exhibited all the characteristics described above, despite the fact that Jesus, its founder, is recorded in the holy book of the movement as being opposed to the adoption of any programme of temporal action. The same is true, it seems, of all universalist religions, at least at some stage in their history. Naturally, such movements can be of considerably different scope. The Jewish 'sects', as they are usually and very inadequately referred to, also seem to have been of this type, although all but the Essenians and probably the Zealots had rather weak forms of organization.[9] Both the Eastern and the Western mediaeval heresies, as well as the various Protestant movements, also fit into our category. And there is a profusion of intermediate examples on the scale between the vast totalitarian ideologies, with their ambitiously universal social programmes, and the more restrained ideologies, such as those of most present-day political parties, whose aims are more modest.[10] These issues call for a much more detailed treatment than we can devote to them here. Let us note, however, that these differences in scope do not have merely cultural causes; they may also stem from the nature, structure and aspirations of the social strata which correspond to the organizations and their ideologies.

Pertinent Historical Variations Within the Two Movements

Before we come to a more precise definition of the two movements whose present relationship we are examining, we must first point out their divergences from the definitions given above. Towards the middle of the Abbasid period, Islam ceased to be characterized by a specific and particular programme established by a single authoritative body whose task it was to realize the programme. It became a pure ideology, as opposed to the militant ideological movement it had been. It is important to remember, however, that a return to the movement's primitive aims, the building of the 'Muslim city', remained the ideal for the Muslim masses, an ideal which tended to shape reality and which remained very much alive, as L. Gardet has shown, albeit possibly with some exaggeration.[11] Various revivalist groups recurrently and more or less successfully took up this ideal, identifying themselves with the real Islam. The Ishmaeli movement is a typical example. Powerful states have also claimed to incarnate the Movement Triumphant, in the face of more or less blatant and profound scepticism on the part of their masses. Examples include the Ottoman Empire and the Sefevid regime. Naturally there was a transition from the utopian stage to the ideological stage, (in the Mannheimian sense), as is the case, at least to some extent, after every triumph.

Islam has been totalitarian to an extreme. Indeed, in principle, it dominated every act and every thought of the faithful. This domination was symbolized, for instance, by the reciting of the *basmala* during even the most trivial actions, and by the *hadith's* universal relevance. All actions, even those arising out of the most elementary biological needs, such as excretion and coition, were regulated by the ideological system. Even social actions of the kind which other cultures considered outside the realm of religion, be they technical, economic or artistic, were integrated into the system and interpreted

41

in terms of it. Any action, institution or idea foreign to the system was either rejected or, when this was not possible, integrated and Islamicized. This did not necessarily exclude a certain level of co-existence with non-Muslim ideological systems, especially when the Muslim character of the state was firmly established; such co-existence was acceptable during the Middle Ages, for example. The point, however, is that national or social struggles were interpreted in terms of Muslim ideology instead of developing their own ideologies. It was as a Muslim opposed to Christianity that one was against the Europeans during the Crusades. It was as an Ishmaeli, as the keeper of the true faith of Islam, that one sought to restrict the privileges of the mighty. The role of the *hadith* in this Islamicization of foreign ideas and values is well known.

This totalitarian aspect of Muslim ideology persisted for a considerable time. One of the best examples is the relatively recent Islamic re-interpretation of Confucian values in China. In 1878 a Chinese Muslim author explained that Fou Hi, the legendary first emperor of China, was a descendant of Adam and had brought the pure Muslim doctrine to China. This doctrine had later degenerated, but important vestiges survived and Confucius had restored the true principles. Confucian ideas, which were taken in China as the expression of the true and the good, could thus be sanctified by linking them to Islam.[12] In the same way Plato has reappeared through the centuries as a disciple of Moses, a precursor of Jesus or of Mohammad.

Today Islam is beginning to lose this totalitarian aspect, just as other religions have lost it. In the last century it has become more and more acceptable that the Muslim people's actions, principles, ideas and values are substantially non-Islamic in origin. A good Muslim can now be inspired by theories and ideologies which have some value aside from Islam, Islamic values and the Muslim ideological system. This became clear the moment people sought to account for the basis of their ideas. Such an issue never arose when non-Islamic systems were simply incorporated into Islam. Today, people are *both* nationalists and Muslims, and their struggle as nationalists to defend national values against Euro-American imperialism, is not necessarily an aspect of Islam. Nonetheless, the old ideal is still prevalent amongst considerable sectors of the population. The Muslim religion retains its totalitarian aims. Movements which are very much alive, the Muslim Brotherhood especially, seek to completely restore Islam's primitive character as a militant ideological movement, and to reimpose its totalitarian hold. States such as Pakistan set themselves the same goals. To a lesser extent several contemporary states express the same aspirations in their constitutions, in a generally less potent form, insisting on their 'Islamic' character and playing on the masses' tendency towards the same ideal.

As for communism, if one traces its origins to the organizations founded by Marx and Engels shortly before 1848, it was not originally totalitarian. It became a little more so in its Leninist form. Something in its particular dynamic, probably in its very nature as a militant socio-ideological movement with its inevitable universalist outlook, increasingly led it towards this outcome.

The Stalinist period, and especially the period of Zhdanovism, brought this trend to its peak, and expressed itself in telling slogans, such as 'Be a Communist 24 hours a day'. The Chinese seem to have gone even further in this direction. On the other hand, there have been phases during which totalitarianism has been minimal. In principle, one cannot be a communist and embrace another ideology at the same time. But the doctrine never took over all the areas of life affected under Islamic totalitarianism. Indeed, values and systems of ideas originating outside communism have very often been accepted as compatible with it.

The Two Movements Face to Face

In the light of what has been said above, we must now examine more closely the two movements whose confrontation we wish to understand.

What does the term Islam mean today? Firstly, from the organizational point of view, it can only refer to: (a) those states having Islam as their official ideology, together with the organized body of religious functionaries whose job it is to represent and express that ideology; and (b) those communities, organizations, fraternities and parties, to a greater or lesser extent independent of the state, whose adopted aim is to defend and propagate this ideology as they understand it, such as the Muslim Brotherhood or Ahmadiyya.

Secondly from the ideological point of view, the term Islam could refer to the set of ideas, beliefs and modes of thought, conscious and subconscious, of contemporary Islamic populations, to the extent that the latter do not consider themselves to have completely broken with the Muslim religion. In this context it is important to note that distinctions must be made according to geographical area and social class; and that contemporary Muslim ideology, or ideologies, only partially stems from the Muslim ideology of the 7th Century. The latter has undergone constant re-interpretation over the centuries. In fact the contemporary condition of the Muslim consciousness or sub-consciousness has two sources: firstly, the ideological tradition; secondly, ideas, beliefs and ways of thinking derived outside that tradition. The ideas, beliefs and ways of thinking which embody the current ideology are a selection both from the range originally embodied in the tradition and from various foreign ideas. This selection has been in response to two main pressures: the inertia of the tradition and, to a far greater extent than most Islamic thinkers realize, the pressure of the contemporary social political and economic situation. The tendency is to retain only those traditional ideas which answer the needs and aspirations of the day, and to re-interpret ideas which have become unusable in their original form so as to fit these new needs. Such re-interpretation is often inspired by completely foreign ideas. The constant re-interpretation of ideologies is one of Mannheim's favourite themes, and the history of ideas in Islam bears him out completely.

What we are dealing with is thus not 'Islam' as a catalogue of dogmas established once and for all during the Middle Ages. The real subject of our enquiry is a sort of *implicit ideology* created by the needs and aspirations of today's Muslim populations. Generally speaking, such implicit ideologies tend to become explicit either by giving birth to a new ideology or, as is more often the case, by transforming and re-interpreting the meaning of ideas, symbols and notions from the national cultural tradition or from outside ideologies whose prestige is on the rise.

There is thus an implicit ideology of the present-day Muslim world. An example which may serve to illustrate what we mean by implicit ideology can be drawn from the contemporary United States of America. A recent book by an American sociologist, Will Herberg, shows clearly and in great detail that the American way of life has transformed the three great religions practised in the U.S.A. from the inside.[13] Thus the dogmas and precepts of Catholicism, Protestantism and Judaism have been re-interpreted to the point where these three religions have become three languages, three very closely related formulations which express more or less the same ideology.

It is crucial to note that Muslim society, even before it had to take up a position *vis-a-vis* communism, has been influenced by scientistic rationalism, or by liberal-humanitarian utopianism, to use Mannheim's terminology. Of course, the effect and intensity of this influence has varied markedly from country to country and from class to class. Nonetheless it has paved the way for the 'introduction' of communism in the Muslim world, as elsewhere.

What we are to understand by 'communism' is not a simple notion either. From the organizational point of view, one must take into account those communist parties which, although no longer institutionally linked since the dissolution of the Comintern, nonetheless still do, to a considerable extent, maintain a common policy, a common ideology, and common practices, rites and symbols. One must also take into account the communist states, those led by a communist party, but which nevertheless enforce a state policy somewhat different from the policy of the corresponding communist party, when necessary.

From the ideological point of view, communist ideology is also something more than a catalogue of dogmas, to be unearthed in the works of Marx, Engels, Lenin, Stalin or Mao Tse-Tung. It is made up of a series of very complex ideological layers. The ideology expressed in the works of Marx and Engels has itself undergone an evolution, even during their lifetimes. It was also later re-interpreted by Lenin, and here too a certain evolution took place during his lifetime. Then there was the Stalinist re-interpretation, or rather re-interpretations, and the more differentiated post-Stalinist re-interpretations.

Three points must be remembered here. Firstly, all these ideological layers act simultaneously through readings of certain texts, which are all treated as classics, with the possible exception of some of Stalin's writings. Just as a Christian can be struck by a certain passage in the Gospels which may seem to him to contradict the ideology of his Church, so a communist may rediscover a text by Marx or Lenin which will set him off on a heterogeneous course.

Secondly, these re-interpretations express themselves in different ways according to the social strata they are aimed at. For instance, the intellectuals and the 'lucid' or 'aware' cadres create for themselves more or less rationalist interpretations of the ideology and the programme, which they express amongst themselves esoterically and not without a certain cynicism. E. Morin has rather oddly referred to this as the Vulgate.[14] A simplified and catechismal version of the doctrine is then offered to the masses, who interpret it in terms of the implicit ideologies already circulating amongst them.

Thirdly, the 'introduction' of communist ideology in underdeveloped countries takes place quite subtly. Certain selected themes and actions of communist propaganda are presented to the people, who then spontaneously select those themes, ideas and actions which answer to their own aspirations.

The Modalities of the Confrontation

I have tried to give an idea of the factors which must be taken into consideration in studying the issue. I will now sketch a brief outline of the problem, which will allow us to see its articulations, its particular difficulties and the lacunae in our investigations.

The first step is to examine the relationships between organizations: states and ideological groupings. This has often been done in the past, albeit not always satisfactorily. A full inquiry would be very involved. We will restrict ourselves to some general conclusions which will hopefully one day be justified in more detail. The relationships between Islamic and communist states and ideological groupings have always been determined by strategic considerations affecting the social struggle within each country and by considerations of international strategy. Ideology has mainly served as an *a posteriori* justification, and has been used to justify diametrically opposed attitudes within the span of a few years. Hostile relations have generally aggravated ideological clashes, friendly relations have generally furthered efforts at ideological conciliation and trends towards peaceful co-existence between the ideologies, be they theoretically expressed or not.

Furthermore the communist organizations' propaganda efforts, and their successes in other areas and on other levels, on top of the friendly relations between organizations, have tended to bring the communists' conceptions to the attention of Muslim populations seeking to formulate their own implicit ideology. Communism has turned out to be particularly well suited to this function, as a result of a series of coincidences and specific compatibilities which I cannot go into now. And yet the dynamic particular to these two movements and their traditions is more likely to promote hostile relations between them. Here, we will consider only the ideological aspect of these relations. As it happens, in the last forty years of history, during which the problem has arisen, there have been a variety of outcomes: clashes, efforts at ideological conciliation, and a trend towards peaceful co-existence.

Clashes

Clashes are the particular effect of this much-talked about and indeed undeniable doctrinal incompatibility between the two ideologies. They represent a first reaction, a normal and natural response which precedes any deeper knowledge of the other. In this sense they are particular cases of the way the normal, general propaganda of each of the ideologies operates. Such clashes are noticeable in two forms.

Firstly there is communism's struggle against Islam. This is a particular case of communism's struggle against all religions, a struggle to which the communist organizations believe their doctrine commits them. In their eyes, religion, as a false ideology which serves the interests of the ruling classes, undermines or mystifies the potential revolutionary consciousness of the oppressed classes. In a society which is in the process of building socialism, religion is a left-over of class society. It diverts the masses from constructive tasks and can serve as a disguise for suspect manoeuvres by the remnants of the expropriated ruling classes or by foreign capitalist enemies. But communist doctrine can also supply another thesis, whose consequences are diametrically opposed to the above conception. Religion is only an ideology, a superstructural phenomenon. It is thus dependant on the infrastructure. Therefore to struggle against it only on the ideological, or even administrative, level would be an idealist method, the practice of fundamentally non-Marxist petty-bourgeois rationalists. The only valid method is to destroy religion's infrastructural base by demolishing class society. It is only once this has been accomplished that propaganda and other superstructural methods can succeed; their role is to clear up the vestiges of the old structure. Furthermore, in the case of a non-socialist society, any programme which puts the struggle against religion in the forefront is based on a fundamental idealist and petty-bourgeois misapprehension. The social struggle must be carried out on the basis of the infrastructural divisions between classes, on the basis of the camps which delimit economic classes and their political and social options. Not on the phantasmagorical basis of ideology, which establishes false and mystified distinctions.

These two positions, which either emphasize or play down the struggle against religion, can both find corroboration in the works of the classical Marxist authors. One or the other is therefore chosen according to the political opportunities available, with the usual *a posteriori* ideological justification.

In non-communist countries the struggle against religion is ideological. In communist countries it can be both ideological and practical or administrative. The particular case of Islam has given rise to numerous well-documented debates in the Soviet Union.[15] Is it a more or a less noxious religion than others? Is it more vulnerable to attack than others? Is it linked to different social strata than others? In the Soviet Union there is a great temptation to resort to arguments drawn from the specific national situation, and this has proved irresistible. Supposedly, Islam has served as a camouflage for the enslavement of the Turkish and Tadjik peoples by the Arabs and it is assumed that it served as an instrument of British imperialism. In the Soviet Union various indices show that the old struggles between Muslims and Christians, notably in the Caucasus, are by no means over, and that they have been used to back up anti-Muslim propaganda. This has been particularly notice-able in the discussion about the historic role of the Shamil.[16]

In the Muslim countries the original minority recruitment of the commu-nist parties allowed for the growth of an anti-religious trend. But this brought a certain unease, since the communists did not wish to perpetuate old religious conflicts, nor to side ideologically with the colonizers. Furthermore, in their desperate effort to reach the Muslim masses, they could not afford to be saddled with an off-hand proclamation of the sort of basic atheism which would be both incomprehensible and repulsive to the population. In the French Maghreb, the French communists, imbued as they were with enlighten-ment ideology, allowed themselves to indulge in an anti-religious polemic which brought them closer to the ambient implicit ideology of the non-communist French, who had nothing but contempt for Islam; the French communists' attitude was in some sense a justification of their reticence as privileged persons to adopt clear anti-colonialist attitudes.

Difficulties soon emerged at every level. The struggle against religion was soon ousted by a compromise, imposed both by religious ideology's mainly passive resistance at home and by its strength abroad. The fact that anti-religious campaigns were useless in general, and even harmful, finally sunk in. There was also a clear temptation to make use of the very ideology which was under attack. In the Soviet Union the incompatibility between anti-Muslim attitudes at home and efforts to sway Islamic governments and masses abroad became a serious issue, which could no longer be avoided. Also there was the problem of reconciling the anti-Arab argument used at home with the efforts to influence Arab governments and masses abroad. Naturally enough, it has always been the anti-Muslim, anti-Arab and anti-religious campaigns which have been sacrificed. Anti-Soviet propaganda, however, has been quick to exploit the after-effects of such campaigns as there were.[17]

The other side of the coin is Islam's struggle against communism. Here, too, we find an immediate response to a first impression. The encounter with communism fitted perfectly naturally into the established context of the Islamic religious cadres' struggle, first against the mediaeval heresies, irreligion, 'debauchery' and the *zandaqua*, then against European-inspired religious indifference and secularism. Islam's past contained a great many precedents justifying a struggle to the death with an ideology such as com-munism. Some thinkers were clearly aware of this continuity, despite the imperfections of their perspective on history. For instance, in August 1953, Sheikh Hasanayn Makhluf, the High Mufti of Egypt, could be heard to say, in his testimony to a tribunal before which communists were appearing, that the communist doctrine was nothing but a continuation of the ideas of mediaeval Ishmaelism, which were themselves based on 'that so-called Greek "philosopher", Plato, who supported the idea of holding women in common'.[18] Just so, in his doctoral thesis, Sheikh Abdurrahman Tag (Taj) denounced the

Babist heresy as a deplorable precursor of communism, in that it 'attempted to achieve purely material goals under the cover of a so-called religious movement . . . to establish an anarchic state of affairs, both in social morals and in the ownership of goods'.[19] This eminent Azharist's viewpoint is curiously close to the thesis of Soviet historians on the subject. His argument is the classical one of all religions, and just as classically finishes with an *ad hominem* argument. Atheism becomes a thesis which apparently justifies debauched behaviour and casting aside of all moral constraints.[20] Once this is established, a political argument can then be tacked on: communism destroys the Muslim people's 'moral fibre' (President Eisenhower's phrase) in order to deliver them to Soviet imperialism. Despite all this, these various arguments are not often invoked in practice. They do have a certain effect on the masses, but to assess the depth and strength of that effect would require a painstaking investigation. The practical weapons of the Muslim religious organizations are also quite effective, apart from their use of propaganda and their constant calls for the state to bring a secular arm into action. For example, in Iraq, it was only recently that a father obtained the right to disinherit his son because the latter was a communist.[21] On the whole, however, the bristling arsenal which the Muslim religion could have deployed against communism seems to have been relatively little used, and with little effect, as is clear on a world scale from the periods of enthusiastic acclaim which the communist states, and even communism itself, occasionally enjoy in the Arab world. This would seem to confirm the Marxist thesis. The ideology inherited from the past has not prevailed against the influence of the implicit ideology imposed by the situation.

2. Ideological Conciliation
As it happens, the indubitable doctrinal incompatibility of these ideologies gives way before various processes of conciliation whenever strategic considerations, both abroad and at home, incline the two movements towards friendship with one another. This conciliation may even sometimes take place without the promptings of strategy. Muslims will willingly borrow ideas from communist ideology whenever such ideas tally with the requirements of their implicit ideology, even when no friendly attitude towards the communist movement is involved. One well-known example of this is the idea of imperialism-colonialism, *isti'mar*, an idea which has been accepted, Leninist connotations notwithstanding, by groups in no way close to communism. The fact is that the Leninist theory, as expounded in *Imperialism, the Highest Stage of Capitalism*[22] is the only theory which can coherently explain to the peoples who have experienced European colonization the main problem they find themselves confronted with.

To take the point further, Muslims commonly re-interpret Muslim ideas and symbols as the equivalents of current communist ideas and themes. This re-interpretation is often made by the communists themselves, as part of their efforts towards an alliance. Where the push towards this re-interpretation has been particularly energetic, there emerges what has been called a form of

Concordat. The term could be generalized to cover a systematic set of re-interpretations.

It is important to remember that Islam has been going through a period during which this type of *Concordat* has been particularly prevalent. There has been systematic re-interpretation of mediaeval Islamic knowledge in the light of European ideas, values and knowledge. The phenomenon is well known and has often been described. The *djinns* become microbes and the mediaeval *ilm* becomes modern science. Islam becomes an advocate of democracy, which should be clear from the *sura* established by the Prophet. The mediaeval Muslims were aware of existentialism and, of course, one only has to look at the Koran to see that it preaches monogamy; the effect of the authorization to have several wives (Koran 4:3) is in fact cancelled out by the exhortation to behave equitably towards them, since another verse (4: 128/129) declares equity towards spouses impossible. The aim is a double one. New ideas can be Islamicized, and thus made accessible to the faithful. At the same time classical Islam is credited with ideas and discoveries which are usually believed to be of European origin. In those cases where the incompatibility is just too obvious, the superiority of Muslim principles is proclaimed ... but again, according to European criteria. Certain contradictions remain inescapable, however, as they did in the numerous previous forms of *Concordat*: for example, in Philon and the Church Fathers' re-interpretation of the Old Testament in the light of Hellenistic thought; the re-interpretation of Christian and Muslim texts in the light of Aristotelianism during the Middle Ages; and the Catholic theologians' re-interpretation of the Bible in the light of 19th-Century science. Thus, the Koran both condemns polygamy and recognizes its occasional usefulness.[23]

Muslims can just as well use the same process in an anti-communist sense, and they do so to a considerable extent. The goal is then to propose social systems and solutions which are proclaimed as authentically Muslim, of Muslim origin or even as the very essence of Islam. Such systems or such solutions are presented as transcending the antinomy between capitalism and communism, as contributing an authentically Muslim line of thought and action. This line, supposedly available ever since the 7th Century, but only recently rediscovered, is treated as both divinely inspired and as the best possible solution to all the problems of social life. However, a careful examination of these solutions, and especially of their translation into practice, quickly reveals a type of thesis which is very current in the Western world, the so-called 'third force' thesis, complete with its typical proposed solutions such as the association of capital and labour. We cannot go into its origin here. We need only point out that such ideas have been canonized by being linked, often quite sincerely, to an authoritative Muslim source. Organizations such as the Muslim Brotherhood, or states such as Pakistan, are particularly inclined to make such re-interpretations. It is on this basis that people are saying that there is 'Muslim Socialism' which one can describe in the same terms one uses to describe the 'French socialism' of a certain period, 'national socialism', etc. The ambiguity and vagueness of the Arabic word *ishtirakiyya* have encouraged this usage. Students of Islam have sometimes been tempted into helping Muslim theoreticians to further the concept, because to do so flatters their own belief in their chosen field of study's specificity. Other contributors have been those economists determined to find a third path which is neither capitalism nor communism.[24] In just this way, Muslim religious elements which are sympathetic either to the communist social system or to the foreign policy of the communist states have favoured an Islamo-communist *Concordat*, re-interpreting the classical ideas of Islam as the equivalents of certain themes from communist propaganda. A certain number of declarations by Syrian, Egyptian and Iraqi Sheikhs have pointed in this direction. Islam is described as seeking the well-being of the people, as opposed to monopoly, and as condemning usury and hence capitalism. But it is usually the ideas of foreign policy put forward by the communist states which attract the most attention. Islam is presented as in favour of peace, and against nuclear tests, foreign bases, racism and colonialism.[25] The point is to show that Islam is not hostile to the values defended by communism, values which evoke the greatest sympathy in the Muslim world because they are the closest to its implicit ideology. The Muslim thinkers who develop such re-interpretations are, in general, religious men, often fervently so, who have no intention of adopting the communists' fundamental atheism. How they react to this atheism, and how they find a way to excuse it, varies from case to case. They can simply refuse to believe that it really exists, or they can see it, as Christians have often done, as a mere appearance beneath which lies a profound attachment to God's designs, and a profound, if distorted, apprehension of the divine. Naturally not everything in such theses is historically incorrect. But the way ideas from the past are declared to be equivalent to contemporary ideas, without any concern for important points of difference, is entirely contrary to the historical approach.

The communists themselves also indulge in similar efforts towards a *Concordat*, although the themes are somewhat different. For communists in Muslim countries, and for those Muslims in the Soviet Union who have adopted communism, the point is to discover an appropriate Islamic tradition. Some make efforts to show that Islam is not essentially hostile to ways of thought analogous to that of communism, or try to defend the Muslim peoples against ideological European right-wing – and sometimes left-wing – accusations, which depict Islam as fatalist, opposed to progress, static, even stagnant. A common procedure is to exalt great Muslims of the past. Sometimes those exalted are ancestors, whose example serves to condemn wealth, and the morals of the rich and the ostentation which highlights the misery of the poor; Abou Dharr, the Prophet's companion, is often cited in this connection.[26] On the other hand, sometimes it is wealthy aristocrats, famous as sceptical philosophers or free thinkers, who are exalted. Such individuals are put forward as having upheld humanitarian, even socialist ideas, and liberal principles, which are equated to communist principles by a prior process of re-interpretation. Furthermore, they are portrayed as advocates of the creative optimism which is the highest value in the communist world, and which is always much appreciated by rising classes, as Max Scheler has shown. *Navoi*, a novel by the Soviet Muslim Aybek, is a highly significant example, the title being a Russian transcription of the Tadjik pronunciation of *'Ali Shir Newa'i*. The hero, a Timurid minister, is cast as a precursor of progressive thought. Naturally there are truthful elements in such a portrait, but the synthesis into which they are integrated turns them into anachronisms.[27] Others, including the present writer, have put Avicenna forward as a communist before his time.[28] The implication is that these great Muslims of the past were part of a great Islamic tradition, and that one aspect of the Muslim religion has a radical content.[29] Islam is presented as a progressive movement, not exactly socialist of course, but democratic, opposed to the wealthy and the oppressors (in whose role the Arab communists cast the Sassanids and the Byzantines, taken as equivalents of present-day imperialists).

It would perhaps be useful here to recall that, for a long time now, the communist parties, the Arab ones at least, have given up presenting the transition to socialism as something other than a distant ideal. Take, for example, this fine piece of bravura by a Lebanese writer, Raif Khoury, a Christian by origin and a faithful Communist Party fellow-traveller, despite his disgrace, during the last few years, as a 'Titoist deviationist'; the extract is from a conference at Damascus on 11 July, 1942:

> How often we have heard the call of the muezzin from the minarets of this eternal Arab city: *Allaho Akbar! Allaho akbar!* How often we have read or been told that Bilal, the Abyssinian, was the first to make the air of the Arabian Peninsula ring with this call, at the time when the Prophet's mission was in its infancy, when he was enduring the persecutions of the persecutors and the obloquy of stubborn conservatives. Bilal's call was a summons, a fanfare sounding the beginning of a struggle between an epoch which was drawing to an end and an age whose sun was just rising. But have you ever dwelt on what was linked to that call, on what it contained? Do you remember, each time you hear the echo of that pristine call, that *Allaho akbar* means, in plain language: punish the greedy usurers! Tax those who accumulate profits! Confiscate the possessions of the thieving monopolists! Guarantee bread to the people! Open the road of education and progress to women! Destroy all the vermin who spread ignorance and division amongst the community (*omma*)! Seek out science, even as far away as China (today's China, not just the China of the past). Let the stars of freedom, of free counsel (*sura*) and of true democracy shine forth![30]

The Arab communists willingly blend appeals to the Arab tradition with appeals to the Muslim tradition. One of the most eloquent texts, in any sense of the word, expressing this point of view is credited to the Syrian communist leader, Khaled Bekdache, a remarkably gifted orator.

And, in the field of national culture, (*ath-thaqafa al-qawmiyya*), we [the Syro-Lebanese communists] have done our duty to the utmost of our ability. We have sought inspiration from the Arab patrimony of freedom (*at-turath al-horr al-arabi*) and we have cherished, in the bosom of our national liberation movement, the best elements of our Arab forefathers' wisdom and tradition. In our political struggle we have adopted that illustrious verse (*al-'aya al-karima*): 'And their concern is the deliberation between them' and that noble *hadith*: 'He who helps the oppressor will have the power of Allah against him'; we have made our own the words of Khalid ibn al-Walid, whose abnegation and devotion are an admirable example to posterity: 'I do not fight for Omar!', and the words of the Arab Caliph, Omar ibn Abd al-Aziz: 'Allah sent Mohammad to show the true path, not to levy taxes', and the words of Jubran Khalil Jubran: 'My idol is freedom' . . . and many other Arab maxims and sayings which have become our mottoes. We have begun to grow because we, unlike some others, do not fear the possibility that such mottoes will reach into the life of the people, that the masses will assimilate them and call for their practical applications in national and social life.[31]

One can see how skilfully Khalid Bekdache uses Arab nationalism to introduce references to the Koran, the Tradition and the Muslim saints. This does not mean that he adopts the religious credo, of course. But the atmosphere created for his audience by such quotations flatters the more traditionalist elements, and shows that the Communist Party, far from brutally opposing the religious tradition, respects and honours it, and even considers itself in some sense the heir of that tradition. A closer look at the quotations in the passage reveals that they are all 'commonplaces' or *testimonia*, which have already been used by the liberal bourgeois generation to show the compatibility of Islam and democracy. Indeed it is generally true that communist ideology has followed in the footsteps of the liberal-humanitarian ideology which preceded it, and from which it was born. This liberal ideology put a great deal of effort and virtuosity into finding precursors from various periods and civilizations, without worrying too much about a correct historical approach.

Faith remains the main difficulty. Of course one can imply that these great Muslims did not believe in God, or not fervently at any rate, and at the very least, they are represented as anti-clerical. But doesn't this implicitly advise the masses to abandon the faith; is it not therefore a piece of anti-religious propaganda, at a time when such attacks are inadvisable, since efforts towards a *Concordat* are being made? One can claim that faith was a necessary illusion at the time. But doesn't this imply that such an illusion is no longer necessary? There is also the danger, especially in the Soviet Union, of a nationalist deviation. Since these great national figures were so close to Marxism, could not the Muslim peoples have achieved socialism without Marx, without Marxism, without Lenin, and without the Russians? Bennigsen is a useful source of further details on this subject.[32]

3. Peaceful Co-existence

In principle, this is the solution preferred by communists and also, probably, by the Muslim faithful. The ideologies remain intangible, no syncretism is attempted, peaceful co-existence and competition prevails. The organizations form an alliance to realize common goals, without going into the intrinsic value of their ideas and principles. This was very much the solution stressed by the French communists at the time of the Popular Front and then during the Resistance and under the tripartite Liberation Government. Thorez and Garaudy referred to it as the 'outstretched hand policy' and Aragon put it into fine verse: 'Celui qui croyait au ciel, celui qui n'y croyait pas'.

Such a solution naturally presupposes a certain number of common aims, negative ones at least, such as the struggle against fascism, foreign domination and colonialism. Despite all the precautions and principles, once the first step towards a political alliance has been made, at least some supporters will feel a strong temptation to go further, towards a *Concordat*. This is what happened amongst the European Christians, as is borne out by the 'Red Dean' of Canterbury, or the pro-communist 'Terre Nouvelle' Christian movement in France around 1936.

Such tactics are fraught with dangers and difficulties. The common goals are justified by each of the two allies in terms of their particular ideology. Supporters may come to add the justification of the ally to their own. This is another temptation which may sometimes lead to syncretism and towards a *Concordat*, in spite of all the precautions taken. The supporters of each camp may, in particular, be troubled by the realization that there are qualities in the other camp which they assumed to be characteristic of their own commitment only. Hence there are temptations to shift sides. The masses, the greatest number of whom are generally not totally committed, may become disoriented. They are called to action in the languages of two partially contradictory ideologies. Of course, they may not perceive such a contradiction, and their ignorance of it may be voluntary, involuntary, or even more or less maintained by the parties concerned. On the other hand the masses may unconsciously resolve the contradiction of a partial re-interpretation of one of the ideologies in terms of the other, or of both in terms of an amalgam, a synthesis, one or the other ideology always being the more influential.

Furthermore, the zig-zag course of international communist strategy from time to time causes sudden changes in the common ideas and goals on which alliances are based. The result has often been a crisis for the communists, since many of them have supported communism on the basis of what were often in fact very different ideologies. To give a well-known example, the German-Soviet Pact of 1939 provoked such a crisis. Many communists supported the aims set by the Communist International in the previous period, namely the struggle against fascism, defence of the French homeland and so forth, on the basis of ideals drawn from the liberal-humanitarian ideology, such as the defence of democratic or even 'bourgeois' rights, and the struggle against inhumane political methods; or from the nationalist ideology, rather than on the basis of the communist ideology with its defence of the socialist state, which could justify such an about-face. *A fortiori*, one can imagine what a crisis this posed for communism's allies. There have been many similar crises in the Middle East, because support for communism or alliances with it have often been made as a function of 'nationalist' aims which were by no means consistently acceptable to the communists.[33]

In the Middle East the implicit ideology developed by the situation has inclined the broad masses (who have remained Muslim), some religious Muslim organizations, and some Muslim states to adopt positions particularly favourable to the foreign policy of communist states and organizations, and to some of the values highlighted by communist ideology. The more lucid elements have generally seen agreement on these options as a sort of alliance, a treaty of peaceful co-existence. But amongst the less enlightened masses, who still keep to the faith and piety of their ancestors, curious reinter-pretations have often been made. It has been assumed that communism could not possibly be contradictory to the Faith, and that those who claimed that it was were slanderers. Many have even assumed that communism was in favour of the Faith. One can imagine how rude the admittedly rare awakening to the reality could be. The absence of any atheistic propaganda by commu-nist organizations in the present period safeguards against such shocks. Only a small intellectual section of the population is aware of dialectical materialism and its implications.

In principle, peaceful competition between the ideologies requires that the two competitors should be on an equal footing and should have access to equi-valent means of propaganda. Obviously, this is not the case in the Soviet Union where, as is enshrined in the 1936 constitution, anti-religious propaganda is a right but religious propaganda is not. But it is quite clear that there is a more general practical impossibility, even given the best possible intentions on both sides (which is not always the case). One ideology always attracts more mili-tants and propagandists than the other, and is better served by the prevailing historical and sociological situation. One could even take up Lenin's termi-nology and speak of a 'law of unequal development' as applied to ideologies.

4. Contact between Ideologies and Relations between Organizations

Above, we have talked very briefly about the relations between Muslim and communist organizations, then a little more thoroughly about the way their ideologies come into contact with one another. Logically, we should now investigate how this relationship between organizations affects the contact between ideologies.

Friendly relations, alliances between states and organizations have obviously been favourable to mutual ideological penetration and to the formation of *Concordats*, despite all the precautions taken by those who sought to go no further than an external alliance and who wanted to avoid any correlation between a strategic alliance and ideological propaganda. The opposite case, that of struggles between states and organizations, has on the whole been unfavourable to such inter-penetration. However, those in opposition within the Muslim countries have often been attracted to the ideology of the foreign opponents for the additional reason that this ideology was under attack from the very state they had set themselves up against. Just so, anti-Muslim propaganda in the Soviet Union has quite possibly brought more-or-less lapsed Muslim opponents of the regime closer to their original faith.

But ideological contact runs deeper than the vicissitudes of political relations. To the Muslim peoples, communist ideology in its present form can largely be interpreted as in conformity with their implicit ideology, as a systematization of their own tendencies. It is therefore quite successful, given certain re-interpretations and difficulties.

Perspectives for the Future

What are the possible outcomes of this confrontation? Several alternatives need to be considered.

1. Firstly, there is the possibility of communism dying out in the Middle East. I hardly think this is very probable in the present period. Indeed Muslim society seems to be evolving towards a stage of class struggles, the battle to decide which sacrifices will be made by which classes in the effort to develop the economy. If this is so, the communist ideology, perhaps in a modified form, perhaps detached from its links with communist states or with some of them at least, seems perfectly suited to serve one section of the population in the struggle. This section may be defeated but can never be annihilated. Furthermore the victorious class may itself be forced to make use of elements of communist ideology.

2. One could also consider Islam dying out. But even if communism were eventually victorious, it seems extremely improbable that Islam would die out. The peoples of the Middle East may perhaps be converted to certain communist values and principles, as has already partly happened, but this does not mean that they are likely to give up their 'organizational' dedication to the Muslim religion, which may even turn out to be due to certain specifically religious values not taken into account by communism. Another factor is the likely value of Islam as a national symbol in an area where secular national symbols are rare, have little tradition behind them and can draw on very few affective values. For instance in the Soviet Union staunch communists of Muslim origin, who have rejected and despise the dogmas of Islam, nonetheless have their boys circumcised, as a symbol of national origin.[34] Finally, Islam may well be very useful as the ideology and symbol of a conservative party, if there is a social struggle. This does not exclude the possibility that the radical camp will also try to use it in this way.

3. Theoretically, one could also conceive of a fusion between the two ideologies. Can one imagine an Islam more deeply communised than is the case today, even in the Soviet Union? Perhaps, but it would still be faced with atheist communism, which would continue to exist. The same problems would still arise. In this context one could even imagine two parallel Islams, one communised and the other anti-communist, in keeping with the state of

the class struggle. In other words, the basic situation would not be essentially different.

4. For the sake of argument, one could even talk of both ideologies dying out. In that case we might be moving into a world with neither utopia nor ideology, the world of *Sachlichkeit* (matter-of-factness) conditionally predicted and dreaded by Mannheim. But this is hardly likely in the foreseeable future.

5. The most probable outcome is therefore the continuation of the present state of co-existence, coupled with a process of mutual influence.

Methods of Study

In conclusion, it seems that the study of the relationships between Islam and communism must take into account various levels which have generally not been understood by those who have written on the subject. We have seen that these levels overlap constantly. I have also tried to show that the study requires the application of sociological theory and perhaps the constitution of new categories. I believe I have demonstrated the necessary distinctions to be made: distinctions between the organizational and ideological levels, distinctions between the phases of organizational strategy, which are often drawn, and distinctions between the evolutionary stages of the ideologies, which are not. I have tried to show that above all one must take into account what I have called the implicit ideology of the present Muslim world, an implicit ideology which is in no way identical to classical Islam, the latter not even being its main source.[35] There are many facts especially in the ideological field, which must be gathered, classified, explained and situated in terms of the categories and types of contact I have attempted to outline. Such facts may, of course, bring about complete or partial revisions of the categories in question.

References

1. B. Lewis, 'Communism and Islam' in *The Middle East in Transition, Studies in Contemporary History*, W.Z. Laqueur (ed.), Routledge and Kegan Paul (London, 1958), pp. 311–24.

2. M. Parmelee in H.P. Fairchild (ed.), *Dictionary of Sociology*, Philosophical Library (New York, 1944), p. 149.

3. See K. Mannheim, *Ideology and Utopia, an Introduction to the Sociology of Knowledge*, Kegan Paul, Trench, Trubner and Co. (London, 1936), for instance, pp. 173–6. I doubt whether the distinction drawn by W. Stark in *The Sociology of Knowledge, an Essay in Aid of a Deeper Understanding of the History of Ideas*, Routledge and Kegan Paul (London, 1958) between ideology (materially self-interested thought) and thought conditioned by social life (but disinterested) takes us very far.

4. W. Montgomery Watt, *Islam and the Integration of Society*, Routledge and Kegan Paul (London, 1961).

5. The early communism of Marx and Engels' days was naturally quite highly organized. But in 1852, after the dissolution of the League of Communists, and in 1873, after the effective dissolution of the First International, the founding fathers joyfully went back to the stage of relying on their intellectual prestige alone to diffuse the ideology.

6. Right from the start, or almost, one must take into account the fact that whole families, clans and tribes would join together the community.

7. The similarities have been noted by J. Monnerat in *Sociologie du Communisme*, Gallimard, (Paris, 1949).

8. Hence the failure of the French 'Colonels' in Algeria, when they tried to apply the recipes of Vietnamese and Chinese communist ideology to the local situation. They built up the cadre structure of a similar movement but did not realize that its ideological content corresponded not at all to the aspirations, tendencies and demands of the masses it was aimed at.

9. Cf. the difficulties faced by Marcel Simon (in *Les Sectes Juives au Temps de Jesus*, P.U.F., (Paris, 1960), p. 5 ff), where he tries to justify it.

10. Cf. the typology established by M. Duverger, *Les Partis Politiques*, A. Colin, (Paris, 1954). The Communist Party prides itself on 'not being just an ordinary party like all the others'.

11. L. Gardet, *La Cite Musulmane, Vie Sociale et Politique*, J. Vrin (Paris, 1954). cf. my critique in *Annee Sociologique* 3rd series, (1960), P.U.F., (Paris, 1961), pp. 365–9.

12. Cf. A. Vissiere, *Etudes Sino-mahometanes*, I.E. Leroux, (Paris, 1911), pp. 120–1, 2nd series, (1913), pp. 45–6 (extracts from *Revue du Monde Musulman*).

13. W. Herberg, *Protestant, Catholic, Jew*, Doubleday, (New York, 1955).

14. E. Morin, *Autocritique*, Jalliard, (Paris, 1959). cf. also Czeslaw Milosz, *The Captive Mind*, Knopf, (New York, 1953).

15. W.Z. Laqueur, *The Soviet Union and the Middle East*, Routledge and Kegan Paul, (London, 1959), pp. 56–60, 175–9; N.A. Smirnov, *Otsherki istorii izutsheniya Islama v S.S.S.R.*, Academy of Science, (Moscow, 1954), summarized by N. Elisseeff, 'L'islamologie en U.R.S.S.', d'apres un ouvrage recent' in *Melanges Louis Massignon*, Vol. II, French Institute, (Damascus, 1957), pp. 23–76.

16. Cf. P.B. Henze, 'The Shamil Problem' in *The Middle East in Transition, Studies in Contemporary History*, W.Z. Laqueur (ed.), Routledge and Kegan Paul, (London, 1958), pp. 415–43.

17. For instance the virulently anti-Muslim pamphlet by L.I. Klimovitch, *Islam, ego proishojdenie i social'naya sushtshnost*, Znanie, (Moscow, 1956), reprinted by Anglo-French propaganda agents during the Suez crisis to fan Egyptian hostility towards the Soviet Union.

18. Agence France Press report from Cairo, (11 August 1953), reprinted in *Le Monde* on 12 August.

19. Abdurrahman Tag, *Le Babisme et l'Islam*, Pichon et Durand-Auzias, (Paris, 1942), pp. 492–3.

20. One example amongst many: the preface to *'Abd al ghafour 'Attar Abbas Mahmoud al-Aqqad, al 'abqariyyat al islamiyyd*, Dar al-fotouh

li-t-tiba'a, (n.d.), (Cairo, 1376/1957).

21. Ner (Jerusalem), Vol. XII, 1/2, (Nov.–Dec. 1960), p. XXVI.

22. Cf. V.I. Lenin, *al isti'mar a'la marahil ar-rasmaliyya*, translated by Rashid al-Barawi, maktabat an-nahda al micriyya, (n.d.), (Cairo, circa 1946), IV, p. 188. Significantly enough, the translator dedicates the work to his 'two sons and their comrades everywhere, that they may grow up inspired to work for the liberation of their homelands from the yoke of isti'mar'.

23. This was put to me by an intelligent, cultured and religious young Algerian Muslim, who was later to become the Algerian Minister of Education. Since then he has published the letter he wrote to me on the subject of Ahmed Taleb, in *Lettres de Prison*, Edition Nationales Algeriennes, (Algiers, 1966), pp. 162–6.

24. For example, J. Austruy, *l'Islam face au development economique*, Economie et Humanisme, Editions Ouvrieres (Paris, 1961). The work is generally rather poorly informed. cf. my critique of this kind of thesis, on historical and sociological grounds, in *Islam and Capitalism*, Penguin, (London, 1974).

25. There have been many declarations on the subject. Many sheikhs have participated in the Peace Movement; for instance, those who participated in the 7th May 1954 feast in Damascus to celebrate the Movement's fiftieth anniversary, cf. *at-Tariq*, (Beirut, June 1954), pp. 1–35. cf. also the sermon pronounced in a Damascus mosque by Sheikh Abdurraziq al Homsi on his return from a journey to the Soviet Union which had obviously filled him with enthusiasm, *Orient*, No. 7, (1958), pp. 177–84. As a final example, let us take the address delivered by the Iraqi Sheikh Abd al Karim al-Mashita to the Iraqi Congress of the Partisans of Peace in April 1959. 'In the name of merciful God, peace be upon you, O partisans of peace. You who seek the good of humanity as a whole and of the men of your country in particular . . . I pray that God may help you in your endeavour and enable you to serve all human children in the world. You must love God and all his servants, for he who loves God also loves his works, and God Almighty rejoices in you because of the succour you bring to your brothers and because of your efforts to put an end to war and to free humanity from the calamities which the Atomic and Hydrogen bomb represent.' (*at-Tariq*, April-May, 1959, p. 86).

26. The Muslim Brotherhood also claim him as one of their own, as an early representative of their 'Muslim socialism'. cf. *'Abd al-hamid Gom'a, al-ishtiraki az-zahid Abou Dharr al Ghifari*, 4th ed., preface by Hasan al Banna', Misr. (Cairo, 1943).

27. Aybek, *Navoi*, a novel, translated from the Uzbek by P. Sletov, Sovetskiy Pisatel, (Moscow, 1946). French translation by Alice Orane, Foreign Language Press, (Moscow, 1948).

28. M. Rodinson, 'La pensee d'Avicenne', *La Pensee*, (Paris), No. 45, (1952) pp. 83–93; No. 46 (1953) pp. 51–7; No. 47 (1953), pp. 85–99.

29. M. Rodinson, 'Allah est-il americain?', *Democratie Nouvelle*, (Paris, May 1955), pp. 28–37.

30. Raif Khoury, *at-torath al gawmi al-'arabi, nahno homato-h, wa mokammilouh*, at Tariq Editions, (Beirut, 1942), p. 7. cf. also an article

by the same author published in 1946 in *at-Tariq*, Vol. 5, No. 23–4, pp. 3–4, summarized by M.S. Agwani, *Communism and the Arab East*, Asia Publishing House, (London, 1969), p. 52.

31. Khaled Bekdache, *al-hizb ash-shoyou'i fi n-nidal li-ajl al-istiqlal wa-s-siyada al wataniyya*, (Beirut, 1944), p. 58. (Speech to a Congress of the Syro-Lebanese Communist Party held in Beirut, 31 December 1943 to 2 January 1944).

32. Notably A. Bennigsen, 'Les peuples musulmans de l'U.R.S.S. et les Soviets', *l'Afrique et l'Asie*, (1952), No. 4, pp. 10–26; (1953) No. 1, pp. 13–30; No. 2, pp. 21–32; No. 3, pp. 15–34.

33. See 'Marxism and Arab Nationalism' in this volume.

34. H. Carrere d'Encausse, *Cahiers du Monde Russe et Sovietique*, (April-June 1962), p. 222 ff. cf. V. Monteil, *Les Musulmans Sovietiques*, Seuil, (Paris, 1957), p. 162. A similar attitude is often a stage on the psychological road to renewed faith. It is fairly common in Israel, for example.

35. J. Berque's *Les Arabes d'Hier à Demain*, Seuil, (Paris, 1960), contains a great deal of subtle and sharp analysis of this implicit ideology. My only reproach is that he does not distinguish clearly enough between the psychological level and the ideological level, in other words between mentality and social idea-forces endowed with a vigorous dynamism of their own. (cf. also my review in *L'Annee Sociologique*, (1960), 3rd series, P.U.F., (Paris, 1961), pp. 371–4.)

4. Problems Facing the Communist Parties in Syria and Egypt

Syria and Egypt occupy a very special position in the Arab world at the moment. Within very different contexts and as the result of very different circumstances, the governments of these two countries have adopted an international policy characterized by a desire for independence from the two great powers which dominate the world scene. This desire for independence is especially manifest in relations with the Atlantic Alliance, for the simple reason that it has been the member countries of the latter which have recently made the greatest efforts, by all and every means available, to bring the Arab countries of the Middle East into the Western political and military system. The so-called neutralist policy of the Syrian and Egyptian governments has quite clearly evoked enthusiastic approbation from large segments of the population in their respective countries. Indeed, such a policy touches deep-seated and ancient aspirations amongst the Arab peoples of the Middle East. Given that these tendencies had been kept down for years, often by the roughest of methods, as they still are in many parts of the Arab world, it is hardly surprising that when they surfaced in Egypt and Syria, they did so with an almost irresistible force. Hence an effervescence, an ebullience on every level, and a type of intellectual activity characteristic of the major revolutionary periods, periods when great masses, whose aspirations have long been ignored, finally see these aspirations being recognized by new leaders. Such leaders soon find themselves both followed and pushed onwards by the masses, whether or not they owe their rise to power to them.

Syria and Egypt are united by a common political line and by the deep-seated feeling that they thereby give exemplary expression to the real tendencies of the Arab population of the Middle East. The leaders of these two countries know that their words and actions find an intense echo amongst all the peoples of the area, who follow, admire and passionately comment on their every gesture. And the leaders of Iraq, Lebanon and Jordan, are well aware that the Syrian and Egyptian leaders enjoy far more support amongst the Iraqi, Jordanian and Lebanese people than they themselves do. They are therefore conducting a desperate rear-guard action, and from time to time are forced to find ways of diverting the constant pressure from the masses. But they know full well that they will not be able to stand against so unanimous a popular opinion for long – given that the general situation remains the same, of course. Currently, the common destiny of Syria and Egypt finds its fullest expression in the presently successful project of federal unity. Such a union is open, having no reason to reject applicants from other Arab countries where the popular will has finally found the means to come to the fore. There now exists a core, around which, given favourable circumstances, the dream of several generations may come true: the dream of a united Arab state.

Naturally enough, the real meaning of these facts has been distorted and misunderstood in Europe, especially in France. Prejudices, prevalent enough even before the official propaganda campaign, and now aggravated by the latter, prevent any positive appreciation of Arab nationalism. The most absurd colonialistic cliches, a mixture of traditional missionary literature, espionage novels and Israeli propaganda, still have an extraordinary influence, even on the left. Much is made of 'Muslim fanaticism', a particularly revealing cliche, whilst a whole movement of intellectual and social renovation is ignored, despite the fact that it dominates the Arab world.

This is the framework of ignorance within which vested interests' particular version of events, according to which a communist conspiracy has determined the direction of events in Syria and Egypt, may actually find an audience. There is indeed some truth in the assertion that the communist movement has played a certain role. But there is a big gap between the legend and the facts; we shall concentrate on the latter.

The Syrian and Egyptian Communist Parties: Some Differences

The backgrounds of the Egyptian and Syrian communist movements are very different. The Syrian Communist Party, which is now once again Syro-Lebanese, after a short separation,[1] is a Communist Party on classical lines. It was formed on the basis of strong links with the international centres of communism, and it has already enjoyed long periods of legality or semi-legality, during which it was able to form its cadres and formulate its principles of action. Several of its oldest leaders studied in Moscow. It has long been treated as an equal by the great Western and Eastern communist parties. It grew without major internal problems, splits or large-scale purges, and without much theoretical discussion. It became a serious, solid, enduring body, which was the envy of all the other communist parties of the Middle East.[2] Its leader, Khaled Bekdache, today the first and only communist deputy in the Arab world, is a powerful personality, an orator whose talent is recognized even by his enemies, an intelligent and flexible individual, devoid of any sentimental attachment to ready-made formulas, rigid conceptions or out-of-date positions. He has nothing of the bureaucrat or the dogmatist about him, and has a far-seeing readiness to initiate new ventures.[3]

In contrast, the 'United Egyptian Communist Party', founded only in June 1957, was born of the fusion of several groups, including the 'Egyptian Communist Party' and the 'Unified Egyptian Communist Party', which were themselves the outcome of a complex and troubled history.[4] The communist groups in Egypt have a long history of mutual bickering, slander and virulent sectarianism. They have been through an endless series of splits, purges and partial re-unifications. Locally formed, in the context of almost permanent illegality and particularly merciless police persecution, they have often sought in vain for contacts with the major foreign communist parties. The latter tended to view these apparently sectarian and inefficient groups of petty bourgeois and intellectuals with suspicion and some disdain, especially as each group was always clamorously denounced by all the others. Throughout, the Egyptian communists made great efforts to elaborate a strategy and tactics in keeping with their general Marxist principles and their own analyses of the local situation. This was not accomplished without a measure of violent controversy, which was generally conducted in the prisons and concentration camps. From their own account, they have been guilty of every error, of every deviation, as is borne out by the frequency and number of their self-criticisms.[5]

The Decisive Choice

The fundamental approach of the Syro-Lebanese Communist Party was set down around 1936. In the Egyptian communist movements, on the other hand, the main tendencies only crystallized in the period 1942-50. This difference was to have serious implications.

Everything revolved around one fundamental option, which depended on the answer given to a particular question: was it possible to prepare a socialist revolution in Syria and Egypt, or at least a revolution led by proletarian forces, workers and peasants, and bring to power a group of men determined to work towards the country's transition to socialism? Or was it the case that any efforts in this direction — which implied a break between the proletariat and the nationalist bourgeoisie and petty bourgeoisie, and furthermore ran the risk of provoking foreign intervention — could in fact only lead to a defeat, a reinforcement of imperialist influence and the endangering of existing socialist countries?

Under the conditions prevailing in 1936, there was no doubt as to which answer the Syro-Lebanese Communist Party would choose. Stalinist pessimism excluded the possibility of proletarian revolution anywhere in the world, even China. Fascism was so menacing a danger to the existing socialist world, limited at the time to the Soviet Union, that all forces had to be directed against it. Above all, the one established bastion of socialism could not be allowed to fall. In France, Popular Front policies prevailed and the Syro-Lebanese Communist Party was very closely linked to the French Communist Party at the time, as Syria was under French mandate.

In France, the Communist Party appealed to national feeling, showing how the traditional goals of French foreign policy coincided with the aims of the anti-fascist struggle. In Syria and Lebanon the Communist Party also geared the essential part of its offensive to the achievement of a national goal, which, paradoxically, was independence from French imperialism. This position implied various nuances: the maintenance of friendly relations with Popular Front France, the avoidance of any indiscriminate anti-French chauvinism, and of course a total rejection of any attempt to seek out the aid of Anglo-French imperialism's main enemy, German-Italian Fascism. Many Arab bourgeois nationalists favoured such an alliance with fascism. The party, by contrast, relied on the Soviet Union, theoretically an ally of France.

Such a line was not always easy to keep to. It only became so as the fascist bloc lost more and more ground, then collapsed, as the Soviet Union came to the fore and was seen to be protecting the independence of the countries of the Levant. The Syro-Lebanese Communist Party, the champion of national independence and of the anti-imperialist struggle, was to benefit more and more from this increasingly popular platform, and soon lost any reservations about claiming that this platform was a complete expression of the Party's ideas.[6]

Was there any opposition to this basic orientation? Were there elements within the Party who argued for a policy of class struggle and action geared to a rapid revolutionary seizure of power? The Party's monolithicism denies us answers to such questions. Some reshuffling did in fact take place within the leadership, but in general very little is known about why some fell from grace, temporarily or permanently, whilst others were promoted. There was talk, about 1950, of some comrades' criticisms of Party policy, and also of Titoist demands for more democracy within the Party; the latter, however, were unmasked as the work of elements who were typically described as 'spies having close links with the Anglo-American and Yugoslav embassies, as well as with circles dependent on the Deuxieme Bureau and the Surete Generale in Syria and Lebanon'.[7] In a November 1955 interview, Khaled Bekdache referred to colonialist agents and Zionist elements who had sought to divide the communist movements, 'by detaching them from the soil of their country, by separating them from the popular republics and the national patriotic movement'.[8] In any case, even if there was some sort of opposition, it was easily defeated and the Party seems to have suffered very little from the whole episode.

In Egypt, on the other hand, the ideas of the communist groups crystallized during a very different and more recent period of history. The Soviet victory of 1945, the Chinese and Yugoslav revolutions, the setting up of other people's republics within the Soviet sphere of influence, not to mention the hopes raised by the internal evolution of other countries such as France and Italy, all made it possible not to exclude out of hand the hypothesis of an imminent revolution.

One must also remember that the social situation seemed much more revolutionary in Egypt than it did in Syria or, especially, in Lebanon. Egyptian social problems were more manifestly tragic, urgent and catastrophic; class divisions were much sharper. No serious reformist movement had ever managed to gain even the beginnings of a mass audience. The poor, the mass of the peasants, the petty and middle bourgeoisies had reached the point where they viewed any proposed revolutionary solution favourably, since no other programme could be taken in the least bit seriously. They welcomed the prospect of communism without fear or agitation.

Naturally the primary aim was still the struggle against Western imperialism. But certain highly influential communists felt that this could rapidly turn into a struggle for power, leading up to a transition to popular democracy. This perhaps partly explains why the 1952 putsch, which brought the 'Free Officers' junta to power, was seen in some quarters as a mere episode in the imperialists' struggle amongst themselves – an American coup against the British, for example; others, without denying this aspect categorically, saw it mainly as an event in the social struggle, a victory of this or that fraction of the bourgeoisie (the 'middle' bourgeoisie, they called it) and therefore as a stage on the road to the revolution. However, the choice was not a clear and explicit one. Practically none of the several rival communist tendencies excluded the possibility of revolution, hence they could all think of the current struggle as being, at least to some extent, a step towards a more or less imminent revolution. The contrast with Syria, where Khaled Bakdache had long ago rejected the possibility of any socialist outcome for the near future, was particularly marked.

The Evolution towards Neutralism and the Communists' Role in Syria

Syria and Egypt's evolution towards neutralism was a slow and complex process, full of backward steps and changes of heart. We will not go into all the internal and external factors which conditioned it. Suffice it to say that the main ones were the Western politicians' almost total lack of understanding of the Arab bourgeoisie's aspirations, and their frenetic and clumsy efforts to press-gang this bourgeoisie into a crusade for which it had no stomach whatsoever. The Arab bourgeoisie did not feel threatened by any Soviet menace on the foreign policy level, as perhaps the Iranian and Turkish bourgeoisies did. At home the fact that the communist movements stressed almost exclusively national demands reassured it, and the possibility that, perhaps eventually, in the distant future, the bourgeoisie would have to struggle against a move towards socialism, hardly seemed to justify any serious sacrifice in the here and now. The many bitter experiences of the past put Britain and France in the worst possible light, and the same applied to the U.S.A., to the extent that the latter supported the former. The Soviet Union, on the other hand, generally had backed Arab demands. The straw that broke the camel's back was the Baghdad Pact, that clumsy attempt to give faithful satellite Turkey a dominant position within the Middle East. The move aroused considerable anxieties amongst all the Arabs, who had, after all, until only recently been under Turkish domination. Syria was both resentful and irredentist on the subject of the Sanjak of Alexandrette, granted, in Syria's name in 1938, by France to Turkey. There were also constant Turkish threats and claims upon the Aleppo region. The officers in power in Egypt were furious at the idea of being subordinated militarily, as was proposed. And as for the religious and patriotic masses, they were nothing if not leery of this recently secularized Turkey which had allied itself with Israel.

These attitudes could, of course, have been counter-balanced by the dread of a proletarian revolution. But — and it is in this way that one can say that the communists influenced the orientation towards neutralism — this was not on the cards. On the contrary the communists supplied the ideas, the methods, the slogans and the cadres which were so necessary to an emerging fundamentally neutralist body of opinion. The two orientations were conjoined to their mutual advantage.

As we have seen, the Syrian Communist Party had long treated the struggle for independence, and its extension, the struggle against imperialism, as its main priority. Using tried and tested formulas developed elsewhere, it had succeeded in building the only mass party worthy of the name in the country. It had attracted a considerable number of efficient and disciplined militants, under the banner of a leader who enjoyed considerable prestige even amongst non-communists. The Party's commitment to the national struggle had never been compromised. The Soviet Union's acceptance of a Jewish state, in the United Nations in 1947, caused a momentary setback and made it possible for the party to be outlawed. But the Soviet Union's subsequent support for the Arab cause soon cancelled out this effect.

As for the party's attitude towards social problems, it was quite comforting for a sizeable part of the bourgeoisie, at least. Khaled Bekdache has often said that his party was not at the present stage struggling for socialism. In a speech in the Syrian chamber of deputies, on 18th January, 1955, he could still be heard to say that socialism was a higher stage of the struggle which would only come much later. To my knowledge, his clearest declaration on the subject is his report to the Party Congress at the beginning of January 1944:

Anybody who reads our 'national pact'[9] will find it devoid of any mention of socialism. It contains not a single expression or demand tinged with socialism. It is nothing more and nothing less than a democratic national pact. And this is our programme for the stage of national liberation, on which we shall concentrate all our efforts and all our struggles until our country has accomplished it and realised it completely. This is no climb-down from our principles . . . Far be it from us to formulate recipes to be learnt by rote or cliches supposed to apply to every situation and valid for every country . . . It is clear that our country, which still suffers under the imperialist yoke and from an economic, agricultural and industrial backwardness, cannot aim to set up a socialist regime. The only goal it can set itself is that of national liberation and the rejection of those vestiges of the Middle Ages which still prevail in its economic and intellectual life . . .

We are a revolutionary party, it is true. That means that we want to see a revolution in our lives and in our society. But the revolution which our country must undergo is not a socialist revolution, but a national democratic revolution.

We have heard claims, from both well- and ill-intentioned people, that our party is only a party of social reform. This expresses a definite lack of understanding, be it real or feigned. Our Communist Party of Lebanon and Syria is, above all and primarily, the party of national liberation, the party of freedom and independence.[10]

In order to achieve this goal, Khaled Bekdache calls on all classes to form a sacred union. He elaborated on this theme in an interview given on 25th May, 1945 to the Party's main journal:

> The Syrian Communist Party, which is the party of the workers and peasants, believes that the new era which is called for in Syria will require the enforcement of a policy which, on the one hand, aims to protect workers' rights and, on the other hand, protects and encourages national enterprises. The great path which lies before the workers leads to the organization of their own trade unions, to the setting up of a democratic labour legislation, which will serve as the starting-point for a harmonization of industrial relations and solutions to the conflicts between workers and employers, solutions based on social justice and the general national interest . . . The present demands of the Syrian workers, such as shorter working hours, freedom to organize trade unions democratically, compensation for industrial accidents and for dismissal, unemployment benefit and social security, are all demands which are in no way extremist and which national employers have no need to fear. The best course for the national employers is not to reinforce industry by the exploitation of their workers — this is a method which in no way guarantees the blossoming of industry — but by demanding that the government protects their production, facilitates their access to raw materials and the importation of modern machinery.[11]

Later texts did not go back upon this fundamental orientation; in fact they promised landowners, industrialists and shopkeepers that there would be no nationalization of their businesses, be they large or small.

One may wonder in what way such a party is communist. But it is. The next stage, however distant, is still conceived of as that of the socialization of the means of production. Efforts are still made to defend the interests of the working class, as far as everyday demands are concerned at any rate, although no structural reforms which would extend such struggles are called for. The methods of organization and propaganda are still very much those of the classical communist party of the Stalinist era, complete with all the advantages and inconveniences which they entail, notably a remarkable efficiency in agitation. There is still a passionate interest in the defence of the socialist world on a world scale. Finally there is the fact that the struggle against Western imperialism is still conceived of as linked to the long-term interest of the

Syrian working classes.

Naturally some contradictions do emerge. The suggested harmonization of relations between workers and employers is not easily put into practice. What is one to do when the exploiting employer or landlord is a firm supporter of national liberation? 'Stand by the exploited, despite everything,' says Khaled Bekdache. But this is not always without its drawbacks, especially in the context of general measures 'supporting national industry'.

Nevertheless, this Communist Party has succeeded in reaching significant portions of the masses. Popular enthusiasm for the national struggle, of which the Party seemed the staunchest defender, cancelled out any minor contradictions. The intelligentsia and the middle classes were seduced by the fact that the communists provided an ideological and economic vocabulary within which the national struggle could be expressed. Marxist and Leninist ideas on the imperialist tendencies of capitalism made considerable headway at every level of society. The result was extensive wariness towards any Western manoeuvre, and a certain open-mindedness towards Soviet initiatives. The Soviet Union's respect for 'young' nationalities, contrasting so strongly with the Atlantic powers' attempts to press-gang them, could only reinforce such attitudes.

The only factor which threatened this favourable situation was the 'two camps' policy elaborated by Zhdanov and pursued during the last period of Stalin's life. It was never in fact strictly applied in the Soviet Union's relations with the Arab Middle East. But its formulation and its repercussions were enough to cause considerable damage. Although the Syrian and Lebanese communists were in no way servile towards Moscow, their understanding of the situation was influenced by Zhdanovist principles. They thus, from time to time at least, came to take a sectarian attitude towards any neutralist elements amongst their compatriots, especially when these neutralists dared to call themselves socialists. To the communists this seemed to be a demagogic encroachment on their own territory, a dangerous and suspicious manoeuvre. It is possible, as W.Z. Laqueur suggests — though this needs checking — that during this period the defence of the workers' claims against the employers, and of the poor and middle peasants' claims against the feudalists, took a more radical turn. It must be appreciated, in any case, that such struggles were never abandoned. This is probably the sense in which the following extract from the important 1951 report by Khaled Bekdache, already quoted from, is to be interpreted.

The progress we have made amongst the working class and the peasantry has been slow, and were it to continue at such a rate it could not produce the required results quickly enough to meet the needs of the international and internal situations' development. We must thus make some fundamental changes in our political and organizational approach and in our work amongst the masses; this is a decisive turning-point, which some comrades have called a revolution.[12]

In the post-war years, essentially petty-bourgeois and intellectual parties and political tendencies developed, whose declared ideal was socialist and whose foreign policy programme was neutralist. The history of these parties — the most important of which is the Ba'ath Party, the party of the Arab renaissance — and their relations with successive governments, their more or less underhand dealings, and their ideological toing and froing is extremely complex. The Communist Party denounced them and at one stage even considered that one of its most important tasks was to 'expose them', as subtle exploiters of the growing popularity of socialist ideals, as denigrators of the 'peace camp' in that they called on the masses to support a 'so-called third force' rather than the Soviet Union.

Quite possibly the new orientation marked by the 1951 report was, at least partially, a response to the fear that by insisting on exclusively national aims the Communist Party was losing touch with those of the popular masses who were particularly concerned with social demands and were thus particularly susceptible to the intensely 'socialist' propaganda of the non-communist left-wing movements. Hence Khaled Bekdache's insistence that no compromise be made with the nationalist exploiters which might damage the Party's prestige amongst the masses.[13]

This did not prevent these 'socialist' movements from becoming more and more successful. Amongst other things, they benefited from a certain wariness towards the communists amongst the not strictly proletarian part of the masses. As the national and international situation changed, the communists were forced to change their attitude towards these groups. The new ideological atmosphere which prevailed in the international communist movement after Stalin's death, and especially after the 20th Congress of the Communist Party of the Soviet Union, tended to facilitate this change of attitude. A *de facto* alliance between the communists and the neutralist socialists was established, and doubtless played a considerable role in the Syrian domestic situation's evolution towards a victory of the nationalist and neutralist forces. The Soviet Union's own attitude was naturally crucial in this respect.[14]

At the moment, the Communist Party is supposedly illegal. But its general secretary, Khaled Bekdache, sits in the Chamber of Deputies, where he has considerable influence. Most recently the course of events seems to have forced the Party to work more for the implementation of its ideas, albeit by its adversaries or by dubious characters, than for the strengthening of the Party as such. Although we have no specific information on the subject, it is probably safe to assume, knowing something of the Syro-Lebanese Communist Party, that the latter objective is nonetheless not being completely neglected.

The Influence of the Egyptian Communists

In their own way, the Egyptian communists were moving towards similar positions. We have already noted the factors common to both Egypt and

Syria, which pushed the national bourgeoisie towards neutralism. We have seen that the Egyptian communist groups adopted contradictory attitudes towards the 'Free Officers' movement. Their internal struggles over the characterization of this movement, their hesitations, critiques and self-criticisms could fill a whole volume.

The core of the military movement, in which all the contradictions of an ardently nationalist bourgeoisie were reflected, had to find its way through a maze of fluctuating ideas. The communists quite clearly had a definite influence on some members of the Council of the Revolution, but this influence was not exclusive, and varied from person to person. The new rulers were, in fact, young and rather ignorant. Here again, the communists supplied a nascent nationalist anti-imperialist force with the arguments and ideological cadres it needed. According to one story, when the most senior leaders of the military movement were on the verge of accepting a considerable American loan, they summoned a Marxist theoretician, the translator of Marx and Lenin into Arabic, who gave them a lecture on imperialism as the highest stage of capitalism. They refused the loan. The story is typical.

When Nasser recaptured the monopoly of power by ousting Neguib, who sought to bring back parliamentarism and political parties, he did so after a press campaign which had used all the Marxist arguments as to the merely formal character of bourgeois democracy. Marxism had permeated the movement.

This did not stop Nasser persecuting the communists, sometimes cruelly. Certain communist leaders suffered barbaric torture in Nasser's jails. But, as the military became increasingly disenchanted with Western policy and as they gradually and naturally moved closer to neutralist positions, the pressure was taken off, and more and more communists were released and granted a certain freedom of action, albeit under close surveillance.

There were several very valuable technicians amongst the communists, economists especially. These were appointed to various posts and some went almost directly from the torture chambers to the ante-chambers of power. Nasser set up his own 'constructive' pet opposition, with two newspapers, one of which was directed by Anwar es-Sadat, a member of the Council of the Revolution, whose ideological stance had in the past tended towards Fascism. The other paper was directed by the Council's youngest member, Khaled Muhieddine, an ultra-left sympathiser who had been instrumental in bringing Neguib back to power after the latter's sacking in 1958 and who had himself been inconspicuously exiled to Geneva after Nasser's final victory. His stay in Switzerland gave him the opportunity for a formative period of study. Both papers were edited by teams full of Marxists and socialist sympathisers of every sort. Meanwhile communists were still incarcerated under the most horrible conditions in the Kharga Oasis concentration camp. Recently, after a long break, a few communists have again been arrested, tried and sentenced. The regime still wants to show that it has a line of its own.

Faced with this evolution, after a long period of confusion and division, the communists have finally come round to an attitude of increasingly firm and uncritical support for the regime. Nasser's attitude after the U.S.A.'s refusal of credits for the construction of the Aswan Dam, and his national leadership during the Suez Crisis have accentuated this support and made it more apparent. Clandestine or semi-clandestine communist publications, as well as legal publications inspired by communists or by communist sympathizers, are full of extravagant eulogies. Nasser has become the national leader rather in the way that de Gaulle was, during the Resistance, when the French communists could think of themselves as 'the most committed Gaullists'.

This development was accompanied, as we have seen, by a quasi-total unification of the various communist groups. This does not mean that the new 'United Egyptian Communist Party' does not contain several more-or-less divergent tendencies. Although apparently all are now agreed on the broad lines of the policy to be followed, there are still nuances. The old leaders of the original 'Egyptian Communist Party', who saw the military movement as essentially an episode in the struggle between imperialists, now seem to have a considerable degree of influence in the new central committee. Ironically enough, and logically perhaps, they are now the strongest advocates of committed support for Nasser. By contrast, it is those elements who were on the look-out for any opportunity of social revolution, and who thus paid much more attention to the movement's potentially progressive character, who are now the most critical, who stress that their support for Nasser is conditional, and who reiterate the need to think of the next stage, of how to reinforce the Party as such, and of the road to socialism. At the moment, however, they do not have major influence.

Pragmatism and Theorization

The Syrian Communist Party was formed, as we have seen, in the communist tradition of the Stalinist period. It does not tend to make any changes in its outlook particularly explicit, and is proud of the somewhat artificial continuity of its line. Its leaders, especially Khaled Bekdache, are essentially men of action, who have no liking for profound ideological re-evaluations. They lead a mass party whose main appeal has been its national policy and which has to some extent neglected the theoretical education of its members, as has been officially noted. The Marxism they use to justify their political positions, and the adaptation of the latter to circumstances, is a simplified and somewhat static version, which they have themselves received from outside. This does not mean that they are incapable of a more intense level of theoretical investigation, nor even that they might not have carried out such investigation in the secrecy of the Party council chambers. But I know of no evidence of such efforts. By contrast, the new Egyptian Communist Party, which was born in such unusual circumstances, has few adherents, at least if one takes into account only the paid-up members and not the masses whose enthusiastic support is readily available but who play no active role within the party. On the whole, what members there are are mainly intellectuals who have joined essentially because of the social possibilities opened up by communism, and who have spent years discussing the future of socialism in Egypt, and the strategies and tactics needed to accomplish it. At least some of its leaders, for all that they are political militants, are also very cultured men who have undertaken original research into various subjects. From a difficult start has come a certain superiority in theoretical enquiry.

It is thus not surprising that the more significant attempts at a theorization of the present phase have been made in Egypt. The internal bulletin of the new United Egyptian Communist Party, which is duplicated, contains a particularly interesting article signed 'Khaled', the pseudonym used by the old secretary of the Egyptian Communist Party, which is now perhaps being used by a different member of the Central Committee.[15]

By means of some skilfully chosen quotations from Stalin and Zhdanov, Khaled demonstrates yet again Marxism's living ability to mould itself to an endlessly changing reality. He lays great stress on the importance of the 20th Congress 'whose lessons we have not yet fully grasped'. 'It represents' he adds:

> a revolution in the parameters of our thinking about Marxism-Leninism, a revolution which frees Marxism-Leninism from all dogmatic petrification and from all empiricist inertia, which frees it from all isolationism and from all dead primitivism. The 20th Congress is an appeal to all the communists in the world to re-examine critically and self-critically all their erroneous, petrified or primitivist ideas of Marxism-Leninism . . .
>
> The 20th Congress has proclaimed that today's world is a new world. Socialism is this new world's essential force, which grows stronger every day, whilst imperialism is a force which is constantly fading; capitalism and imperialism are heading for their allocated stands in the museum of history. Have we really grasped this, or shall we say, like the reactionaries, the reformists and the opportunists, like all the enemies of the 20th Congress, that the latter only repeats the ideas of Bernstein, Millerand, Kautsky and Trotsky? [Such a fundamental change of outlook obviously required a new approach to Egypt's problems.] The 20th Congress has signalled the end of the time when a single thinker did all the thinking for the Marxists of the whole world . . . We Egyptians must now forge our own theory of our country's progress, based on our daily experiences . . . We must work out solutions whose roots lie in our own heritage, and let ourselves be guided by the theses of Marxism-Leninism as applied to the contemporary world.

Starting from this idea of the need for a new approach to Egypt in the light of Marxism's fundamental teachings, Khaled stigmatizes both empiricists and dogmatists, and suggests to his comrades that they ponder 'a few facts concerning the Egyptian revolution, our national bourgeoisie and our working class'.

'The Egyptian revolution', he argues, 'is a new kind of national democratic bourgeois revolution which took place in advanced international and local circumstances.' It can be compared to no previous revolution. The Egyptian national bourgeoisie too is of a new kind: 'It is progressive, in a world where capitalism is in its death-throes.' Whilst it is true that this bourgeoisie bases itself on the exploitation of wage-labour, it nonetheless cannot achieve the primitive accumulation of capital in the same way that the French or English bourgeoisie did, at the expense of the working people. Similarly it neither can, nor seeks to, establish monopolies; on the contrary it opposes monopolies and puts spokes in their wheels.

> It is a bourgeoisie through which socialist thought percolates, a bour-
> geoisie linked to world socialism because the latter is the only regime
> which can and wishes to help it develop its country. It is not a class which
> tends towards socialism or which fights for it. But it is a class which has
> learnt by experience that it cannot progress in its own country without
> the support of the socialist camp abroad and of the popular classes at
> home. Its future growth lies neither in capitalism nor in socialism but in
> state capitalism.
> Between the national bourgeoisie and the working class there will
> always be class struggle, but this struggle takes place within the bounds
> of a national alliance between the two classes.

This struggle and this alliance are two aspects of the same phenomenon. In the course of the struggle the working class educates the bourgeoisie, even while defending its own interests. Gradually it asserts its leading role in the national front, strengthens its necessary alliance with the peasant masses, and paves the way for the passage to socialism under its leadership and that of its Communist Party. This leadership role will not be achieved by any amount of futile chatter about the necessity of working class hegemony but

> by our calm and indefatigable struggle within and at the forefront of the
> masses, appearing in every domain in our capacity as patriots just like all
> other patriots, distinguished from those others only by the fact that, thanks
> to the teachings of Marxism-Leninism, we are firmer, more courageous,
> more far-seeing patriots, who have greater confidence in the masses.

The Grand Alliance . . . and After?

The stage of a grand alliance with the national bourgeoisie had long ago been defined in Syria, by Khaled Bekdache, as the Communist Party's policy for the time being. His analysis of Egypt (published under a pseudonym) set out, a little rashly perhaps, not only to establish the theoretical foundations of such a stage but also to initiate a study of its dynamic and its long-term perspectives. Perhaps it was that the Egyptian communists had more confidence, rightly or wrongly, in the continuity of their Government's political line than did the Syrians. It would then make sense for them to study more closely the consequences of a line which in the Syrian perspective was more to be imposed than debated. Let us assume that today's essential problem will be resolved, that Western attempts to press-gang the Arab world will be totally repulsed, as has happened in India. What then will be the role of the Communist Party? If it wants to avoid the restricted horizons implicit in a struggle confined to the defence of the everyday interests of the working classes, without any broader or more far-reaching perspectives, if it is not content with the diminished influence which would go with a limitation of its agitation to the defence, on the chessboard of world politics, of socialist countries abroad, then only one course lies before it. This course, which furthermore is in keeping both with the party's vocation and with its tradition, is to work towards the socialist transformation of society.

But how is it to do this, with whom must it work, and against whom? Khaled Bekdache (in Syria) has called the question premature. But the Egyptian Khaled believes that one can put forward a partial answer at least. It is quite clear that the answer must, to some extent, stem from an economic analysis. In this world where socialism plays a more and more prominent role, how will the economies of countries such as Egypt and India develop? Both Arab leaders are agreed that it is unlikely that the Communist Party will come to power in the immediate future and thus have the opportunity of preparing the complete socialization of the economy through a carefully controlled but still semi-capitalist process of growth, (as in China, or in Russia under the N.E.P.). It is therefore in the interests of both the capitalists and their gravediggers that the economy should develop. But what directions can this development of national capitalism take?

The recent conclusions reached by a young Egyptian, in his thesis on political economy defended last summer at the Paris Law Faculty, may be of interest here. [16] His very well researched study of economics seeks to show that the impact of the advanced capitalist economies on pre-capitalist economies is effectively to push the latter further and further into what has been called under-development, which he thus defines as something quite different from simple economic backwardness. He argues that under present conditions, given that the pre-capitalist countries are closely tied to the advanced capitalist world, there can be no question of the national bourgeoisies of the under-developed countries playing the same progressive role as did the French and English bourgeoisies, for instance, during the period of capitalism's youth. These 'under-developed' bourgeoisies' investments are restricted to sectors having little influence on a country's economic progress, and indeed often amount to little more than hoarding. If this is true, it is clear that the only possible way such countries can develop is through linkages with the socialist countries abroad and through state capitalism at home.

Will this then be the path chosen by the national bourgeoisie? Will all its elements be able to adapt to it so easily? Or will they be tempted to seek renewed political and economic support from the Western powers?

It must be remembered that none of this excludes class struggle. Can even the regulated development of national capitalism proceed without provoking the opposition of the masses? Will the Communist Party always be able to preach patience and moderate labourite-type struggle without losing the masses' confidence, especially when the imperatives of the national struggle are no longer so pressing? It cannot be denied that these visions of a more-or-less harmonious collaboration between the classes seem not a little optimistic to anybody who takes Marxist teachings seriously. The point surely requires further theoretical investigation, of the kind so brilliantly initiated by the Egyptian communists.

It is clear that these problems have far-reaching implications. It is not only the present situation of Syria and Egypt but the whole future of what is called the 'Third World' which is at issue. These are the problems which pre-occupy the communist leaders whose direct or indirect influence over the destiny of their countries is definitely growing. Much depends on how they will respond to them.

References

1. This was the picture I had come away with after the December 1943– January 1944 Congress; conversations with Party leaders from 1944 to 1947, when I left Lebanon, and publications I saw later all pointed in this direction. But in fact things were taking a slightly different course, as was publicly revealed later on. The 1943–44 Congress had indeed decreed that there would be two separate parties, each with its own name, flag, hymn, and title for the secretary; but the two parties continued to share the same Central Committee and the same Political Bureau. cf. *Qararat al-mo'tamar al watani lil-hizb ash-shoyou'i fi Souriya wa-Lobnan*, (Beirut, 1944). According to the report of the Central Committee of the Lebanese C.P. to the Second Congress, in July 1968, separation did not become effective until the middle of 1964, despite a further set of decisions taken in 1958. cf. *Khamsa wa'ishroun am min nidal al hizb ash shoyou'i al-lobnani . . .* (Beirut, 1968), p. 6 ff.

2. When I wrote this article, there was only one overall history of the Communist Parties of the Middle East: Walter Z. Laqueur's *Communism and Nationalism in the Middle East*, Routledge and Kegan Paul, (London, 1956). For all that it is open to criticism, erroneous in places and often lacking in understanding, the work is still valuable, if only for the mass of rare documentation the author has sifted. There are now several other books on the history of Arab communism: S. Ayoub's *al-hizb ash-shoyou'i fi Souriya wa-Lobnan 1922–58*, Dar al-horriya li-t-tiba'a wa-n-nashr, (n.d.), (Beirut, 1959), dealing mainly with the Lebano-Syrian C.P.s; Al-Hakam Darwaza's *ash shoyou'iyya al-mahalliyya wa- ma'rakat al-'Arab al-qawmiyya*, Dar al-Fajr li-t-taba 'a wa-n-nashr, (Beirut, 1961), is a more general, nationalist polemic, but a well-documented one; another general work is Elyas Morqos' *ta'rikh al-ahzab ash-shoyou'iyya fi l-watan al-'arabi*, Dar at-tali'a, (Beirut, 1964). Finally, there is a work in English by an Indian professor,

M.S. Agwani: *Communism in the Arab East*, Asia Publishing House, (London, 1969). All these works should be read critically, as they are inspired by different ideologies and sometimes have a polemical intent. For details of the communist movement in Mandate Palestine, see Y. Berger-Barzilay, *hat tragedyah shel ha mahpekhah ha-sovyetit*, 'Am 'oved, (Tel Aviv, 1968).

3.   I would not be so unreservedly laudatory today.

4.   This group soon fused with the last other communist group, to form the 'Egyptian Communist Party'.

5.   For the history of the Egyptian communist movement, see Jean et Simone Lacouture, *L'Egypte en Mouvement*, Le Seuil, (Paris, 1956), pp. 242-57. On recent developments, see *Le vie del socialismo*, (10 December 1957), pp. 10–11, and other articles emanating from the Italian C.P. which is on the whole well informed if somewhat severe.

6.   According to its 1968 Report the Party in Lebanon had 1,500 members in 1941, 6,000 at the end of 1943, 15,000 at the end of 1945 and 20,000 in the middle of 1947.

7.   Khaled Bekdache, *Report to the Plenum of the C.C. of the C.P. of Syria and Lebanon* (January 1951), translated in *Middle East Journal* (Spring 1953), pp. 206–21.

8.   *Al-Mokhtar*, 28 November 1955, Damascus.

9.   This was the name the Party gave its fundamental charter, drawn up during this congress (Beirut, 31st December 1943, 1st and 2nd January 1944).

10.   Khaled Bekdache, *al hizb ash shoyou'i fi n-nidal li ajl al-istiqlal wa-s-sidaya al wataniyya*, Sawt ash-sha'b, (Beirut, 1944), p. 71 ff.

11.   Khaled Bekdache, *ahdaf al-hizb ash-soyou'i al watanniya wa-l-ijtima'iyya wa-l-iqtisadiyya*, Sawt ash-sha'b, (Beirut, Damascus, 1945), pp. 7–8.

12.   Khaled Bekdache, *Report, op. cit*, in *Middle East Journal*, (Spring 1953), p. 208.

13.   *Ibid*, p. 210, p. 211.

14.   Cf. my *Israel and the Arabs*, and its bibliography.

15.   It can now be divulged that 'Khaled' was Fo'ad Morsi, an economist who had been imprisoned in 1958. Since then he has moved closer and closer to the regime. In January 1972, he figured as Minister of Trade and Supply in Sadat's Cabinet.

16.   Samir Amin, *Les Effets Structurels de L'Integration Internationale des Economies Precapitalistes*, thesis presented on 20th June 1957 in Xerox form. See also his later *Accumulation on a World Scale*, Harvester, (London, 1972).

5. Marxism and Arab Nationalism

Foundations and Development of Arab Nationalism

The problem of the relationship between the national struggle and the class struggle is one of the key problems of our times, and perhaps the problem with the greatest bearing on the global evolution of humanity today. It is thus of the greatest interest to study it in the light of the methods of Marxist analysis, and to attempt to raise the level of enquiry a little above that of elementary and vulgarizing theorizations, aimed at justifying transitory political attitudes, even if the latter are, in themselves, valid. Our point of departure here will be the study of Arab nationalism, which happens to provide a typical example of nationalism in under-developed countries. Its historical development is quite well documented and rich in lessons. We shall look at its basis and evolution, and at the attitude communists have historically adopted towards it. Then we shall attempt a Marxist critique of this attitude.

The Arab Ethnic Group

There is an Arab ethnic group,[1] which grew to its present form over the centuries following the great period of conquests by the Arabs of Arabia, who had converted to Islam following the teachings of the Prophet Mohammad. These conquests, which began in 633, the year after the Prophet's death in 632, reached a provisional peak during the years 710 to 715. The Arabization of the Empire thus constituted ensued. Many of the conquered peoples learnt Arabic and became more or less completely assimilated with their Arab conquerors. There has thus developed a vast domain, stretching from Mesopotamia to the Atlantic Ocean, the majority of whose inhabitants are Arabic-speaking. The spoken language is divided into a variety of regional dialects, each of which is easier or harder for an Arab from a different area to understand depending on his area of origin. The written language, on the other hand, is constant throughout.

Linguistic traits are, in this case, as so often elsewhere, the clearest indication of membership of the ethnic group in question. It should be pointed out, however, that some members of the group are only marginally Arabized. Some communities continue to speak other languages, but without the status of a written language or a language of culture. To study, to move up the social ladder, one must learn Arabic, rather as the Bretons of Breton-speaking Brittany learn French. This applies to the North African Berbers, to the Aramaens of Iraq, and, to some extent, to the Kurds of that country. Roughly speaking, one could say that there are 75 million members of the Arab ethnic group, occupying a territory of about 14 million square kilometres.[2]

There are other unifying factors which link these people together: a common history and culture. But there are also certain regional differences, which are only normal in so vast and geographically heterogeneous a territory. The Arab world can be divided into clearly defined geographic units and into definite, actual or potential, economic units. The spoken language varies somewhat from place to place, and so do the mores. Each area also has its own particular history and has been exposed to different influences over the centuries.

Arab unity, therefore, expresses only one aspect of the question, however important that aspect may become. There is no manifest destiny in the facts, there are no objective features of the existing social conditions which make the unification of the Arabs into a 'nation' as inevitable as some thinkers, Arab and non-Arab, Marxist and non-Marxist, have sometimes claimed. In the effort to 'prove' such a thesis, much use has been made of the Stalinist definition of the nation, which, as we have shown elsewhere, is generally inadequate.[3] However, it should be obvious that this definition is particularly inappropriate to the Arab case. One can at most talk of a potential economic unity, and even then this is proving to be particularly difficult to establish. In one sense it is true that there is a definite unity of language, culture and 'psychological formation'; but as we have seen above this is not the whole truth. As for unity of territory, a concept developed by Stalin in order to disallow the national character of scattered groups such as the Gypsies and the Jews, or that of ethnic groups separated by great distances such as the North Americans and the English, its relevance to cases other than these specific ones is at best ambiguous. One can draw a line round any given geographical area on a map and decree that the enclosed area enjoys territorial unity.

The Arab nation is a tendency, an aspiration, the realization of which depends on many factors; sociologists and historians are still debating the relative importance of each of these factors. This tendency has been embodied in a specific movement historically, from a given period onwards. Certain objective features of the existing social relations have obviously been necessary for such a movement to emerge. But the reality history presents us with is not so much that of a nation, or even that of a nation 'in formation', as that of a nationalism.

The Evolution of Arab Nationalism

At the beginning of the modern period the factors mentioned above had been present, in more or less the same form, for over a thousand years. The relevant area of territorial unity, if one must introduce the concept, was the same as today. The relationship between the single written language and the various spoken languages was not substantially different from what it is now. The same is true for the cultural and historical characteristics, some of which were common to all, and some of which were more specific. Could one talk of an Arab people even then (a *narodnost*, to use the Soviet term)? Perhaps. But in that case one must recognize that this people's ethno-national consciousness and its unity were virtually non-existent.

On the other hand, one can talk of an Arab ethno-national consciousness during the century of conquest, up to about 750. The Arabs were a conquering ethnic group which had kept its homogeneity, held together by the Muslim religion, an ideology alien to the mass of its subjects; they dominated other peoples politically and exploited them economically. There was an 'Arab Empire' (*Arabisches Reich*), as J. Wellhausen has shown in his classic work. In 750 a political revolution, namely the overthrow of the Ommayid Caliphate and its replacement by the Abbassid Caliphate of Baghdad, signalled a drastic change in these conditions. The conquered peoples had become increasingly Arabized, and to an even greater extent had converted to Islam. They demanded and obtained equal rights with the descendants of the conquerors. The Empire became a *Muslim* Empire incorporating an Arab ethnic group (made up largely of recently Arabized individuals) as well as a Persian ethnic group, a Turkish ethnic group, and so forth. There were no real conflicts between these groups. Indeed, the disintegration of the Empire, and the fact that from about 1050 onwards Turkish dynasties came to dominate most of the states which emerged from this disintegration, seemed to create very little conflict between these groups, although right up until 1800 there were endless *social* revolts. Foreign aggression, for instance the European Crusades in the Middle Ages, roused the populations to defend themselves. But the ideology which inspired or guided such defensive reactions was a purely religious one. There was nothing which could justify one talking about the ethno-national factor as a significant feature of political movements.

Nationalism only appeared in the 19th Century, having emerged from a specific situation. Practically the whole Arab ethnic group was directly or indirectly incorporated into an immense empire dominated by a Turkish ruling class, the Ottoman Empire. This despotically governed Islamic empire was being undermined by the growth of Europe's political, economic and technological power. The rising quality and falling prices of European industrial products quickly made their impact as European goods increasingly penetrated the Empire, ruining local artisans. And European investment came to play an increasing role. In short, the capitalist economy intruded more and more directly into this archaic society whose traditional structures it dissolved. At the same time, on the political level, the Ottoman Empire was being eroded by the European powers, increasingly controlled, supervised, patronized as it was as the 'sick man'. Ideologically, this process appeared as the triumph of European values, be they Christian or materialist, over the indigenous Muslim values.

These events engendered a profound feeling of humiliation amongst the population of the Ottoman Empire, populace and elite alike; and this was particularly bitter in that it replaced a previous sense of superiority. Such humiliation naturally led to hatred and suspicion of Europe, and an intense desire for liberation and revenge, clearly expressed in the jubilation which met the news of any European defeat, such as that inflicted by Japan on Russia in 1905. The fact that the upper classes imitated the West only accentuated this feeling. The suffering masses could find a close target for their hatred and envy: their Europeanized exploiters, by their very lifestyle, came to epitomize the often inaccessible, almost abstract, distant enemy. The rulers of the Empire, faced with the day-to-day task of choosing between political options, could offer only a barely theorized response to the new situation and the new emotions it aroused. Some adopted a reactionary attitude, others a reformist attitude. At this stage, the only possible reforms were measures imposed from above by an enlightened despotism. The problems encountered by this sort of reform are well known. In this case, they weakened the existing structures even further, and prepared the masses to take the next step.

The Old Ideologies

The new situation and the new emotions also gave rise to new ideologies which could take them into account, but these evolved in a very roundabout and gradual manner, thereby arousing the scorn of the 'realist' politicians. In the early stages, of course, people attempted to fit the new situation into the old framework of thought. As in the Middle Ages, people turned to religion. The traditional explanation blamed the woes of the period on the loss of the religious purity of the past. But the man who first embodied this tendency, Jamal ad-din al-Afghani (1839—97), went even further. As in all the countries attacked by Europe, people were looking for the secret of European success. Jamal ad-din believed that the key to this secret was modern science and technology. He argued that a return to primitive Islam, the rational and reasonable religion which had subsequently been so grossly distorted and rigidified, would enable the Muslim world to adapt to the new conditions. But the old political structures prevented this purification of Islam — and these structures were upheld by the European powers who benefited from their sclerosis. The independence of the Muslim world and a struggle against the European imperialists were therefore necessary if Islam was to be purified.

This Muslim religious nationalism sometimes opposed and sometimes supported an Ottoman political nationalism which modelled itself on European nationalism and attempted to arouse loyalty towards the existing political framework. Inspired first by mid-19th Century romantic liberal nationalism, then by French rationalist positivism, this Ottoman nationalism mainly reached those who benefited from the political framework, namely the Turks. It became embodied in various structures and secret societies, and culminated in the 1908 Young Turk revolution. The revolution itself was greeted with universal enthusiasm; it seemed to resolve everybody's problems. A parliamentary regime was to pave the way for all other necessary developments. All ethno-national discrimination within the Empire was to be abolished. Perfect integration from Macedonia to the Yemen, from Skopje and Durazzo to Basra and Al Mukha, seemed imminent.

The New Ideology

The two nationalisms mentioned above, elaborated within the traditional ideological and political frameworks, both failed. They failed because the Turkish bourgeoisie and landowners would not give up their dominant position in the Empire. The Muslim people's United Front proposed by the religious nationalists was thus undermined. The Young Turk Government could not hide the fact that in practice its Ottoman nationalism was only a facade, a disguise for Turkish domination. The bourgeoisie and much of the aristocracy in the Arab countries of the Ottoman Empire were no longer prepared to accept this domination. They demanded ethno-national rights and a decentralization of the Empire. When this was not forthcoming, they adopted a new ideology: Arab nationalism.

The first theoretician of Arab nationalism was Abdurrhaman al-Kawakibi (1849—1903), liberal Syrian freemason, who still believed in a Muslim Empire but an Arab-dominated one. The ideology was available, the situation was ripe; secret societies were set up between 1904 and 1911, laying the ground-work for a new structure. The 1914—18 war provided the opportunity for the first of the secret societies' ideological projects to be realized: in 1916 the Arab revolt broke out, led by Sherif Hussein of Mecca. His own motives were mainly dynastic, but he was backed by the Syrian and Iraqi nationalist secret societies and by Britain. On 29th October 1916, he proclaimed himself King of the Arabs, a title, however, which the Allies did not recognize.

The Arabs, urged into revolt by the Allies, participated in their eventual victory. We all know how their hopes were dashed and the promises made to them broken. During the inter-war period, their disappointment, amongst other things, led to a profound modification of their ideology.

The inter-war period in the Middle East was characterized politically by a sort of compromise between Britain and the dynasts of the Hashemite family. One sector of the territory , Syria and Lebanon, was given over to the French; the other, Palestine, to the Zionists as a homeland for them. Britain maintained a pre-eminent role through a system of mandates and unequal treaties. In exchange, the dynasts received material advantages and important concessions in terms of power. The big landowners who had participated in the Revolt were handsomely provided for and increasingly began to play the role of agents of British power. Meanwhile the Arab peoples of those Asiatic regions which had been under direct Ottoman domination before 1914, namely Iraq, Syria, Lebanon, Palestine and Transjordan, saw all their hopes frustrated. Instead of granting the promised independence, the Mandate powers arrogated the right to supervise or, more often, to govern directly. Instead of promoting unity, they artificially split the area up into fragments, thus the Syrian-Lebanese region, which is about one-third the size of France, was at one stage divided up into five different states. Furthermore, part of the country was exposed to foreign immigration by Zionists who made no secret of their intentions to set up their own state. Meanwhile Arab Egypt was conducting its own struggle for independence from British imperialism. But the Maghreb, Arabia and the Sudan, all colonized or still independent Arab countries, remained quiescent.

It was in Arab Asia that the development of a nationalist ideology went forward. It was there that hatred of imperialism, especially of British imperialism, reached its peak. The big, medium and petty bourgeoisie took up arms against the landowning aristocracy and seized control of the nationalist movement which the aristocracy had betrayed. The influence of worldwide ideologies began to make itself felt. We will return to Marxism's contribution later on. At the time, fascism's influence was more important. The nature of the enemy alliance between Anglo-French imperialism and Zionism was particularly significant in this respect. But racist ideology, which is so ill-suited to the Arabs, was only sporadically taken up, and then only by atypical groups such as Antoun Sa'ad's Syrian Popular Party which created a Syrian racism implicitly opposed to Arab unity. The unified Arab nationalist ideology was clearly predominant, and gaining ground. About 1936 it gained a hold in Egypt, and spread towards the Maghreb and the Sudan. This ideology tried to equip itself with a rational basis; theoreticians discussed the foundations of the Arab nation, its links with the Muslim religion and the federal or unified character of the state it would set up. People tried to define nationhood, and of course they did so in terms of characteristics compatible with the particular traits of the Arab countries' situation. German influence, in addition, pushed people to think of the nation as an objective entity which imposed duties and demanded unconditional devotion from its members.

Some characteristic traits of this Arab nationalism were beginning to emerge more clearly:

1. Both for the theoreticians and for the masses whose aspirations and feelings they expressed, the main contradiction remained the struggle between the oppressed Oriental world and Western imperialism. The contradictions with other Oriental nationalisms, Turkish nationalism, for example, seemed quite secondary. Although it was hoped that one Western imperialist power might be played off against another, this was purely a matter of tactics, except for the few genuine agents, of course. British efforts to make France bear the whole brunt of Arab nationalism were doomed to fail.

2. It was a nationalism which for a long time continued to make some use of religious feeling. This was natural enough, seeing as Islam, which was created by an Arab and reveres a book which God revealed in Arabic, is an Arab cultural phenomenon, a feature of Arab culture despised and threatened by non-Arabs. Even the Arabic-speaking religious minorities, the Jews and Christians, think of it in these terms.

3. As we have seen, it was a nationalism led by the bourgeoisie; the landed aristocracy had been exposed as untrustworthy and had discredited itself. The nationalist movement minimized class struggle in favour of national unity. It was nonetheless accepted by the proletarian masses with little or no resistance. As long as national independence had not been achieved, class struggle quite

easily turned into national struggle. The ruling class which oppressed and exploited its compatriots were denounced mainly as traitors to the national struggle, as collaborators with the imperialists. All miseries, difficulties and conflicts were explained in terms of imperialist domination.

4. It was a unified nationalism, for the reasons we have mentioned. There were no fears that membership of an Arab federation, or even of a united Arab state, would result in the threat of domination by one regional element over others, except perhaps amongst the governing elements and certain business circles. The divisions imposed by the imperialist powers had managed to create relatively specific economic units and particular interests within frontiers, despite the gross artificiality of the latter. But this was quite insignificant compared to the great trend towards unified solidarity.

Recent Achievements

Shortly before 1939, the British realized how very unpopular they had become and set out to remedy the situation. In Palestine, the May 1939 White Paper attempted to put the brakes on the transformation of the Zionist colony into a predominantly Jewish state. In May 1941, Sir Anthony Eden publicly declared that Britain sympathized with the cause of Arab unity. From 1943 to 1945, British influence played a considerable role in the eviction of the French from Syria and Lebanon. On 29th May 1945, the charter setting up the League of Arab States was signed, with British blessings. During the 1947—48 war in Palestine, the British gave their more-or-less discreet support to the Arabs.

All this was far from sufficient to make Arab public opinion more favourable to the British cause. The ulterior motives behind such manoeuvres were all too apparent. The discredited Hashemite dynasty and the much hated landed aristocracy remained in power thanks to British gold and British troops, still stationed in Suez and Jordan. The Arab League, with only administrative and cultural achievements to its credit, had shown itself to be so incapable of dealing with any even slightly contentious issue that it seemed at best to be no more than a useful framework for the future, when conditions had changed. Activities directed against French imperialism and against Israel were bringing Arab national feeling to a pitch.

The Atlantic powers' stubborn and waspish insistence on integrating the Arab countries into an anti-Soviet military coalition did the rest. The May 1950 Tripartite Declaration in which these clumsy efforts culminated went directly against the main current of Arab aspirations. Arab opinion was in no way hostile to the Soviet Union, did not consider communism to be a danger and was very suspicious of the imperialist powers, of their partisans in the Arab aristocracy and of the foreign elements, the Turks and Israelis, being given a leadership role in the association into which the Arab states were being pushed. Ideas of Arab unity and independence, linked as they were with aspirations to economic and social progress, benefited considerably from the contrast.

The Egyptian Revolution of 23 July 1952 was the first victory of international importance for the Arab middle classes. It represented those elements of the bourgeoisie who sought independence and the economic and social progress which would guarantee it. At first, these elements enjoyed the sympathetic support of the Americans and tried to come to some arrangement with the Atlantic powers.

But the latter's stubborn insistence on conscripting the Arabs, and into the junior ranks at that, blew all such hopes sky-high. At the beginning of 1955 the Baghdad Pact countries were Britain, Turkey, Iraq, Iran and Pakistan. Arab national pride was affronted; anger and indignation reached boiling-point. The only possible important outlet on a state level for this feeling of outrage was the about-turn of the Egyptian rulers. In April 1955, Nasser had been to the Bandung Conference, where he had been strongly influenced by Chou-En-Lai, Nehru and Tito. The Western powers refused to help anybody who would not join their coalition. The die was cast. On 26 September 1955, Nasser announced that he had just signed a contract for the purchase of Czech arms. The Egyptian masses responded with their first show of enthusiasm for an official decision.[4]

From then on the course of events accelerated. The pan-Arab ideology reigned supreme and without any serious opposition, except in Lebanon, in all the countries of the Fertile Crescent (Syria, Lebanon, Iraq and Jordan) and in Egypt. To a greater or lesser extent, it penetrated westwards into the Maghreb and Libya, to the south-west into the Sudan and even into parts of Islamized Black Africa, and southwards into the archaically structured feudal states scattered around the Arabian peninsula. This pan-Arabism became linked to a whole range of social and foreign policy ideas which could not fail to be popular. As we shall see, it borrowed from Marxism the characterization of its main enemy as imperialism. Often it accepted the idea of a necessary evolution towards various rather vaguely thought-out socialist structures of ownership, at least in certain sectors of the economy. It linked this socialistic tendency with the notion of national independence, it being recognized that the latter could only be achieved by creating a solid economic infra-structure; since the investments involved in such a project were not very profitable, capitalist financing was unlikely to be forthcoming.

However, bourgeois opinion, which played a leadership role in the national movement, was obviously not in favour of an evolution towards social structures on Soviet lines. In international affairs it had become clear that all that could be expected from the Western powers was hostility or rather cheap-skate aid, conditional on the Arab countries accepting conscription into an anti-Soviet military coalition, in which they would in any case only play a footslogger's role, thereby giving up their right to determine their territories' military dispositions in exchange for a mess of pottage. By contrast, in many Arab circles there was widespread sympathy, both for the Soviet Union, which had nearly always been on the same side as the Arab countries, and for China, where the creation of a sizeable economic and military power base, under conditions quite similar to those prevailing in the Arab countries, could be taken as an impressive example. This attitude tended to express itself in a 'positive neutralist' foreign policy which the Soviet Union, having abandoned the attitudes of the Zhdanovist period, was prepared to consider as friendly. All concerned could therefore establish some common ground on the basis of such a position, despite various reservations.

This neutralist, socialistic and popular pan-Arabism, which enjoyed the support of the masses, found its spokesman in Nasser and its incarnation in the Egyptian and Syrian states. Elsewhere, although public opinion supported it, the governments remained reticent and hostile. From 1955 onwards, events were to increase Nasser's popularity and the power of the ideas he represented; gradually more and more states were brought into line with popular opinion.

The abortive Suez expedition, in late October, 1956, made Nasser the great man of the moment. The evolution of the Algerian Revolution, the accession to independence of the Sudan in 1956, of Tunisia and Morocco in the same year, all strengthened the Arabs' confidence that history was going their way. Pretty soon it was merely a question of which form and which overall direction unity would take. Given the prevailing circumstances, it is quite clear that the creation of the United Arab Republic, on 1st February 1958, was a manoeuvre by non-communist elements who feared Syria's increasing alignment with the Soviet Union. However, it is also clear that it answered a profound mass aspiration. During the next six months, the trend became irresistible: Yemen joined the Republic, Saudi Arabia and many Maghrebians were sympathetic; there was a civil war in Lebanon; finally, and most importantly, on 14 July 1958, the Iraqi Revolution overthrew the 'policeman of reaction' in the Arab countries.

The Communist Attitude

Before the October 1917 Revolution, Marxist theoreticians had paid little attention to Eastern countries, or to colonized countries in general.[5] It seemed obvious that the socialist revolution would start in the highly-developed countries of the West. And then one could foresee a difficult relationship between the proletariat, which had seized power in such countries, and the colonized peoples who, it was assumed, would not have progressed beyond the previous social stage. The reactions of the latter could well be very unsocialist and might even threaten socialized Europe, as Marx and Engels foresaw in 1858[6] and 1882[7] respectively. It would then be absolutely essential to apply democratic principles. There was just one moment, however, when Marx, who had been struck by the Taiping Revolt (1851–64), thought that perhaps the Chinese Revolution, the democratic revolution at least, might precede the European one.[8]

The October Revolution, coinciding as it did with a wave of revolutionary movements in the East, was to modify this perspective. Apart from the expected socialist revolutions in the West which had still not materialised, these Eastern movements were the only ones which could assist the young

Soviet state by struggling against their common enemies. Furthermore, the socialist revolution had succeeded in a rather under-developed country; why then should it not also succeed in even less developed countries, skipping the stage of bourgeois revolution altogether, or going through it very quickly? Such a bourgeois revolution would necessarily also be a national revolution, a conquest of that national independence which was the primary demand of both the bourgeois and the proletarian masses in the country concerned. The struggle for national independence, the struggle for socialist revolution, and aid and support for the bastion of socialism were the three themes around which the communists' various strategic and tactical concerns were to pivot during the next forty years. The problem of which specific forms the national struggle in the Arab countries should take was examined in terms of the specific characteristics of each particular strategic phase, and only attracted significant attention during the very latest phase, which is under consideration here.[9]

Imminent Revolution and the United Front

The first strategic phase in the communists' attitude towards the national struggle in colonized or dependent Arab countries was characterized by a double preoccupation: to help the Soviet Union and to prepare the proletarian revolution. The first period, immediately after the October Revolution and up to 1920, was dominated by one slogan: 'Help the Russian revolution through revolutions which are both national and proletarian'. This was the period of the Civil War and War Communism in Russia, of the struggle for national independence in Turkey, in Egypt and elsewhere; in China, Sun Yat-Sen was leading a flourishing nationalist and socialistic revolutionary movement. Optimism abounded. At the first inaugural Comintern Congress, on 4 March 1919, Zinoviev declared that:

> We already have a victorious proletarian revolution in one great country. A powerful revolution is already on the way in two others (Germany, Hungary). How can we say that we are still too weak? Our slogan is the International Republic of Soviets, and nobody can call it utopian. We are convinced that this is the main question on the agenda for the immediate future.

The communists believed that the problems and difficulties were fading away. In July 1920, the invitations to attend the Baku Congress, issued by the International's executive committee, called upon the peoples of the East, including the specifically mentioned 'peasants of Syria and Arabia' and those of Mesopotamia, to form Soviet republics:

> Workers and peasants of the Middle East! If you organize, if you arm yourselves and unite with the Russian workers and peasants' Red Army, you will be able to confront the British, French and American capitalists,

you will be able to get rid of them, you will liberate yourselves from your oppressors and will be able to manage your own affairs by allying yourselves freely with the other workers' republics in the world. Then the wealth of your country will really belong to you. In your own interests, and in the interests of workers throughout the world, the products of labour will be exchanged equitably and we shall all aid each other.[10]

At the Baku Congress itself in September,[11] Zinoviev had re-adopted a religious vocabulary,[12] calling for a holy war against British imperialism and thereby arousing wild enthusiasm. The Eastern delegates stood up, brandishing their weapons and swearing to carry out the struggle against imperialism. This same appeal was reiterated in lyrical terms in the final manifesto, addressed to the peasants of Mesopotamia, Arabia, Palestine and Egypt amongst others:

What has England ever done for Egypt, where the whole indigenous population has groaned under the heavy yoke of British capitalism for eight decades now, a yoke even heavier and more ruinous for the people than the old yoke of the Pharoahs who built the enormous pyramids with the labour of their slaves? . . .

People of the East! You have often heard your governments calling for holy war, you have marched under the green banner of the Prophet; but all these holy wars were deceptive and dishonest; they served the interests of your selfish rulers. You, the peasants and workers, remained enslaved and impoverished, whilst others derived great benefit from your conquests, benefits that you never enjoyed yourselves.

Now we are calling for the first genuine holy war, under the red banner of the Communist International . . .

Arise as a single man for the holy war against the British occupier . . .

Arise, you Arabs and Afghans, lost in the sandy deserts and cut off from the rest of the world by the British . . .

This is the holy war for the liberation of the peoples of the East, so that humanity will no longer be divided into oppressors and oppressed, so that all peoples and tribes shall be equal whatever the colour of their skin, the language they speak or the religion they profess . . .[13]

This appeal bore little fruit in the short term.[14] Its romanticism, its ignorance of the real conditions of struggle in the East were no doubt partly responsible.[15] The same goes for the naively 'skilful' use of the concept of holy war, a concept which had already been shown to be void during World War I. Indeed the calls to holy war issued under the auspices of both sides in that conflict only found an echo in the Muslim world when they tallied with the possibility of national struggle. But, above all, the fact remained that, in the Muslim world as elsewhere, the objective conditions for a socialist revolution were not present. The progress of socialism in the Arab countries was furthered very little by this phase. Baku was mainly aimed at the Persians and Turks. Of the 1,891 delegates, only three were Arabs, none of whom signed the final manifesto. Communist parties or similar organizations were only established amongst the foreigners in Egypt, in Palestine and in the Arab countries as a whole. They attracted few supporters, were entirely cut off from the life of their countries and all in all aroused very little interest.[16]

In any case, this failure was not restricted to the East. The revolutionary wave was being pushed back everywhere; capitalist regimes had stabilized themselves and all the revolutionary movements outside the Soviet Union had been defeated. Only China was still a source of hope. And so at the end of 1921 a new strategic phase began. Soviet Russia embarked on the task of reconstruction, with the application of the N.E.P. In the other countries, the 3rd Congress of the International (22 June–12 July 1921) opted tactically for a united front policy. In Europe and America, it was no longer a question of seizing power but of winning the hearts and minds of the majority of the working class through a programme of demands for bread and peace.

It was during this period that the problems of the national and bourgeois revolution in the East, especially in China, were feverishly debated. For the colonized countries the watchword could be summed up as: 'Help the Soviet Union by struggling for national independence and bourgeois revolution whilst preparing the proletarian revolution.' It was at this time that Stalin and Bukharin, in contrast to Trotsky, and in partial contrast to Zinoviev and Kamenev, laid down the tactic to be adopted.[17] This involved accepting a national united front against imperialism as a necessary phase, at least for those countries, such as India, which did not yet have a very developed proletariat. The more advanced of these countries would then go through a phase characterized by the formation of an alliance between the workers and the petty bourgeoisie against the big bourgeoisie, since the latter would adopt a conciliatory attitude towards imperialism. This alliance was also to include the peasants and the intellectuals, the four class bloc. If necessary, the Communist Party was, at this stage, to join a great nationalist and democratic party, on the lines of the Kuomintang, but without dissolving itself in the process. From within such a movement it was to 'denounce the hybrid character and the inconsistencies of the national bourgeoisie, and to struggle resolutely against imperialism'. But it was only in the countries with a larger proletariat, such as India, where the big bourgeoisie had already come to some basic understanding with imperialism, that one was to make a decisive break with this bourgeoisie, create a revolutionary anti-imperialist, four-class, bloc under the hegemony of the proletariat and take the independence of the Communist Party as one's watchword.[18] All this was itself only a watchword, and not necessarily realizable. The transition to socialism was put off for a considerable time. Stalin and Bukharin denounced the tendency 'to skip the movement's democratic revolutionary stage in order to embark immediately on the tasks of Soviet power and the dictatorship of the proletariat' as an ultra-left deviation.[19]

Thus, during these first and second phases, which might last for a considerable time, the communists were to assist the national movements, even the most anti-communist ones, such as the Kemalist movement in Turkey, and not excluding Chiang Kai-Shek, even after his spectacular about-face in March 1927 and the atrocious massacre of communists which ensued. Shortly after March 1927, Bukharin wrote: 'It would be a big mistake to abandon the Kuomintang banner to the Chiang Kai-Shek clique ... That is why, even now, *especially* now, the tactic of leaving the Kuomintang is absurd. One should even recruit for the Kuomintang.'[20]

Of course, this was not only because Chiang, the torturer, was an inescapable part of history's course; there were also various considerations of international strategy. Stalin made no bones about it:

> Were we right to support Canton in China and, let us say, Ankara in Turkey, at a time when Ankara and Canton were leading the struggle against imperialism? Yes, we were right. We were right and we were following in Lenin's footsteps, for the struggles of Canton and Ankara scattered the forces of imperialism, they weakened and discredited imperialism and thus facilitated the development of the heartland of international revolution, the development of the U.S.S.R.[21]

In 1924 he theorized this attitude in stark terms which were to play a singularly important role:

> The revolutionary character of the national movement does not necessarily imply the existence of proletarian elements within that movement, nor that it has a revolutionary or republican programme, or a democratic basis. The Emir of Afghanistan's struggle for the independence of Afghanistan is an objectively *revolutionary* struggle despite the Emir's monarchic conceptions, for it weakens, breaks up and undermines imperialism ... The struggle of the Egyptian shopkeepers and bourgeois intellectuals is an objectively *revolutionary* struggle despite the bourgeois origin of the Egyptian national movement's leaders and despite the fact that they are opposed to socialism ...[22]

Concerning the Arab world, the French Communist Party followed the general directives; it courageously supported the Rif Revolt in North Africa in 1924–25 and the Uprising in Syria in 1925–26, both national movements against French imperialism. That was enough. Their structure and internal motivations hardly mattered; indeed the French Communist Party knew as little about them as all the other French parties. But it did not hesitate to oppose the other socialist leaders on the subject. After all, the united front policy was geared to win over the masses and not the leaderships of the other parties who, it was hoped, would be outflanked by their own troops, the latter supposedly having been virtually convinced by the communist slogans about bread and peace. But the socialist parties, who quickly reacted to this tactic, were able to use not only the patriotism which dominated public opinion, combined perhaps with appeals to the overall self-interest of the colonizing people, but also a denunciation of the purely nationalist, if not downright reactionary, character of the movements in revolt. Pierre Semard, the General Secretary of the French Communist Party, answered such charges thus:

> Many of those who hope for the defeat of French imperialism fear the victory of Abd el-Krim just as much, accusing him of being a reactionary leader and a violent dictator. They have not yet understood that the first stage in the liberation of the colonized and semi-colonized people is the triumph of movements having a national character.

These French Communist Party campaigns were very much in keeping with the vigorously internationalist approach which was then part and parcel of the communist ideology. The revolts and movements supported were originally regional, but soon became marked by an orientation towards the Arab nationalist ideology, at least as far as the leaders were concerned. But whatever patriotic anti-communist propaganda may have said about it, distance and practical difficulties more or less prevented any effective collusion between the French communists and the insurgent movements, although the latter were able to use the former's publications for their own propaganda.

Very few documents are available concerning how the general line was applied by the handful of communist parties established in the eastern Arab countries. The small communist groups of Palestine and Egypt did their best to follow the directives laid down. In Egypt as in Turkey, the 'bourgeois revolutionaries' did not exactly appreciate communist 'support', and the Party had a very small following. In Palestine, the communist movement was restricted to small Jewish groups whose anti-Zionist position merely made them powerless in a social context which was by definition Zionist or at least Zionistic. In other countries, the Party was even weaker. None of these tiny groups could carry out theoretical studies of the national question — or if they did, nothing remains of them.

One thing is certain, however. Despite their subordination to considerations of world-wide strategy, and despite their call for unconditional support of 'objectively revolutionary' elements, the Moscow directives did not, theoretically, put the class struggle in abeyance. At the very beginning of the period in question, the theses on the Eastern question adopted by the 4th Congress of the Comintern, November 1922, were quite unequivocal:

> To hold oneself aloof from the struggle for the working class's most urgent everyday needs, in the name of 'national unity' and 'civil peace' with the bourgeois democrats, would be just as counter-productive. The workers' communist parties in the colonized and semi-colonized countries have a double task: they struggle for the most radical possible outcome of a democratic bourgeois revolution geared to the conquest of national independence; and they organize the worker and peasant masses in terms

of their specific class interests, thereby exploiting all the contradictions in the democratic bourgeois nationalist camp.[23]

The communist mini-groups of the Middle East, weak as they may have been, nonetheless had a firm grasp of this point. Whatever the dangers of the Bukharin-Stalinist position, the socialist goal and the proletarian struggle were never forgotten. It would have been impossible to do so in any case, with the October Revolution still so fresh in people's minds and at a time when the very name 'communist' was so closely associated with social struggle.

Proletarian Revolution and Faithfulness to the Soviet Union

The Chinese catastrophe was to have particularly important repercussions. Stalin somewhat belatedly drew the appropriate conclusion; events in Europe were pointing in the same direction. It became clear that the united front strategy had definitely failed. The Soviet Union increasingly fell back upon itself. Having eliminated the leftists, Stalin took up the policies they had recommended and sacked Bukharin and the right. He believed that having succeeded in stabilizing itself capitalism would now abandon the idea of peaceful co-existence and launch a new wave of attacks on the Soviet Union. The Soviet Union was also entering a new phase: it was time to abandon the N.E.P. and to concentrate on building socialism, on industrialization, and on collectivizing agriculture. At the Comintern's 6th Congress, in August 1928, the united front's role was described in far more circumscribed terms: it was now to be only 'a means to unmask and isolate the reformist leaders' in periods during which real revolutionary pressure was lacking.[24] The Congress adopted the 'class against class' tactic, which labelled the socialist parties as implacable enemies on the same level as their 'twin brothers', the fascist movements. In France, Maurice Thorez proclaimed that:

> The Communist Party will have nothing to do with the petty-bourgeois ideology of 'republican discipline' and 'the most advanced party'. It gives pride of place to the formidable antagonism between the proletariat and the bourgeoisie: *class against class.*[25]

The programme adopted by the Comintern Congress spelled it out:

> The duty of the international proletariat is to reply to the imperialist state's aggressions and war against the U.S.S.R. by audacious and resolute mass action and by struggling to overthrow the imperialist governments. The watchwords are the dictatorship of the proletariat and alliance with the U.S.S.R.[26]

The catastrophic repercussions which this strategy had in Europe are all too well known. In practice, the Communist Party, in the name of the working class, rejected all alliances, refused to countenance any intermediate programme whatsoever and claimed to be leading the way directly towards an imminent Soviet revolution. The masses were well aware that such a policy was not realistic. In France, they refused to believe that Blum was their main enemy. In Germany, where despair more or less drove them to accept such a programme as a valid option, the outcome was Hitler's rise to power. But in the colonized or semi-colonized countries the same tactic, applied with the same dauntlessness, was to have very different results. For the first time, small but relatively solid communist core-groups were set up in the Arab countries. There were no socialists in the East. The communist parties attracted very little attention.

But the new tactic enabled them to elaborate a specific doctrine, a particular type of nationalism which took into account both the aspiration to national independence and the situation of the classes in struggle. One could call it a Marxist or proletarian nationalism. There could be no question of carrying off some 'victory'; the point was to make the suffering masses aware of their own interests, and how these were opposed to those of the bourgeois or 'feudalists' who were leading the national struggle. The sectarianism, which in the West was leading the masses who were pro-socialism into isolationism and defeat by, probably consciously, proposing mythical and impossible tasks, was not so important in the East. In the Arab world, where in any case socialism was obviously not on the verge of triumph, the tactic in question was necessarily restricted to a possible and, in the long term, very useful task: the development of class consciousness.

It is clearly no coincidence that it was at this time that the communist movement began to gain some importance in India and went through decisive changes in China.[27] Indeed the International's programme had laid down that in the colonized countries the passage to socialism was only possible 'through a series of preparatory stages, through a whole period of transforming the bourgeois-democratic revolution into a socialist revolution'. Short-term tasks were assigned to the communist parties of these countries, tasks which, furthermore, were all quite beyond the capacities of the poor embryonic communist parties of the Arab world, for instance 'organizing a revolutionary workers' and peasants' army!' In any case these countries were supposed to play a secondary supporting role in the world-wide struggle against capitalism. They were thought of as a world-countryside, as opposed to a world-town consisting of industrialized countries. 'The realization of a fraternal and militant alliance with *the working masses in the colonies* is thus one of the main aims of the world's industrial proletariat, the class which exercises hegemony and leadership in the struggle against imperialism.'[28]

The 'working masses' in the colonies — and nobody else. The bourgeois nationalists who had previously been described as 'objectively revolutionary' were now denounced as representatives of 'counter-revolutionary national-reformism'. This applies as much to the Egyptian Wafd as to everybody else. The Egyptian C.P.'s programme of action stated in 1931 that:

The Wafd is the national-reformist counter-revolutionary party of the bourgeois and the landowners. It unites the rich capitalists, the lawyers, the speculators and the liberal landowners who, fearing a popular revolution, support a compromise with Egypt's oppressors and hope to receive some insignificant recompense in exchange . . . The Wafd not only opposes any real struggle for Egypt's independence, for the overthrow of the monarchy, for the expropriation of the landowners and for the eight-hour day; it also *tries to seize leadership of the mass movement*, in order to weaken and crush this movement, to betray it and sell it to its enemies. The whole history of the Wafd since 1919 is the history of its struggle against the revolutionary workers and peasants, and against workers in general.[29]

A resolution adopted in the same year by the communist parties of Syria and Palestine proclaimed that such an analysis was applicable to the Arab world as a whole.

The position of the National Bloc in Syria can be defined by the fact that it only plays at opposition, whilst refusing categorically to participate in any real struggle or revolutionary action. Many of the old leaders of the 1925 Revolt are now content to sit at the feet of the French generals. The National Bloc is preparing for a compromise with the French oppressors. In Palestine the Arab Executive Committee has treacherously accepted to compete with Zionism in a race to make concessions to British imperialism, in exchange for guarantees of 'peace and quiet' for the Arab masses. National reformism is increasingly veering towards counter-revolution and capitulation . . . In Iraq, the National Party issues appeals to the League of Nations but in fact does not lead any real struggle against the English usurpers and contents itself with words. In Tunisia, the vestiges of the Destour are falling under the influence of French imperialism. In Algeria the bourgeois' and landlords' national reformism only demands that Arabs be granted French citizenship.[30]

It was from approaches of this kind that the appropriate tactic was evolved, despite the fact that they were so totally contrary to those which Stalin had formulated some years before, concerning the very same movements; indeed the Egyptian C.P. even condemned the Wafd retrospectively:

In opposition to counter-revolutionary and capitulationist national reformism, we must build an anti-imperialist revolutionary pan-Arab front, involving the great masses of the workers, peasants and urban petty bourgeoisie, a front which draws its strength from the workers' and peasants' movement on which it must be based.[31]

As for working with 'the national-revolutionary petty-bourgeois groups which are struggling against imperialism, albeit with considerable reservations', the general rule was to be 'advance separately but strike together'. One could establish temporary specific agreements geared to militant action with such groups, as long as their lack of resolution and consistency were criticized, thereby preserving the complete ideological and organizational independence of the communist movement.[32]

This revolutionary front was supposed to struggle against all exploiters, be they imperialist or indigenous.

> In Syria, in Palestine and in Egypt, the struggle for national independence and for the national unification of the Arab peoples on the basis of popular sovereignty is inseparable from the struggle for a peasant agrarian revolution conducted simultaneously against the imperialist usurpers and their agents, the Zionists in Palestine, and against the local feudal landowners.[33]

A resolution adopted by the small Palestinian Communist Party in 1931 declared that

> The Communist Party believes that the only solution to the question of the peasantry lies in an insurrectionary revolutionary struggle, waged against the imperialists, the Zionists and the Arab landowners by the fundamental stratum of the peasant masses, under the direction of the working classes led by their Communist Party.[34]

It should be stressed that it was at this time that the small communist parties of the Eastern Arab countries spelled out very precisely their thesis concerning the unity of the Arab nation, a concept which was absent or very vague in the nationalists' ideology at the time. 'National reformism' was accused of 'failing to transcend the political frontiers established by imperialism, which artificially divide the Arab peoples'.

> The communists see it as their duty to conduct the struggle for national independence and unity, not only within the narrow frontiers of the various Arab countries, frontiers which have been artificially created by imperialism and the dynastic interests, but also on a pan-Arab level, for the unification of the entire Arab East. By transcending these artificial frontiers the anti-imperialist revolutionary movement will attain its true strength, will become truly revolutionary in scope, and will become the centre of gravity for broader masses. The Arab popular masses are well aware that, in order to rid themselves of the imperialist yoke, they must join forces on the basis of the common language, the common historical conditions, and the common enemy which they share. The Arab peoples' fusion in the revolutionary struggle against imperialism, and the goal which inspires this struggle indicate that they are adequately prepared to overthrow the imperialist yoke, achieve national political independence and create a certain number of Arab states which could eventually, of their own free choice, unite on a federal basis.[35]

The creation of a common newspaper for Egypt, Syria, Palestine and Iraq was also envisaged.[36]

An interesting incidental point is that the movement's extension to the Arab Maghreb was expected. The communists of these countries were denounced for a 'right-wing opportunism which gives in on the national question to the great powers and bourgeois nationalism', an opportunism which was condemned as 'one of the main obstacles to the development of the communist movement in the Arab countries . . .'

> In Tunisia and Algeria, the communist organizations are growing weaker due to the fact that the communists have proved incapable of presenting the question of the struggle against French imperialism to the people. If they do not overcome this opportunism, and especially this arrant right-wing opportunism on the national question, the communist parties will not be able to develop in the Arab countries.

It was therefore necessary to 'take urgent steps to organize and unify the communists of Algeria, Tunisia and Morocco, and in future to detach the organization in all these countries from the French Communist Party in order to set up independent units.'[37] It is interesting to imagine what would have happened if the eastern Arab communists' ideas had been put into practice. The outcome for the North African communists could hardly have been worse than it was as things turned out.

The tactic prescribed by the C.P.s in the Arab countries could not hope to achieve more than a small part of the goals it had set itself, and only in the very distant future at that. It was abandoned too soon to lead to any concrete results. But its correct, if exaggerated, evaluation of the forces at work – the bourgeois nationalists were not all traitors to the national ideal – and its Marxist analysis of the situation were to have important consequences in the long run. These ideas, and through them, Marxist thought in general, gained an audience amongst the masses, and even in bourgeois circles which did not and would not accept communism. For example, the notion of imperialism, as propagated by Marxists, and complete with Leninist connotations, has become a common theme of all Arab nationalism. Marxism alone could supply a coherent explanation and analysis of a phenomenon which constituted the fundamental problem faced by the Arab nationalists. It is not insignificant that the single Arabic word *isti'mar* has been chosen to express the connected, but not strictly identical notions of imperialism and colonialism.[38] The idea that a social revolution must follow a national revolution has also become a very common and widespread theme. In one of his theoretical articles, Gamal Abdel Nasser himself states that:

> Every people must undergo two revolutions: a political revolution in which it repossesses what the tyrant has deprived it of, or regains the right to self-government by evicting the foreign army of occupation; a social revolution in which various classes come into conflict and which establishes genuine equity amongst all the sons of the country.[39]

The National Struggle in the Context of the Fight Against Fascism

We have mentioned that the 'class against class' phase of strategy did not last long. Its stubborn, and, in view of all the counter-indications, absurd application in Europe, had by 1933 resulted in membership of the French Communist Party dropping to 28,000; in Germany it had prevented the communists from offering any serious resistance to Hitler's rise to power. One or two years after the German catastrophe, Stalin decided to abandon the theory that social democracy was the twin sister of fascism. The International began to apply the Popular Front tactic: starting in France it was ratified by the 7th Congress of the Comintern, July–August 1935. Sectarianism having been carried to extremes, there was now a corresponding swing in the opposite direction. The defence of democracy — the term 'bourgeois democracy' was used less and less — became the watchword in Europe, and any possible alliance against fascism became acceptable. Maurice Thorez declared to his audience in the Salle Wagram, in October 1935, that 'Democracy, and democratic liberties, for all that they are relative and precarious, nonetheless still afford the working class better conditions under which to struggle for its own interests.'[40] Not long before, and ten months after Hitler's accession to power, Thorez had deplored the fact that 'some comrades had allowed themselves to be influenced' by the fallacious idea that 'one should mobilize the masses to defend democracy against dictatorship'.[41]

The struggle against fascism quite rightly became the main aim. More questionably, long-term perspectives and principles were increasingly sacrificed to the immediate demands of efficiency in that struggle. It was not long before any references to the class struggle and the socialist goal were dropped. Just as the previous tactic had been developed as a reaction to a defeat in China and then been applied with catastrophic results in Europe, so the new strategy, designed to regain lost ground in the West, was then extended to the other continents. In France the French C.P. increasingly appealed to nationalist sentiments, which were particularly suitable to the mobilization of French energies against the fascist countries. It was concurrently increasingly difficult for the Party to call on the colonies to struggle for their independence, as this struggle weakened France and the 'strong French Army' desired by Stalin. This was particularly so in the case of the Arab countries colonized by France: North Africa, Syria and Lebanon.

Previously the French C.P. had urged its militants to struggle against colonialism. In May 1931 Maurice Thorez was heard deploring the fact that the Party's anti-colonialist efforts were 'scandalously insufficient . . . compared to 1925'.[42] 'Shameful', he called it in March 1932.[43] The watchword of 'liberation' or 'independence' for the colonies, and especially for Algeria, figured as a goal in Maurice Thorez's *Collected Works* right up until August 1935.[44] In his 17th October 1935 report to the Central Committee, he tried to smooth over the emerging contradictions in a particularly interesting way. He feared, with good reason, that in Algeria the Popular Front policy would be applied only amongst the European masses, to the detriment of the Arab/Berbers:

The comrades are considerably influenced by what goes on in France and tend to copy rather mechanically what is done here. There is thus a possibility that they will abandon the struggle to defend the rights of the people of Algeria. Hostile elements might be able to push us into adopting a sectarian attitude towards the national reformist elements.[45]

And he suggested that 'more be done to establish links' with the very 'national reformists' who had been so reviled during the previous period and against whom the C.P. paper *Lutte Sociale* (Social Struggle) was still advocating struggle and the creation of a 'real Arab Communist Party' as late as September 1934.[46]

This approach contained the seeds of an interesting synthesis of Arab demands and the necessities of the anti-fascist struggle in Europe. But this synthesis apparently implied the renunciation of all national demands. In their enthusiasm for the French Popular Front's victory, which aroused so many hopes, the Algerian elites announced this renunciation. The June 1926 Muslim Congress, in which all the Algerian parties participated, demanded essentially one thing: what we would now call integration.[47]

But what bourgeois Algerians such as Farhat Abbass were looking forward to during this uplifting period was not acceptable to the proletarian elements grouped in the *Etoile Nord-Africaine* (North African Star), despite the E.N.A.'s short-lived participation in the Muslim Congress. As early as 1935, they protested against the assimilationism of those bourgeois and intellectuals who would have been satisfied with the adoption of the Blum-Viollette plan to enfranchise only some 20,000 members of the Muslim elite. Clumsily, but energetically, they proclaimed that:

The people must also know [*sic*] this policy of Farhat Abbass and Bendgelloun's. What do the latter say on the subject? They ask the Arab people to give up their personal status, that is to say to give up their nationality and to break away from Islam in order to join the family of France. And what about the family of Algeria, gentlemen? Do you disown it? Do you abandon it? Do you betray it? . . .

What we say to the Algerian people is that the policy of assimilation, the renunciation of personal status, represents a very serious danger; at a stroke, we would lose our nationality, our dignity and our hopes of reconquering our independence; it would therefore be suicidal. We condemn this policy, we rise up against it unreservedly and call on the entire Muslim population of Algeria to rise up against it unanimously. Algeria is our country, this is our home, and we shall stay what we have been and what we are. The management of economic, political and cultural affairs is our job and we must organize ourselves and form a solid basis on which to manage our own country. We have no wish whatsoever to live as poor relations or as foreigners in our own country. The *Etoile Nord Africaine*, your national organization, calls on you to struggle for your existence and your total emancipation.[48]

The E.N.A. had joined the *Rassemblement Populaire* (Popular Alliance) and had turned out in strength for all its demonstrations. No informed witness can deny Moussali Hage's affirmation that: 'For twelve years, that is from 1925 until 1937, the Algerian national movement collaborated faithfully and honestly with the French democratic parties based in Paris.'[49] In 1935 and 1936, however, a fundamental choice had to be made for or against assimilation, that is, for or against Algeria's national vocation and its future association, to a greater or lesser extent, with the other Arab or Muslim countries. Surreptitiously at first, and then more and more explicitly, the Communist Party, like the great majority in the Popular Front and like the Algerian bourgeoisié, sided against this national vocation and for the assimilationist reforms. This choice, in which principles were compromised so as not to antagonize Communist Party allies and, in theory at least, so as not to weaken the anti-fascist front, was of crucial historical importance. The E.N.A. increasingly resisted the French and Algerian assimilationists and asserted its commitment to the idea of an Algerian nation. It attacked communist policy in violent language. 'You have taken over where imperialism left off, you have become chauvinists of the worst sort, allies of colonialism.'[50]

On 26 January 1937, the Popular Front Government decreed the dissolution of the *Etoile Nord Africaine*. It was the final breaking point between the French democratic movement and the Algerian national movement. Moussali Hage, the undisputed leader of the latter movement at the time, was deeply shaken, as several of us who were there on the day can testify. The Algerian nationalists could legitimately draw the conclusion that the French left could not be relied upon. The Communist Party had just highlighted a vigorously assimilationist motion passed by the Muslim elect of the *departement* of Constantine:

> . . . a sincere and wholehearted expression of loyalty towards the great French nation to which they feel so deeply attached. They declare their unflinching opposition to any form of special parliamentary representation conflicting with their identification with France, with their own interests, or with the best interest of France. They give their total support to the governmental project to enfranchise French Muslims, the only project capable of consolidating the French accomplishments in the country once and for all. They stress that the attitude of those Algerian members of parliament who, whilst asserting that Algeria is a province of France, also oppose any assimilationist policy, is paradoxical to say the least.[51]

The governmental project in question, for which the C.P. was campaigning, was the Blum-Viollette project to enfranchize some 20,000 members of the Muslim elite.

After a fortnight's thought, *l'Humanite* published an article on the dissolution of the E.N.A., written by Robert Deloche, the secretary of the new Communist Party of Algeria. This embarrassed article admitted that it would have been 'more appropriate to apply the dissolution act to the fascist leagues'.

But, he continued, the attitude of 'certain leaders' of the E.N.A. 'towards the Popular Front, the Government and our own party' had been giving cause for concern. It was necessary, he concluded:

> to extend the achievements of the Popular Front to Algeria. Successful measures have already been taken by Monsieur Guillon, the *Resident General* in Tunisia, and in Morocco General Nogues has attracted much support by authorizing the publication of four Arabic-language newspapers.[52]

The article carefully avoided the essential question.

The actual choice, of which the banning of the E.N.A. was the practical expression, had not yet been theoretically recognized. M. Thorez was, at the time, still talking of the 'complete liberation of the colonial peoples' as one of the Party's goals. But this goal could not be put forward for the time being, and in the meantime the Party supported 'any democratic reform in the colonies'.[53] But in December 1937 things were made more explicit. In his report to the 9th C.P. Congress, M. Thorez stated clearly that:

> Our Communist Party's fundamental demand concerning the colonial peoples remains the right to independence and to determine their own affairs freely. One of Lenin's phrases proved apt when we reminded our Tunisian comrades, who agreed, that the *right to divorce* does not imply any obligation to do so. Since the decisive issue of the moment is the victory of the struggle against fascism, the interest of the colonial peoples lies *in their union* with the people of France, and not in an attitude which might further the aims of fascism and place Algeria, Tunisia or Morocco, for example, under Hitler or Mussolini's yoke, or turn Indo-China into a base for the operations of Japanese militarism.[54]

He put it even more unequivocally on 21 September 1938:

> Under the present conditions, it is in the interests of the indigenous populations of North Africa, and of all the French colonies, to remain linked with the metropolis in the effort to defend peace. But, if there is to be a real *Communauté*, the essential demands of the indigenous peoples of North Africa, Syria, Lebanon and all the colonies must be satisfied.[55]

Syria and Lebanon were thus lumped together with North Africa. However, the situation was very different in these countries, the birthplace of Arab nationalism. In principle, Syria and Lebanon were neither colonies nor protectorates. They were countries under French mandate, which France was supposedly preparing for independence, in accordance with the mission entrusted to her by the League of Nations. The Popular Front Government had worked out treaties granting these countries their independence, in exchange for which France would be guaranteed the preservation of many of her entrenched positions. After much hesitation, the nationalist parties had accepted these treaties, but the Senate never ratified them.

This situation enabled the local communist parties to conduct the struggle for national independence without departing from the global anti-fascist strategy. The new leadership which emerged around 1933–34 was made up of intelligent, energetic and capable men, many trained in the Soviet Union. Despite the conservatism of many of the local state officials, the election of a Popular Front Government in France had resulted in a certain relaxation of police surveillance. The Party's paper, *Sawt ash-Sha'f* (Voice of the People), was not prevented from appearing.

The Syrian and Lebanese Communist Parties were thus able to develop a real nationalism, albeit one devoid of any immediate revolutionary social connotations. To further the world-wide struggle against fascism, it was necessary for Syria and Lebanon to gain their independence, and the French democrats would have to agree to this. In 1937, Khaled Bekdache, the leading light of the Syrian Lebanese communists, writing in a pamphlet designed to popularize the cause of the Spanish Republic, put it as follows:

> We do not, for one moment, expect that the Popular Front will automatically grant us our independence. We have no reason to believe that the Popular Front's victory in France necessarily means that the Arab peoples of Algeria, Tunisia, Morocco and Syria will be freed from the colonialist yoke . . . [But] we do believe that its persistence and success in the struggle against fascism will create circumstances and conditions favourable to the Arab people's struggle for total independence and the march towards the most complete freedom.[56]

The demand for immediate independence featured prominently in every Syrian/Lebanese communist text published during this period, including those appearing in *l'Humanite*, such as the article by Khaled Bekdache on 25th January 1938, or the formal address to Maurice Thorez, voted on by a meeting held in Damascus and published in *l'Humanite* on 23rd November 1937. Despite Maurice Thorez's arguments about the inappropriateness of a divorce, the Syrian/Lebanese Communist Party's attitude forced the French C.P. to go much further towards an accommodation with nationalist demands in these countries than in North Africa. Khaled Bekdache, in the article quoted above, talks of 'the alliance with French democracy' as being in his own country's interest, from a democratic perspective. The French communists replied by admitting that independence — other terms were used whenever possible — was necessary to French national interest. Virgile Barel and Jacques Gresa, on the eve of their departure for Syria, declared that:

> Ratification of the Franco-Syrian treaty, which will restore dignity and freedom to the Syrian and Lebanese peoples, is the only means of maintaining French influence and reinforcing existing links at a time when there is a dangerous degree of fascist agitation in the Eastern Mediterranean

countries. We even believe that this is the only way for France to preserve the social and economic advantages and influence it has gained in these countries.[57]

Just before the War, on 11th February 1939, Maurice Thorez took an interesting step forwards, influenced perhaps by the stubbornly nationalist policy of the Syrian/Lebanese communists, and certainly by the growing temptation for the Algerian nationalists to respond favourably to the only offers of support forthcoming, namely those of fascist Italy. In a speech delivered in Algiers he, on the one hand, integrated the Algerians into what he referred to as 'our own France'; he spoke of the Frenchmen of France and the Frenchmen of Algeria, which included 'you, the native-born Frenchmen, naturalized Frenchmen and Israelites, and you, the Arab and Berber Muslims'; he called on them to unite 'to maintain peace . . . for the greater honour and integrity of a greater France'. But he also recognized that the Algerian people as a whole, including its French and European elements, had a certain national vocation. 'There is an Algerian Nation which is also made up of a mixture of twenty races . . . and whose evolution can be facilitated and aided by the efforts of the French Republic.' These Muslim and Christian Frenchmen of Algeria, who would one day become Algerians, should 'draw even closer to the French democracy'. Once again, there was no need to divorce. 'We seek a free union between the peoples of France and Algeria.'[58]

This clearly involved an attempt to reconcile contradictory factors: national aspirations and a solid, perhaps indissoluble link with France. The Frenchmen of Algeria, citizens of the future Algerian nation, would be a crucial part of this link. In any case, evolution towards nationhood was not for the immediate future. The essential thing was the struggle against international fascism, a struggle which Maurice Thorez thought the Algerians would support wholeheartedly if concessions were made to their national aspirations. This contradictory synthesis was used as theory for the next twenty years. But because it did not countenance independence in the near future, it could not but be a rather weak instrument in the face of the rising tide of increasingly impatient nationalism.

Definite stands, which were to be maintained for a long time, had thus been taken in France, Algeria and the Levant. These were clear-cut positions despite the fact that they were couched in subtle language so as not to detract from the image of perfect unity between communist parties. This is why we have dwelt at length on this period, in which the origins of contemporary problems are so clearly discernible.

There was to be a sudden break in the policy and theorizations of the communist parties. It lasted for nearly two years and corresponded with the period during which the German-Soviet non-aggression pact held good. The War was in its first stages and most communist parties had been banned. Suddenly, but temporarily, the themes of the period 1927–34 reappeared; the struggle of the proletariat against the homogenous mass of the bourgeoisie, combined with the uncompromising struggle for independence waged by the colonized peoples, whose allies were the Soviet Union and the proletarians of the imperialist countries (especially those of England and France, whose rulers were responsible for the War, according to Molotov). The Popular Front strategy, for all that it was supposedly out of date in Europe, was still valid 'in China as in the colonized and dependent countries whose peoples are struggling for national liberation'.[59] The programme for an eventual 'people's government', as drawn up by the clandestine C.P. in 1941,[60] enshrined the right to independence of the peoples of the French Empire. All the principles which had been sacrificed to the anti-fascist struggle reappeared when that struggle was itself sacrificed, but they did so at a time when nothing could be done about them.

In June 1941 the Party's international strategy reverted to being primarily anti-fascist, and everything was once again subordinated to this line, which now found its expression in armed struggle. The positions taken up before the War were re-adopted. The national problem in North Africa was carefully avoided by the French Communist Party. Gradually, bourgeois nationalism began to separate itself from assimilationism in Algeria. In Tunisia and Morocco, it was growing in force. The proletarian nationalism which had begun to emerge in rough outline within the *Etoile Nord Africaine* continued to simmer in the background. It found itself confronted with a very serious contradiction. Its demands could not fail to be opposed by the imperialist bourgeois democracies, and the latters' fundamental policies were supported by actual or *de facto* National Fronts which incorporated the working classes and the communist parties of their countries. Furthermore the bourgeois democracies were the allies of the only socialist state, the Soviet Union. Proletarian content or not, any nationalist demands against France or Britain could only help the fascist countries. Hitler and Mussolini were well aware of the fact, and angled their propaganda in the countries ruled by British and French imperialism accordingly. And certain nationalisms, despite their usual general wariness, found themselves quite attracted by the appeals of their enemies' enemies.

The Syrian/Lebanese communists were not faced with this dilemma. Under the very special conditions prevailing in Syria and Lebanon during the War, the demand for national independence did not, in fact, help the fascist enemy. It was directed against a French imperialism locally represented by the very weak forces of the Free French. The British blatantly supported this demand for independence, and so did the United States of America and the Soviet Union, if a little more discreetly. The de Gaulle Government's frequent clumsiness only increased the strength of the demand. The French Communist Party was far away, and its own preoccupations were far closer to home. So the Syrian/Lebanese communists were able to struggle energetically for independence. They showed themselves to be more vigorous, more consistent, and more competent than their bourgeois allies in the National Front. They thus acquired a reputation as fearless and upstanding fighters in the national struggle. All the fundamental social issues were quite explicitly put off till a later date.[61] The Party contented itself with supporting the immediate demands of the underprivileged, circulating Marxist literature in Arabic, and glorifying the socialist organization of the Soviet Union.

In Iraq, Egypt, Palestine and Transjordan, where the communist groups were less united, less coherent, less 'solid', to use the usual phrase, than those in Syria and Lebanon, there emerged a genuine effort to investigate the relationship between national independence and the march to socialism. But the weakness of these groups at the time meant that such research could merely form the basis of future developments. Unfortunately such a detailed study, although potentially fruitful, would be rather difficult given that the sources are scattered and not easily available.

The period of world-wide anti-fascist strategy did not come to an end once Germany had been defeated. It continued until 1947, with the Soviet 'Tripartite' world policy. Stalin hoped for an *entente* between the three or four great powers against a possible resurgence of the German menace. The Peoples' Democracies were conceived of as having state structures intermediate between those of the bourgeois democracies and the Soviet Union. The former, especially France and Italy, were expected to move non-violently, through parliamentarianism, towards this intermediate stage. The Communist Party's participation in the French Government was the symbol of this peaceful road. The French colonies, including the Arab countries of the Maghreb, supposedly had every interest in following the course taken by France. The arguments put forth by Maurice Thorez in 1937 and 1938 concerning the inappropriateness of a divorce were reiterated exactly when the Setif massacres of 1945 were crystallizing Algerian ethno-national feeling and making the Algerian bourgeoisie's assimilationist position quite untenable. An Algerian proletarian nationalism continued to develop within the organizations which had taken up the mantle of the *Etoile Nord Africaine*. In Morocco, it is true, the cadres of the Moroccan Communist Party had been 'Moroccanized' and in 1946, the Party had issued irreproachably nationalist demands. But these demands were indistinguishable from those of the *Istiqlal*, which did not hesitate to exploit the past failings of the P.C.M. (Communist Party of Morocco), such as its condemnation of the January 1944 riots, and its 'zigzags'.[62] The Moroccan masses, faced with a choice between two parties having similar programmes, chose the more completely Moroccan one. Once again, however, Marxist ideas had penetrated the consciousness of the left wing of the *Istiqlal*, a left wing whose influence was soon to make itself felt.

In the Arab East the demand for nationhood continued to be the essential one for most countries. But in Syria and Lebanon, independence had already been achieved. However, the Communist Party maintained its impetus with a programme based almost exclusively on foreign policy and was thus very successful. From a national point of view the political capital gained during the struggle for independence was bearing fruit. Furthermore public opinion was still very wary of a possible re-assertion of Western imperialism against which the Party was conducting an uncompromising struggle. It was also uncompromising in its struggle against Zionism. On the social level, the Party defended immediate demands and proposed the Soviet Union as the model to be admired, thereby implying, albeit only implicitly, a possible evolution towards socialism. As there were no other significant socialist parties, this was enough to attract all those who hoped for a transformation of society, be it a slow or a brutal one.

The Era of Zhdanovism

Strategic ideas in the Centre of World Revolution underwent a considerable change in 1947. The Marshall Plan was rejected and the Communist and Workers' Parties' Bureau of Information, the Cominform, was set up in October, to replace the Comintern which had been dissolved in 1943. There was a definite tightening-up in the Peoples' Democracies, and they increasingly aligned themselves completely with the policy and economy of the Soviet Union. The communists were expelled from the French Government. The cultural and ideological openness which had prevailed during the previous few years came to an end, both in the socialist world and in the communist parties of the capitalist world. The international *Directoire* of the four great powers gave way to the Cold War between the two 'camps'.

The new positions were set out by Zhdanov in his report to the Inaugural Assembly of the Cominform, at the end of September 1947. They are well known. The world is divided into two camps: the war camp led by the United States of America and the peace camp led by the Soviet Union. The U.S.A. seeks to enslave Europe in order to drag it into a war against the Soviet Union. 'The communists must be the leading force which draws all the freedom-loving anti-fascist elements into the struggle against the new American expansionist plans to enslave Europe.'[63] The report was mainly concerned with Europe. It only mentioned in passing that 'Indonesia, Vietnam and India have joined the anti-imperialist camp; Egypt and Syria have expressed their support.'[64] In any case the Bureau of Information consisted only of European communist parties.

The positions adopted during the anti-fascist struggle were thus reiterated. Indeed, Zhdanov explicitly compared American policy to the 'adventurist programme of the fascist aggressors'. But once Zhdanovism had carried the day, all references to the march towards socialism were dropped. The line around which the 'freedom-loving anti-fascist elements' were to be mobilized was essentially the defence of national independence.

Everything was envisaged in this light, especially the subject which concerns us here: colonial policy. The question of the independence of countries colonized by the great powers was resolved in terms of whether or not it would contribute to the general struggle against American imperialism. Divorce was just as inappropriate as in Hitler's time. After all, the liberated colonies might join and reinforce the American camp. The democratic forces in these colonies were in no way trusted to prevent such a seemingly unavoidable evolution. Far better to struggle for the formation of a 'national' government opposed to American overlordship, with the help of whatever allies against Americanization one could find in the metropolis; and more often than not the latter were particularly chauvinistic elements. The colonized 'part' could thus be saved along with the imperial 'whole'. A fierce struggle was to be waged against pro-American governments in the metropolis. All available forces were to be mobilized for this struggle, including the masses in the colonies. The French C.P. realized that in North Africa only 'national' watchwords could attract these masses. The nationalist parties there had become powerful, and were thus dangerous rivals. One should therefore follow in their footsteps and model one's attitudes on theirs. The constitution of a national front would be proposed. But it was necessary to correct and redirect the positions adopted by these nationalist movements. Great stress would be laid on the fraternity between French and autochthonous elements, and on the links which would eventually be established with France. The central issue was to ensure that these movements adopted the correct world-view: anti-American struggles, defence of peace, support for the positions of the Soviet Union. Above all one must combat any tendencies to form a pan-Arab or pan-Muslim, or even pan-Maghreb bloc, which would necessarily weaken the links with France and might become integrated into some American plan. Hence the declarations by the Maghreb C.P.s expressing a determination to 'struggle against narrow-mindedness and national chauvinism' and a rejection of all 'racial blocs'.[65]

The results of this mongrel tactic were unfortunate, to say the least. Since on the national level all the various parties' programmes were more or less similar, the masses tended to turn towards the nationalist parties, whose cadres compromised fewer French elements and whose watchwords did not include references to worldwide goals too remote from their own aspirations and immediate interests, nor any preoccupation with maintaining links with France. The communist parties, having no programme for fundamental social reforms, merely trailed behind the nationalist movement they had previously vituperated against. In no way did they guide it.

As we have seen, the Zhdanov report had mentioned certain independent countries of the under-developed world which were part of the anti-imperialist camp. But in the months that followed, the rulers of these countries seemed to lean towards a *rapprochement* with the U.S.A., or at least to evince reluctance to be prompted by the Soviet Union and integrated into its camp. The logic of the position adopted in 1947 which assumed the existence of a latent world war, a merciless war, albeit it a cold one, meant that no neutrals could be recognized; there could be no middle ground. Tito's schism reinforced this tendency. The victory of the Chinese Revolution in 1949 raised hopes for analogous rapid victories of communism in the whole under-developed world. This optimism, on the surface, at least, fitted well with Zdhanov's high hopes for Europe, where 'the main danger for the working class is the underestimation of its own strength and the overestimation of the enemy's'.[66]

In his speech concluding a three-day research conference on the problems of the national and colonial movement, organized in early June 1949 by the Science Council of the Soviet Institute of Political Economy and the Soviet Academy of Science's Pacific Institute, E.M. Joukov declared that:

The progressive character of this or that social movement, the revolutionary or reactionary nature of this or that party is today to be determined by its attitude towards the Soviet Union, towards the camp of democracy and socialism. Therefore the controversy as to when the colonial bourgeoisie can be said to be playing a reactionary role can only be resolved in the light of the answer given to this central question.[67]

Consequently, the only elements which could be trusted were the communist parties. Considerable stress was laid on their strength, often rather ridiculously exaggerated:

The working class in the colonies and the dependent countries *has become* the recognized leader in the national and colonial revolution. This means that the national bourgeoisie *has been dislodged* from its leadership position within the national liberation movement in nearly all the countries of the colonial East. [my italics][68]

This was supposedly especially marked in the Arab countries. The working class, guided by the communist party, had as its ally the impoverished peasantry. The party had strong links with the masses. And so on. The terms invoked against the national bourgeoisie were the old familiar ones. The bourgeois were denounced as 'national reformists' who had betrayed the cause and sold out to the British and the Americans. In India, for instance, the Independence granted by the British was, in fact, nothing but 'a transaction between British imperialism and the upper levels of the Indian bourgeoisie, a new form of dependence upon British imperialism in these dominions (India and Pakistan)'. As usual the failures of the tactics of the past were blamed on parties which had quite straightforwardly applied the general line of the time. The Communist Party of India was criticized for having regarded Independence as 'a step forwards', for having 'decided to support Nehru's bourgeois government' and for having seized 'the opportunity to form a united national front ranging from Gandhi to the communists'.[69] Similarly the Syrian bourgeois Khaled el-Azem, who was shortly to become a great friend of the Soviet Union, was called a protege of the French and American imperialists who had brought him to power.[70]

Thus the masses of the colonial and dependent countries were supposedly taking great strides towards popular democracy. It is characteristic of such research conferences, where so many Eastern and Latin American peoples are scrutinized, that very little attention is devoted to black peoples, or to the Arab Maghreb. There is obviously considerable respect for the French Communist Party's policy concerning these peoples, which is to draw them along behind it towards some Union of the Popular Democracies of the ex-French Empire. Of course, this means that any possibility of a union between these Arab countries is implicitly excluded from consideration.

The Syrian and Lebanese Communist Parties, separate in name alone since

January 1944, faced a difficult task, despite the fact that they enjoyed the best level of political organization in the Middle East and had accumulated considerable moral capital over the years.[71] On the one hand, they tried for a certain radicalization, a denunciation of the national bourgeoisie. But on the other hand, it so happened that this national bourgeoisie was itself rising up against the American efforts to conscript them into the anti-Soviet alliance mentioned earlier in this chapter. This bourgeoisie signed the Stockholm appeal, often supported the partisans of peace and felt a considerable sympathy for the Soviet Union, especially as the latter supported its positions in various international instances. Hence a variety of contradictions which Khaled Bekdache, still the undisputed leader of both parties, made great efforts to reconcile. Little by little a new political force emerged, especially in Syria: the new socialist, nationalist and pan-Arabist 'Party of the Arab Renaissance', *al Ba'ath*, which sapped some of the support which had been or would have been attracted to the Communist Party. Faced with a competitor willing to outbid it both on the national level, with explicit pan-Arabism, and on the social level, with a programme of structural reforms, the Communist Party entered a phase of much greater activity. It found it necessary to lay much greater stress on its programme of demands. In 1951 Khaled Bekdache recognized that the Party had hitherto mainly reached intellectuals and 'enlightened' workers, without making a deep enough impression on the workers and peasants. The Party's nationalism remained centred essentially on the struggle against any possible reassertions of imperialism, especially American imperialism, and against Zionism, considered to be an agent of that imperialism.

It is rather difficult to work out what was happening to the Iraqi communists during this period. But we do know that in 1953 there was a split. The expelled group was accused of defending too right-wing a policy, of being too willing to make concessions towards the other left groups, in short of being too ready to give up the principle of 'proletarian hegemony'.

The Return to the National Front

The Zhdanovist strategy was far too unrealistic to last for long. Indeed, there is a crucial distinction to be drawn here, between the ulterior motives of those who thought it up and the actual guidelines laid down to put it into effect; one should distinguish between the real effects expected from the application of these guidelines, varying according to time and place, and the goals they were supposed to serve. Given these ulterior motives, these calculations underlying the watchwords issued, certain sections of the world-wide movement could be allowed some latitude of interpretation. Indeed, it would have been difficult and inappropriate not to allow them a relative freedom of this sort, as long as they were always careful not to contradict the general orientation too explicitly. In any case the Zhdanovist strategy had never been applied very strictly by the Syrian and Lebanese Communist Parties. The fear of American aggression against the Soviet Union, which was very much behind this orientation, receded as the latter grew economically stronger, as the communist regime in China consolidated itself, and as contradictions emerged in the 'imperialist camp' itself. As early as 1952, Stalin, in his *Economic Problems of Socialism*, estimated that wars between capitalist countries were far more likely than a war between the 'imperialist camp' and the 'anti-imperialist camp'. Correct or not, such an opinion contained the germ of a revision of the Zhdanovist strategy. Stalin's death (5th March 1953) only hastened this revision. As far as the colonized and dependent countries were concerned, what most impressed the communist international strategists was the growing strength of the national movement, and the visible proof that the countries which had achieved independence under bourgeois leadership had nonetheless not completely fallen in with American policy. The Bandung Conference and Nasser's about-face in 1955 showed this quite conclusively. Khrushchevite empiricism could hardly disdain potential allies of such importance. Furthermore the 20th Congress, in February 1956, foresaw a lasting period of peaceful co-existence, and a plurality of roads towards socialism, including peaceful and parliamentary roads. The colonial bourgeoisie itself might be led along certain specific paths towards socialism.

The change came quickly and was as quickly theorized. Towards the middle of 1955 the journal *Sovetskoe Vostokovedenie* (Soviet Orientalism) was still claiming that:

> The experience of history proves that the national bourgeoisie of the colonized and semi-colonized countries, linked as it is in a thousand ways to the feudal classes and to foreign imperialism, cannot lead a national liberation movement to victory. The anti-imperialist and anti-feudal revolution can only triumph through an alliance of workers and peasants led by the communists. [72]

But in January 1956, an editorial in the same journal was arguing that:

> After the Second World War, because of the radical changes wrought in the international balance of power, the pre-eminent position of foreign capital in various Eastern countries can no longer be taken to mean that imperialism necessarily dominates political life there. Thus, countries such as Indonesia or Saudi Arabia are today making their own policy decisions, for all that they are not yet liberated from Western imperialism. [73]

And further, it argued that:

> The national bourgeoisie is not always prepared to betray the cause of national independence; on the contrary it is the natural and practically irreconcilable enemy of imperialism . . . The facts show that the increasing role played by international capitalism in the East triggers off an aggravation in the contradictions which oppose the local bourgeoisie to foreign capital and to the feudal landowners. [74]

One should therefore form a National Front, led by the national bourgeoisie wherever the working class was not developed enough to seize the initiative. This National Front would be long lasting and communists should support it without asking for any special privileges, and without demanding to participate in its leadership. For a long period:

> the peoples of the East, thanks to this national unity which draws together the democratic and patriotic forces of all parties, all classes and all layers of the population, will be able to accomplish successfully the great tasks of the struggle for national liberty, for the application of an energetic peace-loving policy and for the well-being of the people.[75]

The ensuing transition to socialism would be quite painless.

These theses were received by the various communist parties with the usual automatic respectful attention, barely tempered by Togliatti's ephemeral 'polycentric theory' or by the French C.P.s Molotovian resistance to new ideas. Their repercussions were felt everywhere. Of course the Algerian insurrection made it impossible for the French C.P. to have any clear colonial policy, and with national independence the Tunisian and Moroccan C.P.s were finally free of the French Union policy which had been imposed upon them and which had compromised them for so long.

In the Arab East, however, things were somewhat different.[76] The Syrian and Lebanese C.P.s had accepted only a minimum of Zhdanovism and had remained faithful to the Popular Front line. They now enthusiastically re-adopted it in an accentuated form. An alliance with the socialistic and nationalist Ba'ath Party was established, and the links with 'partisans of peace' in the big bourgeoisie, Khaled al-Azem for instance, became even closer. All the communist groups in the Middle East showered the highest praises on the 'national hero', Gamal Abdel Nasser, who had stood up to Anglo-French imperialism over Suez, initiated certain structural (agrarian) reforms, oriented his trade policy towards the East, and even consented to free most of the communists he had incarcerated. The pan-Arabism so dear to Nasser and the middle classes of Egypt and the Fertile Crescent was also adopted by the communists. Their declarations on the subject were clearer than ever and, if necessary, invoked the Stalinist definition of the nation.

On 7th May 1956, the Central Committee of the Syrian and Lebanese C.P. passed a resolution declaring that 'the Arab countries' aspiration to unity is neither the result of temporary circumstances, nor of a sentimental desire, nor of this or that party or group's ideological propaganda'. Several factors, including 'various Arab countries' victories in the struggle to free themselves from the imperialist yoke and to achieve their independence, and the application by these countries – most notably Egypt and Syria – of a policy of emancipation based on the enjoyment of national sovereignty, and the struggle against foreign intervention and imperialist alliances' had led to 'the practical application of the watchword, Arab unity'. The forthcoming victory of the Iraqi people over its tyrants would 'pave the way for an even speedier march towards *complete* Arab unity'. [my italics] [77]

Similarly, in September 1957, the Egyptian communist groups who had just united to form a single 'United Egyptian Communist Party' explained that:

> There has been a radical change in Egypt's status, a change which has done away with the country's dependence on imperialism, on feudal power and on collaborationist capitalism. Credit for this grandiose transformation goes to all the patriotic and popular classes, especially to the working class and its communist avant-garde. It also goes to the Free Officers led by Abdel Nasser, for the present Government has played a decisive part in the great national accomplishments. On the national level, the Egyptian Communists consider Egypt to be an integral part of the great Arab nation . . . The Arab masses have a growing awareness of this fact, which inspires their struggle for complete Arab unity. [78]

True, the National Front led by Nasser was not gentle with the communists. Quite a few were freed, but others were kept as hostages. The Government's social achievements were often insufficient and warranted criticism. Its international orientation, whilst remaining true to the general line of 'positive neutralism', was nonetheless fairly erratic. The communist groups were in the paradoxical position of having to pursue their action and propaganda in favour of the regime clandestinely and under police surveillance. This did not diminish their ardour. Georges Cogniot caught the spirit of the times in his November 1956 article entitled 'Nasser and Progress'. Basing himself on arguments developed by Stalin, discreetly referred to by the indefinite pronoun 'one', he wrote that:

> The aspiration to full national sovereignty, which is so strong amongst the Egyptian bourgeoisie, intellectuals and officers, has been and still is, for the same reasons, an aspiration which should be supported, even if one can demonstrate that they violate certain democratic principles. And the same would still be true even were one to prove that their declarations as to the *republican* or *socialist* character of their programme are not borne out by the facts. [79]

However, towards the end of 1957 there was a change in the communist attitude. In the Soviet Union, 'liberalization' had been slowed down following the Hungarian and Polish crises of the previous year. Relations with Tito were steadily growing worse. In November he had refused to sign the Communist Parties' common declaration. Syria's evolution towards the left was being accelerated by American and Turkish manoeuvres and threats; the Ba'ath was practically in power. A correspondent in the December issue of *Democratie Nouvelle* described how a programme of economic development was being:

applied by the nationalist Government led by the socialist Ba'ath Party and supported by the influential Communist Party. The agrarian reform projects in the semi-feudal South will be enormously reinforced by the new developments in the North-East. Action by peasant trade unions led by the Ba'ath is already leading to the realization of plans which will strike hard at the old landowning classes by creating an independent peasantry and a better paid agricultural proletariat. The national bourgeoisie can still play a progressive and constructive role here.[80]

The *rapprochement* between Syria and the Soviet Union was proceeding apace. The Communist Party mobilized the masses behind Government policy. But Syria's economic and military links with Egypt were getting stronger. There was much talk of an even closer union. It was than that Khaled Bekdache raised the question of what form the Arab Union should take, a question which had often been debated theoretically, but never very passionately. As against the spokesmen of the Ba'ath, who wanted an organic union, he supported the idea of a federation. He feared that were there to be a union the Syrian C.P. would suffer by the Egyptian laws forbidding all parties except the Government party, the so-called 'National Union'. In this, he enjoyed the support of some of the Syrian big bourgeoisie, who had their own reasons for fearing the economic hegemony of the Egyptian bourgeoisie.[81] The Ba'ath, whose main fear was communist hegemony, hastened the process and convinced Nasser; soon afterwards, on 1st February 1958, the United Arab Republic was established.

Khaled Bekdache left Syria to preach against Titoism at the Congress of the Bulgarian Communist Party, and other such venues. But his real target was his friend Nasser and the Ba'ath, yesterday's ally. National aspirations had to some extent been realized and some Egyptian and Syrian communists were all for pursuing the policy of previous months, with support for Nasser and alliance with the Ba'ath. They hoped for a slow evolution towards social-ization within the framework of a dictatorial state 'even if it does violate certain democratic principles', and in the context of a foreign policy based on positive neutralism. At first the Egyptian laws were applied in Syria very gradually and with great flexibility. And it seems that Nasser and Nasserism continued to enjoy the support of the Soviet Union.

On 14th July 1958, a military movement, backed by the overwhelming majority of the Iraqi population united against the feudal aristocracy and the Hashemite dynasty, overthrew the Iraqi throne and the old British agent Nuri Sa'id. Before long, dissension was breaking out within the Iraqi National Front. The Iraqi communists supported Khaled Bekdache's ideas for a federa-tion; they opposed joining the United Arab Republic. They controlled a vast mass movement. The Party had emerged from a long and terrible period of clandestinity untarnished by compromise and with enormous popular support. As in France in 1936, the communists were given the 'Ministry of the Masses' by the Kassem administration. They supported General Kassem and that important section of the Iraqi bourgeoisie which had much the same reasons as the Syrian bourgeoisie for opposing the union with the U.A.R. In their stand against the Ba'athists and the Nasserist General Aref, they put forth, as an alternative to the Nasserist pan-Arab ideology, a programme of anti-feudal, notably agrarian social reforms, parts of which Kassem applied. One of the Syrian and Iraqi communists' arguments against the union, apparently overlooked previously, was the absence of democratic institutions in the U.A.R.: no parliament, no free trade unions, no parties. Nasserist unitarianism doubtless frightened the significantly large section of the Iraqi population belonging to ethnic or religious minorities: the Kurds, Shi'ite Muslims, 'Sabeans', 'Assyrians', and Nestorian Christians. Furthermore, as the Political Bureau of the Iraqi C.P. declared on 3rd September: 'The idea of joining the U.A.R. worries our people because this union will not give the economy and national capital the opportunity it needs to develop and evolve.,[82]

On his return to Syria in September, Khaled Bekdache continued his propaganda against the U.A.R. and in favour of a federation, democratic institutions and an Iraqi-style policy; he also denounced Nasser's Titoism. Within Syria itself, Egyptian clumsiness and the economic interests injured by the Union ensured that his propaganda was increasingly well received. Nasser, that 'impulsive young man' as Khrushchev described him, became irritated and arrested all his own communists at the beginning of January — although many of the latter did not agree with Bekdache's orientation. Relations between Egypt and Iraq became tense. On 16th March, Khrushchev announced that he thought the Iraqi regime was the more progressive. The prestige of Iraqi-style Arab nationalism rose amongst the communists of the Middle East. But it was quite clear that the conflict was not essentially based on different theories of nationalism. Nasser, yesterday's hero, was vilified all over again. A new era was beginning.

Outline of a Marxist Critique

This long and incomplete survey of the facts was necessary before we could proceed to a theoretical analysis. The contemporary issues are rooted in the attitudes adopted in the past by the various sides.

Let us start from a basic idea which would appear to be incontestable from a Marxist point of view. We have traced the broad outlines of the formation and evolution of an Arab nationalism which grew up within the property-owning classes. It would seem likely that, here as elsewhere, the Marxist contribution should consist in highlighting the aspirations peculiar to the suffering masses, by means of a socialist theoretical understanding, and in organizing these masses with a view to realizing the ideas and perspectives emerging from such an analysis. In this case these aspirations were national liberation and economic freedom from foreign and indigenous capitalism.

Faced with a socially anti-feudal bourgeois nationalism, the Marxists' task was thus to create a socialist, anti-imperialist and anti-capitalist nationalism.

Thanks to their sociological analysis of the facts, and to their practical and theoretical experience, they should have been able to meet the aspirations of the masses, to contribute to the setting up of specific organizations staffed by cadres recruited from the masses themselves, and geared to the realization of their ideological projects.

The historical outline given above clearly shows that, whilst the communist parties did contribute to this task, they did not carry it out fully in several Arab countries, and indeed often had to hand over the reins to competitors, and rather odd ones at that. Why did this happen? One could of course invoke contingent causes: lack of cadres, brutal police repression, difficulties of all sorts. But all these factors have been present elsewhere without leading to the same results. One must therefore look a little deeper.

One of the main causes underlying this admittedly partial failure of the communist parties in the Arab countries is the implacable subordination of the struggle in these countries to the world strategy of communism. True, it cannot be denied that all particular struggles for socialism are necessarily interdependent on a world scale. But this interdependence should not imply that all such struggles have to be rigidly directed, down to the smallest details, by a supposedly omniscient world General Staff. Experience has shown that such hypercentralization has more disadvantages than advantages. Decisions have been taken in the light of events which affected huge territorial areas, but not the whole world, such as the failure of the Chinese revolution, and the rise of fascism in Germany, etc. These decisions have been applied in areas where the situation was profoundly different. All too often no real distinction was made between Western Europe, the U.S.A. and the colonized and underdeveloped world. Generally speaking, despite some declarations of principle, there has been, until very recently, little practical recognition of the enormous importance of the colonized people's struggle for their independence and their right to a better life. With a fine disregard for the dialectical rule set out so clearly by Stalin, no priority of attention was given to that which was growing and developing. The whole 'colonial question' was sacrificed to a strategy centred on Europe. The subordination of the struggle in North Africa to the French Communist strategy was just one instance of a general phenomenon. If just a little more room had been left for the analysis of specific conditions and the elaboration of regional tactics, the results would probably have been considerably better.

I hope I will be forgiven a small digression concerning the responsibility for this state of affairs. It could be argued that there was nothing forcing the local communist parties to toe the Comintern line so rigidly. They often took this to extremes, as we have seen in the case of those groups who ardently desired a close link with the international centre of the Revolution but were denied it, for instance the Egyptian communists who avidly sought 'directives' from supposedly more competent parties. But it would surely be somewhat dishonest to lay all the blame at the disciples' door. The anathema pronounced by Moscow on the smallest 'deviation', the wariness *vis-a-vis* the slightest inclination to independence hardly encouraged an open-minded search for national roads to socialism. The fear of falling into heterodoxy had a paralysing effect. It took all the traditional flexibility, skill and cheerful dissembling of the Chinese people and the exceptional circumstances of the Yugoslav Resistance to ensure successes not conceived of by the great General Staff. Rigid and bureaucratic leadership, and a lack of confidence in the creative spontaneity of the rank and file once again proved harmful to the cause. A notable result of this authoritarianism in global strategy was a constant chopping and changing, a series of sudden about-faces which were particularly apt to dampen enthusiasm, to breed discouragement and disenchantment.

One extremely important practical consequence of this same phenomenon was the frequent abandonment of the very principles of the struggle, an abandonment which was itself a direct cause of catastrophic failures. The conception of the march towards socialism as a struggle directed by a central General Staff, according to an overall world-wide strategy, did, of course, imply that from time to time some sectors would be temporarily sacrificed An example of this from the earliest days of the International is the case of the Turkish Communist Party's struggle. As described elsewhere, in this instance it was decided to tell the truth and give the Turkish communists the real reasons why their sector was being temporarily shut down. To cap it all, they were asked for their approval of the process. Needless to say, future policy adopted a different course. Each transitory tactical phase was theorized and declared in keeping with the eternal principles of Marxist sociological theory, and even with the principles of the fundamental philosophy — and then the same would be claimed for a diametrically opposite line a few months later. From 1934 onwards, the socialist goal seemed too distant and was put into abeyance; the communist movement was thus deprived of everything which gave it its particular appeal amongst the suffering masses. In Syria, in Lebanon, and, far more absurdly, in France, the national ideal was brought in to replace it. The communist parties could obtain a certain success on this basis too. But they soon had to deal with other even more nationalist parties, and, in the context, it was not long before these new rivals became more attractive to the masses, for a variety of reasons. True, the communists' social ideal continued to find some expression in their tradition, notably the pious translation of the classics, in their attachment to the socialist Soviet Union and in the support they gave to immediate demands. But this was not always sufficient.

The deep underlying causes of the communist parties' partial failure in the Arab countries are therefore to be found in that set of deviations in Marxist thought and practice which have been called Stalinism. The consequence was that in a whole series of countries other groups laid claim to a central role in actions which should have been the historical task of the communist parties. The advantages and dangers of this state of affairs warrant closer examination.

Arab Roads to Socialism

This all bears out the 20th Congress theses concerning the plurality of roads to socialism. It would perhaps be best if this advance could be made, as the Stalinist myth would have it, with a high level of awareness, under the guidance of reliable agents and in careful co-ordination with all the other social and national liberation movements. However, the nature of the historical process makes such a rosy future extremely unlikely. One only has to think of the paths taken by the bourgeois revolution, which often broke with its most aware supporters and occasionally triumphed under the leadership of a Prussian Junker or a Mikado, a son of God, to see why. The Stalinist attempt to make reality conform to the myth culminated in disaster in a whole series of countries.

The paths taken by the various Arab peoples will be diverse and, in many cases, no doubt unexpected. Judgements in such cases will be difficult, and one will have to be careful that they are not made with inconsiderate haste, not to say frantically.

Nikita Khrushchev was clearly right to lecture his Egyptian pupils for not having grasped that the class struggle must inevitably come to the fore once the struggle for national independence has been successfully concluded. But he was wrong in his apparent belief that communists affiliated to a communist party will everywhere and always be the only champions of this class struggle and of the march towards socialism.[88]

If one is to make valid judgements, it is essential not to confuse the problems. The march towards socialism is not necessarily linked with a particular course in foreign policy. It does not necessarily imply full membership of the 'socialist camp'. It is not necessarily linked to a parliamentary system which, in the under-developed countries, usually brings the most reactionary elements to power. Sadly, but inevitably, it is not even necessarily linked to the preservation of civil rights. Nor is it necessarily linked to a benevolent attitude towards members of the communist party. The English bourgeoisie, when it was leading the world-wide evolution by which capitalism freed itself from the trammels of feudalism, was not above persecuting even the most moderate British disciples of French Jacobinism. This does not mean that we must sing the praises of police repression, authoritarianism or the strategic meanderings of the movements we believe are, in their own way, building socialism. We must distinguish between the various levels and maintain our lucidity as Marxists.

The march towards socialism will be peaceful or violent, despotic or democratic, pitiless or humane, enlightened or obscurantist, intransigent or adaptable; but it will take place. It will be linked to the struggle for the realization, preservation and intensification of national independence, a struggle which has long since achieved its aims in Europe. This struggle is part of the ideal of liberation dear to all socialists. It must be defended. True, it should not, in itself, detract from the struggle for socialism on the international level. Marx and Engels tried to make this quite clear in their oft-quoted writings about the Czechs and Croats. But those were purely national struggles, devoid of any socialist perspective. What we are talking about now are struggles each and every one of which can be closely linked with the march towards socialism.

Once nearly all the Arab countries had achieved independence, the nationalist viewpoint ceased to be really exclusive. The problem of whether the national movement should opt for a vast united Arab nation or for individual Arab states united into a federation or confederation has become a secondary issue. Two basic facts remain crucial: the masses are above all in favour of freedom from European imperialism; they see no essential national difference between the peoples of the various Arab countries; on the contrary, there is still a strong feeling of Arab fraternity. This creates a vaguely unified tendency, which many other factors may counter-balance. The idea of Arab unity had enormous strength when it was aimed against the feudalists and business operators who were weakening the struggle against foreign imperialism by manipulating particular local issues. This idea, linked as it was to the ideal of national liberation could only lose some of its virulence once that ideal had been largely realized. However, such an idea, which had inspired so much devotion for so long, and which still corresponded to a certain reality, could not just disappear so quickly. It was further sustained by the irredentism of Algeria, Israel and to a lesser extent, Southern Arabia.

It is difficult to give an exact evaluation of how strong and widespread such a feeling remains in the various countries and amongst the various social classes. But it is certain that, where it does persist, it can be used to evoke a powerful and broadly based response. Hence the present Nasserist propaganda based on the 'divisive' work of Kassem — note the pun in his name, which can mean 'divider' in Arabic. Hence also the efforts of the Syrian and Iraqi communists to build up a counter-ideology based on ideas of democracy and federalism. Arab nationalism has of necessity often been unleashed against ethnic and religious minorities, because the latter have been used by imperialism against the liberation movement. This has led to a certain Arab chauvinism which can easily be used to discredit the stress laid by Kassem and the communists on the important role to be played by non-Arab and non-Muslim elements, especially the Kurds. More or less camouflaged attempts at such manipulation have not been lacking. Whatever may happen in the immediate future, it is clear that a principled socialist programme must aim to set up either a highly decentralized but unified Arab state or at least a group of independent states joined together by specific links. The idea proposed by the Israeli 'Semitic Movement' (*Uri Avneri*), which favours a union of Western Asiatic and North African states, seems particularly well suited to reconcile the most important divergences, whatever one may think of its originators.

At the moment the most important question is no longer which form will the Arab national entity assume; it is how to achieve that economic independence which in the mind of the masses, if not, sadly, in reality, is linked, at least for the moment, to raising the standard of living. Economic independence presupposes the construction of a solid industrial infrastructure. Aid from the capitalist countries, with all its attendant dangers, or from the socialist countries, can contribute to such an aim, but can never be sufficient in itself. This independence implies sacrifices; which classes bear the main brunt of these sacrifices will depend on the type of state which is guiding the programme of development.

The dilemmas here are more or less the same as those which prompted the pre-1917 Russian Social Democrats' fiercest debates. Must the socialist revolution follow on immediately after the anti-feudal (and in this case anti-imperialist) revolution, as both Trotsky and, after the April Theses, Lenin recommended? Or should one be prepared for a long phase between the two revolutions, in which economic independence can be built up within the framework of capitalist relations of production?

The social forces necessary for a socialist revolution exist. The middle and poor peasantry who make up the immense majority of the population is ready to back it, as long as it does not mean forced collectivization. The urban proletariat and semi-proletariat see it as the extension of the anti-imperialist struggle, and are ready to support it. The middle classes, who are far more proletarianized than their equivalents in the West, have no interest in supporting a capitalist regime which offers them nothing but destitution. The big bourgeoisie is weak and furthermore is fascinated by the power of the socialist states. But what stands in the way of such a qualitative jump, in today's Iraq, for instance, is the approach to the international situation suggested by the leaders of the 'socialist camp'. This is motivated not so much by a fear of imperialist reactions, as it was under Stalin, as by a lack of enthusiasm for the considerable effort implicit in wholehearted support for very poor countries, where everything is still to be done — and, however things may have changed, the international complications resulting from these countries 'going communist' would still be unwelcome. Indeed it seems that the Chinese leaders have a somewhat less timid attitude to encouraging revolution than their Soviet counterparts. Of course, the Soviet arguments, which can be deduced from an analysis of attitudes and situations, are not completely worthless. But one should also remember that equally pessimistic views on the international conjuncture have often been put forward in the past. Had they been heeded, there would have been no revolution in Russia, in Yugoslavia, or in China.

It thus seems probable that, despite everything, events will impose or at least favour the course recommended in various forms by the Mensheviks and by Lenin before 1917: a lengthy phase of anti-feudal, and in this case anti-imperialist, leadership accompanied by a deepening of the bourgeois revolution. In their time the Mensheviks believed that during such a period the liberal bourgeoisie would govern, with the proletariat and its party as a loyal opposition; Lenin, on the contrary, opted for a ruling coalition which would incorporate revolutionary proletarians supported by the working class and the peasantry. Experience has taught us to draw finer distinctions and not to equate a class — a sociological base — with a party, a means of political struggle. There are movements coming on to the scene whose orientation is socialistic and nationalist but whose cadres are bourgeois and exposed in a thousand ways to the influence of capitalist interests; they are not, however, tied to any given programme. On the other side of the stage we have communist parties, whose cadres are hardly less bourgeois, but whose ideology, doctrine and international links do, on the whole, preclude compromises of this kind. Finally, there may be a third group of organizations, especially in Algeria, whose cadres are mainly proletarian, influenced by Marxism but repelled by the failings of the European communist parties; generally speaking the vicissitudes of war have protected this third group from corrupting influences.

The dangers of deviation during the transition period are obvious. We all have before us the historical example of Turkish Kemalism and its degeneration. In 1920, that movement and its programme of anti-imperialist struggle and anti-feudal revolution enjoyed the support of all the innovatory elements in society, and was strongly backed in foreign affairs by the 'socialist camp' of the time, the Soviet Union. But it betrayed its promise. It became conservative and reactionary, opposed any further steps forward, preserved the capitalist regime by brute force and turned to social, ideological and political reaction. It became a Middle Eastern bastion of Western imperialism, and was indeed encouraged to adopt such a position by national reactions to the brutal Stalinist policy of conquering zones of influence (Soviet territorial demands at the end of the War). It is quite clear that Nasserism could also move into some post-Kemalist regressive evolution of the sort. How can this be avoided?

The structure of the communist parties offers certain guarantees in this respect, as has been pointed out. The only way that their cadres can lastingly come to power is on the basis of a perspective oriented towards a socialization of the economy. Their unconditional ideological faithfulness to the old General Staff of the International Soviet Revolution, or what remains of it, also binds them. The main danger is their latent tendency to bureaucratic deviation; there is also a risk implicit in the fact that they tend to allow themselves to be influenced by the great General Staff's approach to the international situation, and in consequence, may occasionally put the brakes on mass enthusiasms. Other movements may perhaps be safe from degeneration because of other factors: an atmosphere of war, with all energies bent towards the revolutionary goal; thoroughgoing and irreversible structural reforms not confined to the agrarian level; a powerful mass impetus which has been given plenty of room to operate in. We are entering new realms here, these dramas have never been enacted on the historical stage before. Only the future will tell us what can be expected from such movements. In any case the communist parties no longer enjoy pride of place in the favour of the masses in many regions, notably in North Africa. Ideas of national and social liberation have penetrated society quite deeply, and this is largely thanks to the communists, but other groups have taken up these ideas at times when the communists themselves seemed to have betrayed them. The proletarian elements gathered around the *Etoile Nord Africaine*, the P.P.A.

and the M.T.L.D., are a case in point. Many of these militants ended up as an important tendency within the F.L.N. in Algeria. Another example is that of the elements in Morocco who ended up in the Istiqlal left and the trade unions. Tunisia's still disorganized and diffuse opposition is yet another case in point.

Egyptian Nasserism is a very different matter. Its cadres are particularly exposed to the risk of compromise with the capitalist system. Its authoritarian organization does not allow for any mass influence over its decisions. For the moment it seems to be sticking to its proclaimed aims of anti-feudal and anti-imperialist revolution. Its orientation towards socialism is much more debatable. How far will its petty-bourgeois and popular supporters back it up? If this Nasserism underwent a Kemalist-type degeneration, would it be the Communist Party which would replace it as the favourite of the suffering masses? Perhaps it would — but the Party is by no means the only possible successor.

The Syrian Ba'ath is different again. Its structure is less authoritarian, its programme is more socialistic and it enjoys the support of the students and the peasantry of central Syria, whose interests it has defended so efficiently. However, the Ba'ath is being seriously damaged by its alliance with Egyptian Nasserism, with the attendant authoritarianism and predominance of Egyptian interests. The masses and even the big bourgeoisie might well turn to the communists in despair. Already one hears that signs of friction are appearing between the two allies.

The common thread running through all these movements, their most distinctive characteristic, is the fact that they all keep at a certain distance from the Soviet Union and the socialist world. The support of the latter is sought out when the need arises, but in general any overly close ties with general Soviet strategy are avoided, in accordance with the Tito-Nehru line. On the other hand it is precisely such close ties which characterize the communist parties.

The Algerian C.P. now has practically no support; the Tunisian C.P. is not much better off; the Moroccan C.P. is alive and has considerable potential. In Egypt the communists are still an important force, and their achievements will depend both on Nasser's attitude and on their own. Their strength in Syria is greater still. But it is in Iraq that for the time being the C.P. has the greatest chances. Having just emerged from clandestinity, on 14th July this year, the Party has kept a certain virginity, an immaculate reputation as the uncompromising defender of national independence, of the poor, of religious and ethnic minorities, of the revolutionary anti-feudal struggle. The vast mass movement which waged the revolution against the detested *Ancien Regime* provided the C.P., in its role as the most advanced and irreconcilable element in that revolution, with a large, enthusiastic and powerful body of supporters. It remains to be seen whether the Party will avoid disappointing them. It has just put in its claim to participate in the Government, thereby moving from a Menshevik strategy to the first stage of a Leninist one. This represents a definite step forward, in the direction indicated by the masses. But will the

Party avoid bureaucratic deviations? Time will tell.

All over the world there are people inspired by the socialist ideal. What attitude should they adopt *vis-a-vis* all these Arab movements which are leading vast masses towards this ideal, albeit often by rather odd paths? One should surely not stand on principle and condemn them for nationalism. National liberation is as much a part of the socialist ideal as social liberation, and it would be hypocritical for those favoured by the *status quo* to accuse those whom it leaves unsatisfied of disturbing world peace. Nor does it make sense to oppose unified nationalism on principle, or to brand it as racist as Herve, Guy Mollet, various Zionist publicists and, from time to time, the French C.P. have done.[84] We have seen that it has nothing to do with racism; racist deviations are possible, but are hardly likely to make much impact. It is also meaningless to draw alarmist comparisons with pan-Germanism, and in any case there would be nothing frightening about a peace-loving socialist federation of German states. On the other hand, we cannot accept the sort of mystical blanket enthusiasm which has caused so many of us so much harm in the painfully recent past. Of course, one should support all progressive movements, but never unconditionally. We must keep the right to criticize even the movements with which we are most in sympathy, including communist movements. In fact, we should make it a duty to exercise that right and if it were kept up it might put an end to the confusing about-turns which so disorient the masses. By successively presenting Nasser first as a pure and unblemished national hero, then as a reactionary and bloody tyrant — and the show is not yet over — one destroys confidence, enthusiasm and commitment. It is always difficult to mobilize the masses behind a programme which eschews myths and is consistently lucid, but that is precisely the task of Marxists, and they have paid dearly whenever they have opted for an easier course. Movements deserve the support of world socialist opinion to the extent that they are really socialist, and really democratic which means giving as much say to the masses as possible, becoming their interpreter, trying to influence their aspirations, without deforming or constraining them. To be really socialist means doing the utmost possible under the circumstances to eliminate the barriers to human freedom caused by private ownership of land and the means of production. One could add, when talking of Marxist movements, that it means being really Marxist, that is to say making no concessions either to the myths of dogmatism or to the military morality of sectarianism; that it means being inspired by a scientific analysis of the facts, without bending those facts and that analysis to fit the demands of pragmatic opportunism.

References

1. I have recently developed the first part of this essay in my articles for the *Encyclopaedia Universalis*, (Paris, 1968), under the headings 'Arabe: 1. Les Arabes' and 'Arabisme'. At the moment it is being re-worked for

a small book, *Les Arabes*, to be published in the *Que sais-je?* collection, (P.U.F., Paris).

2. This figure is no longer accurate. Roughly speaking, and including the Arabic-speaking minorities in the frontier areas of the region, there are something like 100 million Arabs in the world today.

3. M. Rodinson, 'Sur la theorie marxiste de la nation',*Voie Nouvelles*, no. 2, May 1958, pp. 25–30. See, for example, the answer given by Khaled Bekdache during an interview in March 1957: 'Do you believe that there is an Arab nation, and if so what cultural elements go to make it up? – Yes. The elements which make up the Arab nation are objective historically established elements. Primarily, there is a common language, a common territory, a common history and a common psychological background which is reflected in a unified Arab culture. There is also a clear and growing tendency towards complete economic inter-dependence, despite all the obstacles which imperialism seeks to set in its path.' (*At-Tariq*, Beirut, December 1957), p. 90. These points are developed by the Lebanese progressive, Georges Hanna, in his recent book *Le Sens de la Nationalite Arabe*, significant extracts of which have been published in the July 1957 edition of *At-Tariq*, pp. 1–5.

4. As is noted by those excellent observers Jean and Simonne Lacoutre, *L'Egypte en Mouvement*, Le Seuil, (Paris, 1956), p. 215.

5. For the attitude to national problems characteristic of Marxist theoreticians in general, see especially S.F. Bloom, *The World of Nations – A Study of the National Implications in the Work of Karl Marx*, Columbia University Press, (New York, 1941); Horace B. Davis, *Nationalism and Socialism – Marxist and Labor Theories of Nationalism to 1917*, Monthly Review Press, (New York, 1967).

6. Letter to Engels, 8 October 1858, Marx-Engels, *Briefwechsel*, II, Dietz, (Berlin, 1949), p. 424.

7. Letter to Karl Kautsky, 12 September 1882. cf. Lenin's 'Summary of the debate on the right to national self-determination'.

8. Marx and Engels, Letter to the *Neue Rheinische Zeitung*, 31 January, 1850, in Marx, Engels, *Werke*, Vol. VII, Dietz, (Berlin, 1960), pp. 213–25.

9. *The Communist International, 1919–1943, Documents*, selected by Jane Degras, Vol. I, 1919–22, O.U.P., (London, 1956), p. 16. On 8th November 1918, Lenin declared that 'We have never been closer to the international proletarian revolution.' He was answering Hugo Eberlein, the Spartakusbund delegate, who, on Rosa Luxembourg's instructions, was opposing the immediate setting up of the Third International. For the context of this Congress see, for example, H. Seton-Watson, *The Pattern of Communist Revolution – A Historical Analysis*, Methuen, (London, 1953), p. 68 ff., and the memoirs of Angelica Balabanoff, *My Life as a Rebel*, Harper, (New York, 1938), p. 212 ff.

10. *The Communist International, op. cit.*, Vol. I, p. 109.

11. Cf. E.H. Carr's account and quotations from this Congress in *A History of Soviet Russia – The Bolshevik Revolution, 1917–1923*, Vol. III, Macmillan, (London, 1961), pp. 260–8.

12. Which did not prevent a Communist International delegate, Statshko, who was presenting a report on the agrarian question, from later

attacking 'the Muslim clergy', 'those hypocritical parasites and oppressors who hide their real nature behind a white turban and the holy Koran.' In some senses this delegate's speech was the first attempt at a Marxist compromise with Islam, in that he drew a distinction between current practices and the original spirit of the Koran, which laid down that 'land can only belong to he who works it'. Zinoviev, too, spoke of 'respecting the religious spirit of the masses' until a long process of education had borne fruit; and the Turkestani, Narbutabekov, protested against the brutal anti-religious practices of Bolshevik cadres in Turkestan, although he went on to condemn the ulemas and the 'black gangs of mullahs'. On this whole question of religion, see E.H. Carr's important note in *The Bolshevik Revolution*, III, p. 263, n. 3.

13.   The final manifestos were approved by the Congress before it had even seen them. They were published in *Kommunistitsheskiy Internacional*, (Petrograd, 1920) no. 15, cols. 3141–50. (The reference in Carr, III, p. 267, n.1 is erroneous.) An English translation by I. Spector appears in *The Soviet Union and the Muslim World*, University of Washington Press, (Washington, 1958), pp. 182–8.

14.   Most of the Bolshevik leaders were originally quite sceptical about the relevance of the Baku Congress. The main exception was Zinoviev, whose idea it was and who expected to bask in the limelight. M.N. Roy refused to participate in what he called 'the Zinoviev Circus'. He would have welcomed a great Eastern mass rally at Baku, but saw no use for a 'Congress'. Radek was also fairly enthusiastic, but for reasons which were not particularly political. He attempted to convince Roy by mocking the latter's 'precocious seriousness'. 'It may well not lead to any lasting results, but why pass over the opportunity for such an entertaining spectacle, which is sure to give a few sleepless nights to the British Foreign Secretary, Lord Curzon?' See M.N. Roy, *Memoirs*, Allied Publishers Private Ltd., (Bombay, 1964), p. 391 ff.

15.   As Zinoviev admitted fifteen months later, during the much better organized Congress of Far Eastern Workers. cf. Spector, p. 42 ff., X.J. Eudin and R.C. North, *Soviet Russia and the East, 1920–1927*, Stanford University Press, (Stanford, 1957). cf. also A.S. Whiting, *Soviet Policies in China, 1917–1924*, Columbia University Press, (New York, 1954), pp. 77–86. An extract from Zinoviev's speech appears in H. Carrere d'Encausse and S. Schram, *Le Marxisme et L'Asie*, Colin, (Paris, 1965), pp. 296–9. Analysis in E.H. Carr, *A History of Soviet Russia – The Bolshevik Revolution, 1917–1923*, Vol. III, Macmillan (London, 1961), pp. 33 ff, 73 ff, and Colotti Pischel and Ch. Robertazzi, *L'Internationale Communiste et les Problemes Coloniaux 1919–1935*, Mouton, (Paris – La Haye, 1968), pp. 66–72.

16.   Details in W.Z. Laqueur, *Communism and Nationalism in the Middle East*, Routledge and Kegan Paul, (London, 1956), p. 33 ff, p. 73 ff.

17.   Cf. Stalin, *Marxism and the National Question*, various editions; N. Bukharin, *Problems of the Chinese Revolution*, various editions. On the whole issue of the political struggles within the Bolshevik leadership about China, see I. Deutscher, *Stalin*, O.U.P., (London, 1949).

18.   Stalin, *ibid.*, text of 18th May 1925. This text is modified in the various editions of Stalin's works. For the original, see H. Carrere d'Encausse

and S. Schram, *Le Marxisme et L'Asie, op. cit.*

19. Stalin, *ibid.*, text of 1st August 1927. See extracts in Carrere d'Encausse and Schram, *Le Marxisme et L'Asie*, pp. 320—2.
20. Bukharin, *Problems of the Chinese Revolution.*
21. Stalin, *op. cit.*, text of 1st August 1927.
22. Stalin, *op. cit.*, text of April 1924.
23. See *The Communist International . . .*, I, p. 389.
24. *Programme of the Communist International* (1928).
25. *L'Humanite*, 7 April 1928.
26. *Programme of the Communist International* (1928).
27. I overlooked Indonesia, where communism developed earlier.
28. *Programme of the Communist International* (1928). My italics, although the last sentence is in italics in the original.
29. *Programmnie documenty kommunistitsheskih partii Vostoka,* L. Mad'yar et al (ed.), Porty Editions, (Moscow, 1934), p. 173. Translation in Spector, *The Soviet Union . . .*, p. 100.
30. *Ibid.*, p. 94.
31. Resolution passed by the conference of the Communist Parties of Palestine and Syria in 1931. Spector, *op. cit.*, p. 95.
32. Spector, *op. cit.*, pp. 96—7.
33. *Ibid.*, p. 92.
34. *Ibid.*, p. 116.
35. *Ibid.*, pp. 93, 94, 96.
36. *Ibid.*, p. 98.
37. *Ibid.*, pp. 97, 98. The following year, in March 1932, Maurice Thorez set the French C.P. the task of creating an Algerian Communist Party, *Oeuvres*, Bk. II, Vol. III, Editions Sociales, (Paris, 1951). The goal of forming an Algerian C.P. was mentioned in a C.P. journal in Algeria in September 1934. Ch. A. Julien, *L'Afrique du Nord en Marche*, Jalliard, (Paris, 1952), p. 134. It was adopted by the Villeurbanne Congress in 1935 but was only achieved in 1936, and with a French Secretary at that.
38. There have also been direct borrowings from European languages, notably *imbaraturiyya*, 'imperialism'. In 1957, the Cairo Academy unsuccessfully proposed the word *tasallotiyya* to express this concept, V. Monteil, *L'Arabe Moderne*, Klincksiek, (Paris, 1960) *Etudes Arabes et Islamiques, Etudes et Documents 3*, p. 124. Recently the word *imberyaliyya* has been used by Marxist authors, who have consciously created it to establish a clear distinction between the two concepts. See the recent Arabic translations of Lenin's *Imperialism . . .* published in Moscow by Progress Publishers (1970). A semantic study of the history of how these concepts have been expressed in Arabic, Turkish and Persian would certainly be interesting.
39. *Falsafat ath-thawra*, Dar al-ma'arif, (Cairo, n.d.), pp. 25—6.
40. M. Thorez, *Oeuvres*, Bk. II, Vol. IX, Editions Sociales (Paris, 1952), p. 180. Report to the Paris Communist Assembly, 7 October 1935.
41. M. Thorez, *Oeuvres*, Bk. II, Vol. V, Editions Sociales, (Paris, 1952), p. 147 ff. Report to the Central Committee, (end of October 1933).
42. M. Thorez, *Oeuvres*, Bk. II, Vol. I, Editions Sociales, (Paris, 1950), p. 200. Report to the XIth plenum of the Comintern Executive Committee.

43. M. Thorez, *Oeuvres*, Bk. II, Vol. III, Editions Sociales, (Paris, 1951), p. 141. Report to the VIIth C.P. Congress. The leadership accepted that it bore most of the responsibility for these failings.

44. M. Thorez, *Oeuvres*, Bk. II, Vol. III, Editions Sociales, (Paris, 1951), pp. 74 ff, 170; Vol. V, (Paris, 1951), p. 111 (July 1933); Vol. VIII, (Paris, 1952), pp. 40, 49 (January 1935); Vol. IX (Paris, 1952), p. 126.

45. M. Thorez, *Oeuvres*, Bk. II, Vol. X (Paris, 1952), p. 46.

46. Ch. A. Julien, *L'Afrique du Nord en Marche*, p. 134 (2nd edn., p. 120).

47. *L'Humanite*, 12 February 1937; cf. also Ch. A. Julien, *op. cit.*, p. 131 ff; J. Berque, *Le Maghreb entre Deux Guerres*, p. 292 ff; A. Nouschi, *La Naissance du Nationalisme Algerien*, Editions de Minuit, (Paris, 1962), p. 84 ff.

48. *El Ouma* [sic] national organ for the defence of the interests of Tunisian, Moroccan and Algerian Muslims (Paris, 1935) no. 33, p. 2, (unsigned article entitled 'Algerians, where are you going?').

49. Moussali Hage, *Appel aux Nations Unies*, Chateau d'Eau, (Paris, 1948), pp. 23–4 for details.

50. Imache Amar in *El Ouma*, according to *L'Humanite*, 12 February 1937, article by R. Deloche quoted below.

51. *L'Humanite*, 15 January 1937.

52. R. Deloche, 'La dissolution de l'Etoile nord-africaine', *L'Humanite* 12 February 1937.

53. M. Thorez, *Oeuvres*, Bk. III, Vol. XIII, Editions Sociales, (Paris, 1954), p. 162. Report presented on 22 January 1937 to the National Conference of the French C.P.

54. M. Thorez, *ibid.*, Bk. III, Vol. XIV, Editions Sociales, (Paris, 1954), p. 280 ff.

55. M. Thorez, *ibid.*, Bk. III, Vol. XV, Editions Sociales, (Paris, 1955), p. 204.

56. Khaled Bekdache, *al-'Arab wa-l-harb al ahliyya fi Isbanya*, (The Arabs in the Spanish Civil War), the author, (Damascus, 1937), p. 30.

57. *L'Humanite*, 11 May 1938.

58. M. Thorez, *Oeuvres*, Bk. IV, Vol. XVI, Editions Sociales, (Paris, 1956), p. 171 ff.

59. G. Dimitrov, 'La Guerre et la Classe Ouvriere des Pays Capitalistes', in *Cahiers du Bolshevisme*, (the theoretical journal of the French Communist Party) 1939–January 1940, pp. 16–19.

60. *Cahiers du Bolshevisme*, 1st trimester 1941, p. 13. For texts clandestinely distributed during this period by the Syro-Lebanese C.P., attacking Anglo-French imperialism and supporting independence, see al-Hakam Darwaza's book *ash-shouyou'iyya al-mahalliyya wa-ma'rakat al 'Arab al qawmiyya* (2nd edn.), Maktabat Mneymneh, (Beirut, 1963), p. 444 ff.

61. See 'Problems facing the Communist Parties in Syria and Egypt' in this volume.

62. Cf. R. Rezette, *Les Partis Politiques Marocains*, A. Colin, (Paris, 1955), pp. 162–8.

63. A. Zhdanov's report on the international situation, reproduced in an article by Zhdanov, 'On the international situation' in *Cahiers du Communisme*, 24th year, no. 11, 1947, pp. 1124-51.

64. *Ibid.*

65. Larbi Bouhali, Speech to the Congress of the Algerian C.P., (*L'Humanite*, 27 May 1949). Mohammad Ennafaa, Secretary of the Tunisian C.P., in a speech to the XIIth Congress of the French C.P., (*L'Humanite*, 6 April 1950).

66. A. Zhdanov, *op. cit.*

67. Quoted in *Colonial People's Struggle for Liberation*, People's Publishing House, (Bombay, 1950), p. 98.

68. *Ibid.*, p. 98.

69. V.M. Maslennikov in *Colonial People's Struggle for Liberation, op. cit.*, p. 23.

70. V.B. Luckiy in *Colonial People's Struggle for Liberation, op. cit.*, p. 83.

71. Although it suffered greatly from having followed the Moscow line concerning the Partition of Palestine in 1947.

72. *Sovetskoe Vostokovedenie*, 1955, no. 6, p. 13; translated by A. Bennigsen as 'Le front national dans la nouvelle strategie communiste au Moyen—Orient', *Politique Etrangere*, 21, no. 5, (1956), p. 617.

73. *Ibid.*, 1956, no. 1, p. 7.

74. *Ibid.*, p. 7.

75. *Ibid.*, p. 9.

76. For the factors affecting this change, and their relevance to the Middle East, see Victor Segesvary, *le Realisme Khrouchtchevien*, la Baconniere, (Neuchatel, 1968). (Histoire et Societe d'aujourd'hui).

77. 'Resolutions of the Central Committee of the Communist Party of Syria and Lebanon' (April—May 1956 session), *Bulletin d'Information* (duplicated). For extracts and commentaries see Elyas Morqos, *tari'kh al-ahzab ash-shoyou'iyya fi l-watan al-'arabi*, Dar at-tali'a, (Beirut, 1964), p. 86 ff.

78. Quotes from a duplicated pamphlet in French entitled *Documents d'Egypte (extraits des publications du Parti Communiste Egyptien Uni)*, no. 2, 1957. cf. Elyas Morqos, *op. cit.*, p. 93 ff and al-Hakam Darwaza, *ash shouyou'iyya al mahalliyya . . .*, p. 171 ff.

79. *Democratie Nouvelle*, (November 1956), p. 659.

80. *Ibid.*, December 1957, p. 764.

81. See documents quoted in al-Hakam Darwaza, *op. cit.*, p. 185 ff and Elyas Morqos, *op. cit.*, pp. 102 ff, 256 ff.

82. Manifesto reproduced in *France Nouvelle*, (22—28 July 1959), pp. 16—17.

83. Mohammad Hasanayn Haykal, a friend of Nasser's, replied to Krushchev, in *al-Ahram* on 29 January 1959. There is more than a little truth in his argument. For the text, and Pravda's reply, see *Orient*, no. 9, (1959), p. 129 ff.

84. For example, A.G. Horon's articles in French and English, as in *The Mediterranean and Eurafrica*, (Summer 1958), pp. 11—13.

6. The Bolsheviks and Colonized Muslims

I am honoured to have been asked to introduce a book which I believe to be a work of some importance.[1] It is important in several ways; firstly, as a history of events, a point which I will not develop here, since the reader will find it needs no elaboration. Any book which helps us to untangle the skein of events, which brings out the main lines from a mass of disparate facts in a way which is accessible to non-specialists, to most of us in other words, is obviously useful. A book also deserves our respect and interest to the extent that it has been intelligently and honestly compiled, which is indubitably true of this work by Mme Helene Carrere d'Encausse. Her book is a reliable and readable source of information on a Central Asian state, the Khanate of Bokhara, during the 19th and early 20th Centuries. It describes this state's history and structure, and how its elites and its masses reacted to the upheaval of the Russian conquest and the penetration of the capitalist economy. The book tells of the growth of a reformist ideology in Muslim circles stemming from a particularly archaic society, and of the vicissitudes of its encounter with the Russian Revolution. This is already a significant contribution which will bear close study.

But this book has more to offer. Mme Carrere d'Encausse has not been content to draw out the main threads of history, although this in itself is already an honourable accomplishment. She has sought to pinpoint the underlying causes, and to reflect on their connections and interactions. Her book is thus one of those rather exceptional works which show that human history is not just sound and fury, not just some senseless dream or nightmare peopled by shadows blindly feeling their way towards night. The destinies of men, or of human communities at least, are inseparably bound to central issues, whose modalities are always changing, but which nevertheless remain substantially the same over the centuries and the millenia. 'Even two drops of water are not as alike as the future and the past' wrote Ibn Khaldoun, the great 14th-Century Arab sociologist.[2] In one sense this statement is quite false, but in another it is very true, and it is the sense in which it is true which gives any reflection upon history its legitimacy. It is only on this basis that any instructive, if not always encouraging, consideration of history is possible, Valery and others notwithstanding. If lucidity is a quality which helps us to meet the challenges of individual and collective life, how can we hope to acquire it without referring to history?

The history which Mme Carrere d'Encausse recounts is particularly rich in this sort of lesson for contemporary Man, for what she offers us, especially in her conclusion, is a basic 'model' — a basic representation of the crucial problems of today. And this representation is acted out on a particularly interesting and typical stage. There is an interesting parallel here with the problematic adopted from Philon of Alexandria by the Church Fathers, that conception which treated all the elements of the New Law as having already been depicted in the Old, as having already been 'represented', since each character in the continuing drama merely re-plays a part played by a corresponding 'type' a millenium before. To continue in this vein, one could say that, unbeknown to the world, the prototypes of today's and even tomorrow's *dramatis personae* were already playing out their tragedy in that backwater canton of Asia which concerns us here.

I would like to elaborate on Mme Carrere d'Encausse's reflections, from my own point of view, assuming all responsibility for any failings which may result. As her work shows so clearly, the history of Bokhara during the period she describes is wholly centred on the clash of two ideologies. Half a century later we are witnessing the effects of such a clash on a far broader stage, the whole of the so-called Third World. On the one side we have the universalist ideology which had already taken hold spiritually in Russia before coming to dominate it politically, an ideology of social progress to be universally and ubiquitously realized through the class struggle, an ideology whose bourgeois forms could think of themselves as applicable to the problems of the dependent countries, and whose proletarian form also saw itself, proclaimed itself, theorized itself as capable of playing that role. In the opposite corner a different ideology, at the time still imprecise, untheorized and clumsy, often drawing its conceptual frameworks from the preceding universalist ideological movement, namely Islam, an ideology fuelled however by a thousand implicit feelings, feelings which for all that they were still only barely sketched out, hardly daring to formulate and define themselves, were nonetheless implanted in the depths of every heart by everyday life itself, by the warmth of the family hearth, by the emotions of childhood and by the triumphs, sufferings and bitterness of adulthood. Even in the case of the first of these ideologies, the time had not yet come for precise projects carefully worked out by economists and engineers. Ideals were still all-important, and all the more attractive for being ill-defined. Their existential resonance was all the deeper and the clashes all the fiercer.

In the 19th Century, Bokhara was, for the European, the very picture of stagnation. O. Olufsen, the Danish traveller who visited it at the very end of the 19th Century, congratulated himself 'on having seen every aspect of the country at a time when its character and population remain unchanged since Tamburlaine'. He was pleased to observe that the Russians had been content to establish their authority there indirectly, eliminating only 'the most serious abuses of power and the brutal influence of the old superstition'. 'Thus,' he concludes triumphantly:

Bokhara is likely to continue unadorned by the trappings of the West for a good while yet, and its original Oriental stamp is far from wearing thin. The Emir of Bokhara still lives as in days of yore within his tall battlements, and his vassal kings, the Begs, still maintain their courts in lugubriously romantic castles. The winding streets, with their terraced cobwork houses, the mosques and the medresehs, are as yet undisturbed by Western-style houses. The mullahs, the dervishes, the congregations and the devannahs (feeble-minded beggars) still crowd around the sanctuaries as they have for centuries. Slowly and calmly, the caravans cross the vast deserts and steppes on their camels, the two-wheeled arba bumps down the awful roads and the donkey, laden from head to tail, plods along patiently on his short drumstick-thin legs; the dogs snap at each other in the Muslim cemetries and vultures wheel overhead above the rotting carcasses of camels. The muezzin's 'Allah Akbar' accompanied by the braying of donkeys and the cooing of doves still rings out through the orchards and rice fields of the oases. And the mystery of the closed-off courtyards permeates everything. The city gates are shut at night, doors are locked against intruders and the aversion to any intimate contact with the 'Christian dogs' is as strong as it was in the Middle Ages. It was force, not desire, which brought the Muslims into contact with the Europeans. Probably only the rollers, perched in rows on the telegraph wires, willingly have anything to do with that instrument of European civilization.[3]

This idyllic portrait is typical of the image of the Muslim world dear to the romantic souls of the West, a mixture of sentimentality with a certain self-interested short-sightedness. For an explanation was never far behind the description, the lazy explanation, which is still so common today, based on the good and bad qualities of peoples as a whole: 'Nowhere has the Turkish rule shown itself less suited to guide a country along the road to civilization, for all the many good qualities of the Turks.'[4]

As usual, the romantic souls had got it wrong. They could see neither the mire in the mill-stream nor the hell in the smith's hearth. The Turks of Bokhara were, after all, men, and within the lugubrious castles, in the winding streets, in the cobwork houses, the mosques and the medresehs, on the jolting arbas, through the orchards and the ricefields, there could be heard, if one listened carefully and could understand Uzbek, something quite different from the braying of donkeys and the cooing of doves: the voices of men reacting to their situation as men have always reacted in every part of the world. The struggles for power, for control over men and goods, had never ceased, stagnation had never been complete. But the strength of the monarchy was so much greater than that which any possible opposition could hope for, the chances of any innovatory movement were so slim, the solutions promising change so few and far between, that all had fallen prey to resignation. Europeans could see Csarism as a despotic regime verging on barbarism. For the Bokharans and for all the Muslim peoples of Central Asia, it offered a new model, an alternative. People learnt that another way of life was possible, and for all the unattractiveness of the Russian model, the Russian presence did

127

bring an opening-out towards Europe. At least the new model included some customary limitation of the arbitrary power of the monarch, at least the elites could participate in the control over people and goods. And further-more, this new practice seemed to be organically linked to a constant progress towards power and well-being. The attraction of this European model was general and insurmountable, throughout the entire world. This simple and obvious fact ought to be enough to put paid to all the nonsense about the irreducible originality of peoples and the inability of some civilizations to respond to certain stimulations. But of course our culture, just like any other, is entitled to its share of nonsense.

It was this attraction which in Turkestan, broadly speaking, took the form of the *jadidist* movement, the movement of the innovators and modernists of the 'new' Arab *jadid*, whose development in Bokhara Mme Carrere d'Encausse describes, drawing precisely and intelligently on considerable documentary material. Nearly all the *jadids* remained Muslims. For some, this was the expression of a stubborn attachment to the existential values which the religion, founded by Mohammad, had come to embody. But what this attachment mainly expressed was a desire to remain themselves, to be faithful to a transmitted and accepted identity, not to be detached from the people they came from. Here, again, we see the fundamental ambiguity of the reference to Islam, an ambiguity which is indeed typical of reference to any ideology whatsoever, once a certain stage has been undergone. The traditionalists, the reactionaries, the partisans of the Old Way (*Qadim*) also invoked Islam. But for them Islam was the world of the thoughts, values and customs with which they had always lived and which had been effectively sacralized by the religion, even if originally each element had come from outside and had imposed itself on Islam, or been imposed upon it by some previous *jadid* movement.

The tragedy was that all too often the masses found it easier to recognize themselves in the traditionalists than in the innovators. The slaves of Antiquity, the proletarians of the capitalist world, were sufficiently excluded from the Establishment and its values to give a joyful welcome to anything which might threaten the oppressive *status quo*; they recognized themselves in Eunius, Spartacus, Jesus, Marx, Bakunin or Lenin. But traditional Muslim society has a place for the pauper, it recognizes his worth in God's eyes and his rights to a holy charity, it welcomes him into its fraternities and its corporations and turns him into a guide and a saint. It sanctifies, sacralizes his grime and his misery. At first sight, the pauper sees the innovator as some-body who wants to push him off his mystic throne. And what is he offered in return? Nothing.

Institutional Marxist authors, particularly Soviet ones, have adopted the axiom that any trend of thought which attacks the traditional values of an oppressive society will be supported, or at least accepted, by the masses. Yet no idea has so often been shown to be wrong by history. The thinkers who first attacked tradition came from the privileged social strata, and could have nothing but contempt for the masses still hampered mentally by traditionalism.

This contempt in its turn engendered envy and hatred. The masses always prefer ideological cadres who come from their own midst and remain close to them rather than theorizing innovators, proud of their knowledge and originality and dedicated above all to destroying the world of certitudes by which the masses live. The same phenomenon can be observed today in the communist ideological movement. The *jadids* sought an orientation towards a way of life which the masses, because of their poverty, could not possibly aspire to, whatever political reforms were implemented. The *jadids* were already adopting the life-style of the foreigners, of the infidels, they already benefited from a culture to which the masses could have no access, and they were mainly recruited from the wealthier strata of society. The hatred which at least a segment of the suffering masses directed against them is much more adequately explained in these terms than by any innate Muslim, or Oriental, propensity to fanaticism or xenophobia. The reaction was not essentially different from that of proletarians smashing machines, or from that of the pietist movements of the Renaissance who burned the paintings of aristocratic and enlightened artists.

The victorious Bolsheviks were soon to discover these problems in their own field of action. The texts written by Lenin between his victory and his death abound with bitter references to the backwardness and barbarism of the moujiks. Much like the French democrats of 1848, struggling to set back the date of the elections which were to make the people the real judges of democracy, the *jadids* of Bokhara and the Bolsheviks of Moscow had either to satisfy the masses despite themselves or to perish. The slogan of 1793, liberty, equality, fraternity or death, acquired a new but not unwarranted sense.

The Russian Bolsheviks, faced with the masses whose happiness they sought to ensure, had to cope with the same situation as had earlier confronted the *jadids*. And to some extent this was to condition the encounter of the two groups. Each was linked to its own people. The *jadids* had, in fact, attracted a measure of support from the most impoverished and least integrated victims of the traditional society, such as the dispossessed peasantry. But this support fluctuated, and the leaders had to adapt themselves to meet its demands. Their background had often been a wealthy one and they were terrified at the idea of knocking down a coherent structure without any clear conception of what to replace it with, so they could only countenance the most tentative social reforms. At the very least, the masses demanded a firm stand on the national issue, which remained their main concern. The Russian Bolsheviks could, just about, get their own people to accept the Bolshevik vision of future happiness, and even then they had to use barbarian methods in their fight against barbarism. Perhaps the moujiks saw them, for a while, as new oppressors, as terrifying reincarnations of Ivan the Terrible or of the Anti-Christ. But to the Uzbeks they were, above all, foreigners. At first they had been welcomed as friends, not because of their social doctrine which, it was thought, was their own business, but because they proclaimed their intention to renounce the Czarist policy of national oppression.

But it soon became apparent that the Russian Bolsheviks did not find it so easy to turn over a new leaf in their attitudes to allogenous peoples. The Bolsheviks, following Lenin and Wilson, may have quite sincerely believed in the right of peoples to self-determination. But to let the Muslim peoples choose their own social system in practice amounted to handing over power to somewhat unenlightened reformists, whose practical inexperience would soon allow the indigenous traditionalist bourgeoisie to re-assert itself and to retain its privilege, keeping its contempt and exploitation of the masses well-hidden under the folds of the green banner of Islam. And there was always the distinct possibility that this bourgeoisie, or the landowning aristocracy with which it would ally itself, would call in the anti-communist imperialist powers. Furthermore, it would not have been too difficult to sanctify such an appeal, even one directed to the Giaours, in terms of the defence of Islam. For the Bolsheviks this would have meant allowing the class enemy and the national enemy to establish a base within the very limits of the newly-defunct Russian empire. Out of pure Quixotism, and without the indigenous population drawing any benefit from it, the enemy would have been granted access routes, through the Urals, Siberia and the lower Volga, to the centres of the proletarian revolution, and would then be in a position to help the foes of that revolution and to exert pressure upon it.

It is easily understandable that the Bolsheviks rejected such a possibility. But the other horn of the dilemma was also dangerous. Who can say whether the decision to keep these Muslim provinces within the Russian orbit was motivated more by an unwillingness to put the revolution at risk than by a reluctance to cede lands conquered by Russians? In any case, this is a matter for psychoanalysts and the secular confessional, since God no longer sat enthroned in glory in the Kremlin, sounding out the hearts of the Russian rulers. There were more serious issues. Not all the officials, the military, the police, the managerial personnel in short, who were to be entrusted with enforcing the new policies were Bolsheviks, but they were certainly all Russian or Russified. In practical terms, they necessarily tended to react as Russians, as Europeans putting down backward natives who were incapable of realizing what was good for them, in this case the dictatorship of the proletariat rather than the autocracy of the White Czar. And the indigenous population naturally saw these officials essentially as Russians, as pagan foreign oppressors who arrogated the right to make decisions and who sought to impose their diabolical ways and their foolhardy attempts to change an order sanctified by the centuries and thus by Allah, praised be His name. The traditional tension between dominators and dominated was thus re-established; it had a new form, certainly, but was still in many ways strongly reminiscent of a past which it had been hoped could be transcended.

The same dilemma has reappeared in many colonies, where the dominators were far less justified than the Bolsheviks in claiming to bring new and efficient solutions to the problems weighing on the masses. Above all, it is this dilemma which, in a modified form, is at the root of contemporary Third World problems.

Ever since almost all the Asian and African countries gained their independence, indigenous rulers have undertaken to lead their people towards progress. Some of these rulers are sincere, some hypocritical; some are committed to the future, others are still tied to the past; some are rigid, others flexible; some are intelligent, some are stupidly short-sighted; some are linked with this or that segment of the population, others themselves form a particular segment, with its own selfish interests. But nearly all, be it worthily or out of self-interest, seem to be seized with that very same panic at the idea of an eventual overturning of traditional society which gripped the *jadids* of Bokhara in 1920. One must admit, however, that it would hardly be possible for them to grant the illiterate masses an immediate right to decide their own fate, to allocate investments, or to choose between the most crucial economic and political options. The new rulers have no choice but to adopt the attitude of the Russian Bolsheviks. In doing so they have the incomparable advantage of being indigenous to their area. But they also suffer from the handicap of not being organically linked, by a doctrinal and organizational structure, to a progressive ideology geared to prevail against their own failings in the course of the struggle for social progress.

Almost everywhere would-be substitute rulers are waiting for a chance to make their own breakthrough. They too adopt an essentially Bolshevik position, and if they place less emphasis on the national character of their project, it is only because the national approach of the established rulers is generally not easily criticized. It is far easier, and may well become more and more so, to denounce the established rulers' social compromise, their attachment to economic and political privilege, their slowness in passing on the fruits of development to the masses — who become less and less capable of receiving them — and in sharing their power and advantages. Increasingly those who would use the traditional ploy of turning the exaltation of national values into an excuse for such failings will find themselves confronted by those who fight for the demands of the oppressed under the red or black banners of the social struggle. Meanwhile, perhaps the dissidents in the Communist world will, in an inverse process, take the national emblem as their rallying point.

All these possibilities were barely distinguishable in the old Uzbek Khanate in the years following the upheaval of 1917. In the shadow of the sinister Ark fortress, people still trembled before the 'Emir of the Night'. But the seed had been planted, and Mme Carrère d'Encausse's book is particularly useful in helping us discern it. Balkhi, a 10th Century Arab geographer of Bokhara, said of the area:

> I have never seen, nor even heard of there being any town more pleasantly situated than Bokhara in all the lands of Islam. If one climbs to the top of the citadel, everywhere one looks, one sees the lush greenery of the surrounding countryside, a green which blends into the green of the sky, as if the sky were a green lid covering a green vase; the castles sparkle in the landscape and the fields around the villages look as if they had been polished like mirrors.[5]

131

Mme Carrere d'Encausse's book shows us a less poetic but more instructive face of Bokhara, a mirror in which it is not the sky but the earth which is reflected.

References

1. H. Carrere d'Encausse, *Reforme et Revolution chez les Musulmans de l'Empire Russe, Bukhara, 1867–1924*, A. Colin, *Cahiers de la Fondation Nationale des Sciences Politiques*, (Paris, 1966), p. 141.
2. Ibn Khaldoun, *moqaddima*, translated by F. Rosenthal, Pantheon Books, Bollingen Series, 43, (New York, 1943) Bk. 1, p. 17.
3. O. Olufsen, *The Emir of Bokhara and his Country, Journeys and Studies in Bokhara*, Heinemann, (London, 1911), pp. 1–2.
4. *Ibid.*, p. 1.
5. Istakhri, *Viae Regnorum*, Brill, (Leyde, 1870), Bibliotheca geographorum arabicorum editit M. J. de Goeje, p. 213.

7. A Forgotten Precursor

Sultan Galiev

The book on which these reflections are based has just been published under the auspices of the *Ecole Pratique des Hautes Etudes (6ᵉ section).*[1] It is a conscientious and detailed study of a set of questions which have on the whole been given far more serious attention in the Anglo-Saxon countries than in France, where gratuitous political prophecy passes for scientific research all too often. A book like this is usually received with *a priori* suspicion in militant circles, and even elsewhere. My aim is to offer some counterweight to this traditional sectarianism.

Sultan Galiev is one of the men who played an important part in the early days of the Communist International and the Soviet Union. Most socialist militants are aware of him only through a passing reference made by Stalin,[2] rather an emotional reference, I used to think. Perhaps I was right. To have aroused some emotion in Stalin is already something in the way of an achievement.

Mir Sayit Sultan Galiev was born the son of a Tartar schoolteacher in about 1900. The Tartars were a Muslim minority within the Czarist Empire, with a character all of their own. There were about three and a half million of them scattered throughout the Empire, but they were concentrated to some extent in the 'Government' of Kazan, their political and cultural centre. They were mainly peasants, and the few Tartar industrial workers still kept close ties to rural life. But there was also a bourgeoisie: a few industrialists and many shopkeepers, from which a Muslim 'clergy' and an intelligentsia had emerged. This bourgeoisie and these intellectuals were active, dynamic and ambitious. Many had long been 'modernists' in their attitude towards Muslim dogma, and 'advanced' in their attitudes to the traditional Muslim way of life. Their teaching activities often led them to penetrate and even establish themselves in areas inhabited by their less evolved co-religionists, such as Central Asia, Siberia and the Caucasus. In so doing, they introduced new ideas and modern ways, and generally stirred things up. They can be seen playing this role in the translations of Kazak and Tadjik novels published by Aragon, for instance.[3] All this was naturally viewed with great suspicion by the reactionary Khans.

Then came the October Revolution. An important part of the Tartar intelligentsia supported it, thinking that the socialism established by the new regime would realize and deepen the reformist movement's programme. Naturally enough they particularly appreciated Bolshevism's internationalist orientation. They hoped that this would lead to equality between ethnic groups and put an end to Great-Russian domination, a domination the 'Whites' would re-impose should they be victorious.

Sultan Galiev joined the Bolshevik Party in November 1917, and, thanks to his talents as an orator and organizer, soon became an important figure as the representative of this 'colonial' intelligentsia. He became a member and then president of the 'Central Muslim Commissariat', a new body affiliated to the Narkomnats (The People's Commissariat for Nationalities), a Commissariat presided over by a Bolshevik leader still relatively unknown at the time, Joseph Stalin. With the help of friends, Sultan Galiev created a Muslim Communist Party, and raised Tartar military units which played a key role in the struggle against Koltchak. Despite the opposition of the local Russian Soviets and communists, he extracted a promise from the Central Government to create a large predominantly Muslim state, the Tartaro-Bachkir Republic, which was to have five to six million inhabitants and to cover the vast areas of the Middle Volga and the Southern Urals.

It was during this period that he developed a series of ideas which he hoped to defend and to realize. He saw Muslim society, with the exception of a few big feudal landowners and bourgeois, as a unit which had been collectively oppressed by the Russians under Czarism. There was thus no point in dividing it with artificially created differences and class struggles. Since for the time being the poorer Muslims were too impoverished and uncultured to provide cadres, one should not hesitate to make use of the available ones: the petty-bourgeois intellectuals and even the reformist clergy, who had given some proof of their faithfulness to the Revolution. In fact, the socialist revolution should adapt itself to fit a society so imbued with Muslim traditions. Sultan Galiev, an atheist himself, therefore recommended that Islam be handled gently, through a gradual 'defanaticization' and secularization. The Muslims of Russia, and especially the most enlightened amongst them, the Tartars, would then be capable of playing a tremendous historical role. For on the world scale the Revolution would have to be above all a liberation of the colonial peoples. It was therefore vital to counteract the Comintern tendency to concentrate mainly on the West. The socialist revolution would begin in the East. And who could bear the torch of both culture and socialism into Asia better than the Bolshevik Muslims of Russia?

To avoid confusion it should be stated right from the start that neither religious nor clerical demands were at issue. There were several ethnic groups in Russia whose religion was Islam, which had given them a common culture and tradition, and had similarly influenced many important aspects of their way of life. There was thus a certain incontestable cultural unity amongst these people which went beyond their ethnic particularities, especially as the latter were in many cases not very pronounced. This cultural unity had been reinforced by their resistance to attempts to convert them to Christianity and to turn them into Russians, an attempt which they perceived not as an ideological struggle, but as a colonial aggression against their common cultural heritage.

These ideas worried the Bolshevik leaders. Stalin supported Sultan Galiev against those who wanted to fan class war in Muslim circles and break off all contact with the non-proletarian elements. But unlike the Tartar, he saw the class alliance as only temporary. Once Koltchak and the Czechs had been defeated, the support of the Volga and Ural Muslims, whose cadres had been disabled during the struggle, became less important. The Muslim Communist Party lost its autonomy and the idea of a lasting alliance between the petty bourgeoisie and the proletariat was rejected by the September 1920 Congress of Oriental Peoples in Baku. It was proclaimed that the national revolution had to be led by the proletariat, that is to say, the Western proletariat, and that, as one Congress delegate declared, 'the salvation of the East lies only in the victory of the proletariat'.[4] The project of a great Muslim state was dropped. Instead two small republics were created, the one Bachkir and the other Tartar. Most Tartars lived outside the latter, and its population was only 51.6% Tartar. Its towns were almost 80% Russian. Kazan, the capital, was a Russian centre.

It was at this stage that Sultan Galiev, who still held an important official post, moved into opposition, in an attempt to fight the manifestations of what he called 'Great Russian chauvinism', and sought to infiltrate his Tartar partisans into Party organizations and Soviets. He wanted to make Kazan into a centre for Tartar national culture and a revolutionary seedbed from which 'Muslim Communism' would spread to all the Muslim peoples of the Soviet Union and beyond, to the whole Muslim East. He struggled against the leftists who argued for a more anti-bourgeois policy and were backed by the Russian elements. And he worked towards making Tartar and not Russian the official language of administration.

Having come up against the unflinching opposition of the Central Government and the Russian Communists, especially after the 10th Party Congress had passed a clear resolution condemning the 'nationalist deviation', Sultan Galiev established more or less secret contacts with a number of discontented militants. He wanted to set up a common front against the Russians, whom he accused of readopting Czarist colonial policy. How far did he go in seeking support for this front? Stalin accused him of having gone so far as to contact the Basmatsh, the gangs of insurgent Muslims who were waging armed struggle against the Bolsheviks of Turkestan. But there is no reason to take Stalin's words at face value. Be that as it may, in 1923 Stalin had Sultan Galiev arrested and expelled from the Communist Party. He was released shortly afterwards, but Kamenev was later to regret that he and Zinoviev had given their consent to this 'first arrest of an eminent member of the Party on Stalin's initiative'.[5]

Little is known of Sultan Galiev's life after 1923. He was perhaps exiled, re-arrested, then released. He worked in Moscow in the state publishing houses. But he continued his struggle, clandestinely. He had created a whole underground organization which had attracted a great many Muslim communists, mainly Tartars. He developed his ideas in the light of the evolving situation. As he now saw it, the socialist revolution did not resolve the problem of inequality between peoples. The Bolshevik programme amounted to replacing oppression by the European bourgeoisie with oppression by the European proletariat. In any case, Soviet rule was being liquidated; N.E.P. was in full swing. It would either be overthrown by the Western bourgeoisie or would turn into state capitalism and bourgeois democracy. Whatever the outcome, the Russians as a people would once again become dominating oppressors. The only possible remedy was to ensure the developing colonial world's hegemony over the European powers. This meant creating a Communist Colonial International, which would be independent of the Third International, and perhaps even opposed to it. Russia, as an industrial power, would have to be excluded. The spread of communism in the East, which this new International would promote, would make it possible to shake off Russian hegemony over the communist world.

As the Russian regime grew stronger it became less and less tolerant of dissent. On several occasions the Russians realized they were facing an organized Tartar opposition. Stalin clamped down on it. In November 1928 Sultan Galiev was arrested and sentenced to ten years' hard labour, which he served in Solovski. He was released in 1939 and we lose track of him in 1940 . . .

Lessons of a Forgotten History

Alexandre Bennigsen and Chantal Quelquejay deserve our gratitude for having revived this forgotten history. Their task of sifting, scrutinizing and organizing a mass of documents in Tartar and Russian, was a difficult and important one. Hopefully we can draw certain conclusions from their findings.

The first thing which comes to mind is that analysis of the political struggle over the problem of the Muslim minorities in the Soviet Union clearly demonstrates that there can be contradictions under a socialist regime. This is not new of course: Mao Tse-tung himself has said so — albeit with the quite gratuitous rider that such contradictions can only be 'non-antagonistic'. But that does not change the fact that every time someone highlights one of these contradictions on a practical level everything is done to deny it or to minimize it. Naturally the most dogmatic make no attempt to analyse such contradictions, to explain them or to understand their causes and their repercussions. On the contrary each phase of the policy adopted by the communist leaders is presented as determined by a superior wisdom which carefully follows the twists and turns of the national and international conjuncture, guided by the infallible compass of Marxist doctrine. Of course the reality is quite different: each policy decision is the outcome of constant struggles between opposing tendencies and expresses the balance of forces between them. The social background to these struggles is probably quite different from that in a class society, but the mechanism is essentially similar. In other words, history continues and we have not yet entered the timeless realm of the holy city. Many people will answer that all this is quite obvious, but perhaps they do not grasp all its complications.

Soviet policy could have been different, more oriented towards Asia, for example. Some of Sultan Galiev's ideas could perhaps have been put into practice. But there were very real obstacles to such a programme: the lack of Muslim cadres, the situation in the East at the time. In the interior there was a definite danger of Tartar nationalist deviation, strengthened by harmful Tartar chauvinism. Abroad, even if Sultan Galiev's ideas, which were partly shared by the Indian communist Manabendra Nath Roy and others who defended them during the first Comintern Congresses, had been applied, the benefits would probably have been few and far between. Even Walter Z. Laqueur agrees with this pessimistic view, and nobody could suspect him of being indulgent towards the Bolshevik leaders.[6] But it is clear that the choice of orientation in this respect was also influenced by other considerations: there was the dogmatism of the leaders, the fact that at certain periods the idea that the proletariat was the predominant force in the revolution was applied mechanically and against all commonsense, even to areas in which the proletariat was non-existent. Indeed, on the whole, and until quite recently, the communist leaders have been as obtuse as the capitalists in their approach to the colonial people's awakening. And, although their lack of understanding is excusable on many levels, the fact remains that it has had many disastrous consequences even from their own point of view.

Socialism and the National Question

It is also clear that socialism, by which I mean the socialization of the means of production, does not automatically resolve all problems. Stalinism has shown us that despotism was possible under socialism, and hence that there was a problem of political power. Other events suggest that the national problem also does not necessarily vanish under socialism. 'The fact that the proletariat will have carried out the social revolution will not turn it into a saint' wrote Lenin in 1916. 'But eventual errors (and the selfish interests which push one to ride on the backs of others) will inevitably lead it to realize the following truth . . . By turning capitalism into socialism, the proletariat creates the *possibility* of entirely abolishing national oppression: this possibility will "only" ["only"!] become fact when democracy has been completely established in all fields.'[7]

The example of Sultan Galiev demonstrates that between 1920 and 1928, the Tartars were very wary of the Russian communists, and feared a Russian communist neo-colonialism. The Bolshevik leaders denied that such a fear was justified. Stalin himself declared, in 1923, that 'If Turkestan is effectively a colony, as it was under Czarism, then the *Basmatsh* are right, and it is not up to us to judge Sultan Galiev, but up to him to judge us, as the sort of people who tolerate the existence of a colony in the framework of Soviet power.'[8] But things were not quite so simple. Soviet policy towards the Soviet Union's Muslim minorities has, on the whole, been extremely attentive. The Muslims have been well cared for and their areas have been industrialized. Indigenous cadres were gradually promoted, and this process continues. Muslims are protected by exactly the same laws as other Soviet citizens, and in practice the 'locals' have even enjoyed certain privileges *vis-a-vis* the Russians. But this evolution has been carefully controlled. A tight grip is maintained over all key posts. Furthermore the general tendency of Stalinist *mores* did not favour interpenetration between communities. The situation has nothing in common with colonial situations elsewhere. But national problems persist, as was clearly shown by the behaviour of many minority groups during World War II, and as is borne out by many small incidents even today.[9] And incidentally, such happenings would attract less attention, and might well be less distorted abroad, if the Soviets did not put so much effort into covering them up and attacking the 'slanderers' who dare to suggest that everything is not absolutely perfect in these areas of the Soviet Union.

A Precursor

Sultan Galiev does not seem to have had any real spiritual heirs in the Muslim areas of the Soviet Union. We do not know what would happen today if political pressure groups were allowed to emerge. But what one can surmise about the aspirations held by the peoples of these areas shows them to have little in common with Sultan Galiev. Their demands appear to be much more 'reformist', much less revolutionary. If they could, they would press for slight changes, without questioning the regime's right to rule. The role of propagators of the Revolution in the East seems to hold little attraction for them. It is possible, of course, that the lid of official conformism hides a much more ebullient reality . . .

But it is outside the Soviet Union, in the so-called underdeveloped countries, that the contemporary situation constantly makes one think of Sultan Galiev's ideas. To what extent can he be said to be a precursor of the new line adopted by the Soviet Union since 1954, a line which backs the Afro-Asiatic neutralist bourgeoisie? To what extent can he be said to be a precursor of Maoist communism, which concentrates essentially on the immediate struggle for socialist revolution in the ex-colonies?

The attitude of Sultan Galiev and the Tartar communists in 1918 stemmed from their refusal to serve as a mere back-up for a European proletarian movement, however justified. They wanted the Revolution to be their revolution as well, and to follow a course determined by their own actions, not by those of their somewhat over-paternal elder brother, the Russian proletariat. One should note that one of the latter's methods of intervention, which was later to be used elsewhere, was an insistence that indigenous support should be drawn only from amongst the proletariat. In countries where the proletariat was still embryonic, this amounted to arbitrarily designating the individuals who were worth talking to. The Tartars' essential demand 'to carry out our own revolution' came at the wrong time. The Bolshevik leadership was already taking a very different turn: careful bureaucratic control over every aspect of the mass movement. Both the Soviets and the trade unions at home and allied or communist parties abroad, were being kept on a very tight rein.

Significantly the man of the moment was Stalin, whose universal and petty wariness was later to become quite pathological. The ailing Lenin was ignored when he warned that 'The harm which a lack of unity between the national state apparatuses and the Russian state apparatus may cause is nothing compared to the damage which will result from an excess of centralism; this will injure not only ourselves but the whole International, and the hundreds of millions of Asians who will soon follow in our footsteps and burst onto the historical scene.'[10] In theory the International's purpose was to further the world's march towards socialism. Its task would therefore seem to have been to develop a Marxist nationalism fighting for national independence and socialization in the dependent countries. The social development of the East at the time precluded any more ambitious ventures. In spite of all his mistakes, it is clear that this was Sultan Galiev's basic intuition. The Stalinist system made it impossible for the colonial Communist Parties to accomplish this task. Essentially, it was their rigid subordination to the world strategy of an International centred on the European world which was to blame for this failure. These colonial Communist Parties were sometimes even directly dependent on their European equivalents. A Marxian nationalism did nonetheless eventually emerge, borne on the tide of history. But it did not do so in the framework of the communist parties, and it took American anti-communist imbecility to push the Moroccan and Algerian left, Castro, Sekou Toure and Modibo Keita into the arms of what remained of the Third International.

Today the Colonial International recognized by Sultan Galiev exists. It takes the form of the Afro-Asian bloc, which is beginning to extend to Latin America, and is united against white domination, as the Tartar commissar dreamed it would be. But already there are differences, which do not yet amount to a split, between a Marxist wing committed to rapid advance towards socialism, and a bourgeois wing which favours slow transformation or even no change at all. There are also a number of ambiguous cases which are particularly interesting.

Since 1954 the Soviet Union has supported this Colonial International. But Khrushchev is only apparently and partially following Sultan Galiev's line. The colonial peoples are still seen only as a back-up force whose function is to exert pressure on the Soviet Union's white adversaries, to extract concessions from them, not to destroy them. The Soviet Union does not encourage socialization in the Third World and probably does not even desire it. It would seem that the Soviet authorities finally agree with Sultan Galiev on this point, but their motive is not to strengthen the revolution; the aim is a much more selfish one. The world triumph of socialism is still seen essentially as the result of the more or less revolutionary evolution of the industrially advanced countries. It is only in China, where distance and ancestral Chinese cunning made it easier to sidestep the Stalinist international strategy, that Marxist nationalism was able to emerge triumphant in the framework of a traditional Communist Party. Indeed, Mao Tse-Tung was quite content to apply the ideas defended by the Comintern during its popular or national front phases. But he applied them systematically and consistently. His victory and the ensuing circumstances, the militant hostility of the white nations and the socialization of Chinese society, led him to take the helm of a new type of colonial communism, which he proposed as a model for the whole under-developed world as early as 1949. Since then, events in China have constantly brought the ideas of the new Chinese leaders closer and closer to some of Sultan Galiev's. The primacy of the colonial revolution and the fear that a neo-colonialism, or a neo-paternalism at least, might eventually emerge from within the heart of the socialist world itself have been constantly reiterated themes.

Thus Sultan Galiev's ideas have resurfaced in the two main currents of world communism. Of course nobody quotes this condemned champion of yesterday's obscure struggles. And yet he can be seen as the first prophet of the colonial struggle against white hegemony within socialism itself, as the first to forecast a break between the Russians' European communism and Colonial communism. He could also be celebrated as the man who first proclaimed the importance of Marxist nationalism in colonial countries, and the international relevance for socialism of those national movements which do not immediately envisage complete class war and socialization. Mao himself was still adopting this position at Yenan. The future will no doubt pass its own verdict on this first representative of the Third World within the communist movement. Surely it will not fail to recognize his role as an outcast prophet.

References

1. Alexandre Bennigsen and Chantal Quelquejay, *les Mouvements Nationaux chez les Musulmans de Russie, 1: le 'Sultangalievisme' au Tartarstan*, Mouton, (La Haye, 1960) (*Documents et Temoignages, 3*).
2. In fact, throughout one of the speeches delivered to the IVth Conference of the Central Committee of the Russian Communist Party, extended to include militants responsible for the republics and national regions, 9th to 12th June, 1923. See I.V. Stalin, *Sotshineniya*, Bk. V, (Moscow, 1947), pp. 301–12. For important details of this conference, which had been specially called to condemn Sultan Galiev, who had been arrested in late April or sometime in May, see E.H. Carr, *A History of Soviet Russia*, Vol. IV, *The Interregnum*, Macmillan, (London, 1960),

pp. 287–9; Bennigsen and Quelquejay express some reservations about the passage. A photograph of the participants in the congress, which was only numbered IVth in order to play down its importance, appears in the official *Istoriya Kommunistitsheskoy partii Sovetskogo soyuza,* Bk. IV/I, (Moscow, 1970), p. 283. The accompanying commentary makes it clear that the condemnation of Sultan Galiev still persists in the official ideology, and is indeed reinforced by contemporary considerations.

3. For example, Sariddine Aini, *Boukhara*, translated from the Tadjik by S. Borodine and P. Korotkine, Gallimard, (Paris, 1956); Moukhtar Aouezov, *La Jeunesse d'Abai*, translated from the Kazak by L. Sobolev and A. Vitez, Gallimard, (Paris, 1959).
4. *Premier Congres des peuples de l'Orient, Bakou, 1920*, (Petrograd, 1921), French edn., quoted by Bennigsen and Quelquejay, *op.cit.*, p. 140.
5. As he once told Trotsky. cf. L. Trotsky, *Stalin*, Hollis and Carter, (London, 1947), p. 417.
6. Walter Z. Laqueur, *The Soviet Union and the Middle East*, Routledge and Kegan Paul, (London, 1959), p. 22.
7. 'Summary of a discussion on the right of nations to self-determination' in V.I. Lenin, *Critical Remarks on the National Question*, Collected Works, Vol. 20, pp. 1–34. (4th Russian edn.), (Lenin's punctuation). For an analysis of how Lenin's position evolved, how it differed from Stalin's and how the problem manifests itself in the Soviet Union today, see H. Carrere d'Encausse, 'Unite proletarienne et diversite nationale, Lenine et la theorie de l'autodetermination' in *Revue Francaise de Science Politique*, Vol. XXI, No. 2, pp. 221–55.
8. Stalin, *Marxism and the National Question*, various edns.
9. I was probably minimizing the problem. See A. Bennigsen and C. Lemercier-Quelquejay, *l'Islam en Union Sovietique*, Payot, (Paris, 1968), for an objective account.
10. Remarks on 'nationalities and autonomy'; see *Marxist Quarterly*, October 1956, p. 255. 'National apparatuses' refers to the apparatuses of the non-Russian Communist Parties in the Union.

8. Islam and the Modern Economic Revolution

Today's world is witnessing a tremendous upheaval. Explicitly or implicitly, everybody agrees that the driving force behind this upheaval is easily distinguishable. The evidence is undeniable, even to those who most dislike to recognize the role played by economic factors in history. Large-scale industrialization has reached an unprecedented level. In several countries the forces of production have grown at a rate which has permitted a real qualitative change. What has happened can no longer be described as evolution: we are talking about a revolution.

The nations which have most benefited from this revolution are those which have long been advancing along the path of industrial development. The revolution in question has increased their already considerable power. Potentially or in practice, they dominate the world to an extent which would have been inconceivable to earlier conquerors. The two most powerful of these nations already have the means to annihilate entire countries, the whole planet even, at the touch of a button. The nations which have not undergone this process face a far more dramatic and consequential choice than any they have faced before. They must either industrialize, 'take off', 'develop' as the Euro-American nations have already done, or remain dependent on decisions taken by the world powers. True, they can tack to and fro, play off contradictions and thus to some extent preserve their independence, as many states in the past have done when confronted by powers which could easily have annihilated them. But it has long been recognized that such independence is precarious and limited. The only way to get one's voice heard, to defend one's own interests effectively, is to be a power oneself, or at least to join a group which is a power collectively. In the life of states as in individual life, this is the only way; everything else is just words. Protests against neo-colonialism are certainly justified, necessary even. But until they can be translated into force, they are merely verbal decoration.

Of course, it is not enough just to have the will. The choice must first be possible. Certain natural, geographic, conditions must apply, if at all possible. I assume that natural conditions in the countries concerned here present no insurmountable obstacle to industrialization, even though they may well not be ideal or easy. I will therefore concentrate on social and human obstacles and advantages.

The countries concerned make up what is called the Muslim world. That is to say that in these countries, until quite recently at least, the dominant type of ideology has been the Islamic religion. This does not mean, far from it, that this world was united at all levels, nor that the same social conditions prevailed everywhere within it. But it does imply that a whole series of analogous problems, the ones I will try to tackle here, occur throughout the Muslim world and that some factors are ubiquitously relevant. I will stick to the broad outlines, to what is generally valid for all these countries.

Thus defined, the Muslim world, in common with the rest of the Third World, faces the fundamental problems mentioned earlier. If I concentrate on one particular facet of them, it is because my own specialization enables me to tackle it more competently. I would define these problems as follows:
1. What model of industrialization should one choose?
2. Does the Muslim world's cultural tradition allow it
   (a) to modernize itself, that is to say, to industrialize?
   (b) to choose freely between models of industrialization – or is one particular model favoured or even prescribed? Does the cultural tradition allow for a transformation of structures of the sort which, in one case at least, seems essential?
   (c) to choose, if need be, an ideology which many people believe to be essential if the masses are to be spurred on to the efforts required for modernization, irrespective of the model of industrialization?
3. Does the evolution envisaged allow the Muslim world to keep a certain cultural originality, in continuity with the tradition of the past, in other words to retain its identity or the identity of the peoples which make it up?

How is one to answer these questions? To begin with, by using the only relatively reliable approach available, namely an approach based on the tried and tested methods of scientific analysis. Any other method can at best only produce flashes of intuition, brilliant perhaps, but nonetheless uncontrolled and liable to mislead. Several scientific disciplines have already elaborated relevant research methods and axioms, but these have perhaps not been used widely and coherently enough to supply even partial and provisional answers to the above questions. The economist can give an informed opinion as to the qualities and defects of the proposed models and the economic consequences of the various options. The sociologist also has much to contribute. But clearly the latter must draw on the lessons of humanity's collective experience, as very few sociologists dealing with the problem have done.

It is here that the history of Islam becomes relevant. This tremendous storehouse of varied and instructive experiences is relatively unexplored even by the Muslims (by which I mean the inhabitants of the Muslim world) who more often than not have a mythical conception of it. Out of ignorance or complacency even non-Muslim researchers have been taken in by this mythical conception, which in their case is combined with the myths of the colonial period. These myths must be set aside for any valid scientific approach to these problems to emerge. I do not deny that some have been or still are useful on some levels, or at certain times and I realize that by ignoring or criticising such myths, I will probably offend or upset many of my readers, thus exposing myself to unpleasant suspicions and personal consequences. But lucidity also has its privileges, and I intend to make the most of this opportunity to enunciate truths which many in the Muslim world are aware of but cannot mention and which others feel are better left unspoken. Many of the latter will live long enough to realize that myths are no royal road to an understanding of their world's and their time's problems.

Which Model of Modernization?

Two models are offered by the modern world. Currently they are called the capitalist and the socialist models. Sometimes they appear in apparently intermediate forms and variations. The Muslim world has been seduced by both models in turn. But until now it is mainly the ruling elite which has been susceptible to this seduction. The models have been appreciated especially in terms of their apparent value to development, without too much concern as to their relative values at other levels. Here, as elsewhere, efforts have been made to find a third course, because the two models have seemed too alien to the world which sought to apply them. In their writings, European economists and sociologists have encouraged this search for a variety of reasons, not all disinterested. Two series of comments seem called for here.

1. The Fundamental Options
A wide range of forms is indeed available, and others will no doubt appear. One can also choose one of these forms and give it a particular name, such as solidarism or justicialism, or a particular label such as Arab, Muslim, Argentinian or Christian socialism, in order to camouflage its actual relationship to models current elsewhere. But despite all this variety, the same questions keep re-appearing, and they must be answered with reference to the recurrent major problems, which cannot safely be ignored.

The big question is always the same: Who has the power to take the fundamental economic decisions? Everywhere and always, there are only three possible answers. It is either: the producers themselves, that is to say, in the modern economic context, groups of producers; or autonomous individuals who control the means of production but are not themselves producers, that is to say, in the modern economic context, capitalists; or the state.

Of course, economic decision-making power may be shared between two or three of these elements. Furthermore, the state can itself be dominated by capitalists or by workers or by other groups, and can also be the product of compromises between several groups. In fact the state is probably never, except perhaps during brief transitory phases, that impartial organ of the collective will it is ideally supposed to be. All this makes for a great variety of mixed forms. But what is important is to know which element is dominant. The choice, which cannot be avoided, must be made by the countries concerned. Foreigners such as myself can only sound a warning: Beware of ideologies and nomenclatures which camouflage and disguise this choice. It is quite useless merely to invoke an attractive name or adjective, or to warble on about the advantages of this or that system, its roots in the national tradition or the aura of religiosity which surrounds it. The fundamental question will still arise, and in the same terms.[1]

2. The Universal Value and the Cultural Tradition of the Fundamental Options

The three options in question and their various combinations are not peculiar to any one nation or group of nations. They stem from the very nature of all society and of all possible production. They thus have a universal value. However, if one nonetheless wishes to link these options to local tradition in the presently Muslim countries of the Middle East and Africa, it is quite possible to do so. Indeed, it is probably possible just about anywhere. But in these particular countries one can also show that none of the options is without precedent in the existing cultural tradition.

Co-operation between producers first appeared there at the dawn of history and, under various institutional forms, it has been an important factor in production for several historical periods. For instance, in agricultural production, there have often been agricultural communes in which land was periodically redistributed. In pastoral production, communitarian stockbreeder clans have always played an important role. True, such communities have rarely exercised a strong egalitarian influence on the state. When their influence made itself felt, it was usually at the expense of other elements of the population, particularly the agricultural communes. Furthermore, a high level of social differentiation and hierarchization within the clan was usually prevalent at such times. Nonetheless, it is clear that all these communities often enjoyed considerable autonomy or semi-autonomy. Furthermore, the urban artisans often operated within that mode which Marxists call merchant petty production. In other words, the producer, with the help of his family, sold his goods directly on the market. Sometimes corporations or groups of these independent producers dominated the towns or exercised a strong influence on the municipal council. Small-scale agricultural production by independent farmers who brought their own produce to market also existed at various times and had some influence on the state.

The capitalist private enterprise, controlled by private non-productive individuals, has a long tradition in these countries, a tradition which can be traced back to pre-history. It tended mainly to dominate commercial activity, with occasional ventures into artisan production or manufacturing industry, but sometimes it dominated entire states, especially in the ancient cities of Tyre or Carthage, and it was often preponderant in the mediaeval Islamic cities. It has had far less influence on the state in more recent times.

Contrary to common belief, statism has also been a widespread phenomenon. One only has to look at Egypt where, in ancient times and on several occasions since, the state controlled the whole economy or at least a fair part of it.

The Cultural Tradition and Modernization

Does the Cultural Tradition Allow for Modernization?

It has often been claimed that the Muslim world's cultural tradition incorporated a certain misoneism, a Nicht-progressivismus as a German economist studying 'the economic soul of Islam' put it. It has often been argued that this misoneism, this distaste for innovation, was rooted in the ideology which has been central to the region for thirteen centuries, the Islamic religion.

It is certainly true that what is too summarily called traditional society, not only in the Muslim world but also in China, India, mediaeval Europe and elsewhere, was generally ignorant of the modern idea of progress. It lacked that conception according to which humanity progresses indefinitely through a set of higher and higher qualitative stages, constantly rising above itself by its own efforts. In general, far from putting their hopes in historical evolution, people were frightened of history, as Mircea Eliade has so clearly shown. There was a terrible fear of change, of time's passing and the deterioration it might bring; above all there was an intense desire for stability.

Whilst this picture is on the whole accurate, it should be pointed out that there are a few features which limit its scope. Firstly, there is the fact that the basic document, the sacred text of the Muslim religion, the Koran, favours activity. Its dominant tendency is to oppose fatalism, contrary to the opinion generally held in Europe. It overthrew the idea, previously current, especially amongst the Arabs, that a blind and implacable destiny is all-powerful. It replaced it with God, Allah, a free Will which can be invoked, prayed to, swayed; human action ceased to be foredoomed to failure.

The Koran certainly contains the notion of Allah's omnipotence and even that of the predetermination of human actions. But side by side with this idea, one finds a constant incitement to action. This is certainly contradictory but contradictions of this sort can be found in every religion and perhaps in every ideology. What matters is that those who want to act can find frequent and precise encouragement in the Koran. The logical contradiction is more or less satisfactorily resolved by the idea that the power of God furthers action and enables it to be efficacious. In the Koran, Allah says of David, cast as a blacksmith prophet: 'We have softened the iron for him, saying: "Make solid (chain-mail), measure the links carefully!"' (34 : 10/10–11). These instructions are reminiscent of the way another historical technician, Ambroise Pare, resolved the same contradiction without the benefit of complex theology: 'I looked after him, God healed him!'

As for the dominant theology, it too has always made efforts to reconcile the idea of divine omnipotence with incitement to action. It condemned pure quietism, total surrender (*tawakkol*) to the grace of God. On the whole, it preached reasonable and moderate activity, shunning both excess zeal and listlessness but always giving God His due. It insisted that the leaders and members of the Muslim community accomplish their political duties, duties which were as much part of their religious obligations as the act of worship. In this ideology, which makes far less distinction between the spiritual and the temporal than the Christian West does, the prosperity of the community is itself a religious duty.

Secondly, this cultural tradition has also incorporated ideologies of progress, of human action moving through qualitatively higher and higher stages; revolutionary ideologies, in other words. In the Middle Ages especially, numerous 'sects', or politico-religious parties, preached revolutionary action towards a new order. It is true that, in the pursuit of their aims, they also relied on being in accord with the will of God or of the higher beings. But the fact that modern revolutionary parties believe that the laws of history are on their side does not prevent them from counting essentially on human action. The history of Islam is seen by 'mystified' Muslims and by the mystics as an everlasting submission to God's will. In fact it could far more accurately be characterized as a permanent revolution. The history of the 10th Century Ishmaeli revolutionary international is particularly typical. Furthermore, ideologies of progress linked to an overthrow of the established order are by no means unknown in traditional societies in other parts of the world. The fear of history has in fact not been as general a phenomenon as Eliade, for example, would have us believe. Finally, whilst it is quite true that the religious ideologies, or some at least, have often opposed innovation, and that this opposition has often manifested itself as a feature of traditionalist circles, and even of poor peoples' consciousness in general, it is nonetheless also true that throughout history this misoneism has often been overcome, sidestepped or defeated.

In principle, traditional Islam condemns *bida'*, (singular: *bid'a*), new customs and ways of doing things. The religious ideologues have often vigorously castigated new customs when they first appeared. But when the innovatory thrusts were really strong, they managed to impose themselves despite the condemnation and with the passage of time other religious functionaries have emerged to legitimize what their predecessors failed to prevent. This happened in the case of tobacco and coffee, for example.

Throughout, the deepest transformations have been accepted almost without resistance if they have coincided with the interests of the state or of powerful strata of private individuals, despite any previous theoretical reticence about the type of behaviour they implied. Thus, whilst the Muslim religion was not responsible for bringing about the mediaeval economic revolution, as has been claimed, it is certainly true that the Muslim world did not allow any theoretical considerations to isolate it from this revolution. Just so, in the contemporary period, the Muslim world has unreservedly accepted practices linked precisely to the modernization of the economy in a capitalist direction. For example, as I pointed out in detail in my book *Islam and Capitalism*, it accepted modern banking practice and interest-bearing state loans right from the start and without reservations, despite the formal condemnation of usury in classical Islamic teaching.

It is interesting to see how the Ottoman Empire coped with this sort of situation in the 19th and early 20th Centuries. The Ottoman Empire was by far the greatest independent Muslim power, almost the only one in fact.

Its sovereign gloried in the title of Caliph, successor of the Prophet and God's shadow on Earth. Even beyond the frontiers of his Empire most Sunni Muslims, who formed the largest Islamic denomination, accepted him as such. Yet in 1840, without bothering at all about the formal interdiction on interest, the Ottoman Government issued treasury bonds bearing 12% interest. This was the beginning of the famous 'Ottoman Debt', floating at first then consolidated in bonds from 1857, which played such an important role in the decadence of the Empire. During the same period interest-bearing loans were considered normal practice in the Ottoman Empire, and legislation concerning them was passed without any problem. Thus an Ottoman *firman*, in the year 1268 of the Hegira (1851–52), reduced the rate of interest to 8%, while the Ottoman maritime Commercial Code adopted in 1863 takes interest-bearing loans for granted. The Ottoman Empire, in its somewhat irresolute attempt at modernization, hampered as it was by Europe's economic supremacy, was well aware of the need to set up credit institutions on the European model. One of the great charters of Ottoman reformism, the 18th of February 1856 *khatt-i humayun*, sets out a programme for the creation of banks, a measure which was applied soon after. These banks were supposed to have the same functions as their European models. In 1888 the foundation charter of a state-established bank, the Agricultural Bank, laid down that it was to lend to farmers at 6% and that depositors would receive interest of 4%. The canon forbidding usury is not even mentioned in any of these documents. Possibly the practice had been legalized in religious terms by means of a favourable consultation of the Empire's highest religious authority, Sheikh ul-Islam. Such a consultation would, of course, have been based to some extent on the texts and to some extent on pure casuistry. If it did take place, it certainly seems to have received very little publicity.

The first indication that people were aware of the contradiction between the Empire's official practice and the religious law is a negative one, and comes quite late on the scene. In 1877, the Medjelleh, a new Ottoman statute book strongly influenced by European jurisprudence, attempted to co-ordinate the principles of Ottoman law whilst keeping to the prescriptions of Islam. It quite simply leaves out any mention of interest-bearing loans. Such embarrassed silence is obviously significant. It was only in 1887, about half a century after the first issue of interest-bearing treasury bonds, that the first timid steps to bring Ottoman legislation into line with religious law were made; it was decided that the rate of interest would run at 9% but that the total interest accrued should not exceed the principal loaned. This manouvre was a surreptitious, implicit attempt to play on the obscurity of the passage in the Koran on which the prohibition of usury is based. For thirteen centuries of Islam this passage had been interpreted as forbidding money-lending altogether. Now, without openly saying so, it was being re-interpreted as merely meaning that it was forbidden to double one's capital by lending at extortionate rates.

The first instance of a Muslim religious authority really facing up to the problem and trying to justify the by then well-established practice appears to have been in 1903 in a pronouncement or *fatwa* by the Grand Mufti of Egypt, which was still theoretically under Ottoman sovereignty but governed by a Khedive under British protection. At that time, the Grand Mufti of Egypt, the country's highest religious authority, was Mohammed 'Abdoh', a modernist. And even then, this *fatwa*, which legitimized the practice of interest-bearing savings accounts, was circulated to such a limited extent that even now researchers are unable to find a copy. The act which set up these savings accounts, administered by the post offices, also tried, by means of some rather unconvincing tricks, to keep up the appearance of abiding by the religious law. Interest was referred to as 'dividends', it was specified that the handling of the accounts must not contradict the religious law, whilst in fact the very stipulations of the act violated it, at least in the traditional form in which it had been known for the previous thirteen centuries, and once again the doubling of one's capital was forbidden. At least the religious law was being taken into account; the previous sixty years of Ottoman legislation had quite simply ignored it.

It was only then that the scruples which had been troubling many pious Muslims culminated in some concerted action. Indian Muslims, who wished to put the traditional teachings of Islamic law into practice, but nonetheless recognized the demands made by modern capitalist society, attempted to set up credit co-operatives giving free credit. Such modern attempts to put the religious law into practice were not uninfluenced by the European co-operative movement. However, their size and scope remained limited.

This history of the legislation affecting lending with interest during the contemporary period can serve as a useful illustration. Things often took place in a similar manner. Innovations were first spontaneously accepted in specific circles. Often enough this was followed by scruples, and then, finally, by the decisions of the *'ulemas'*, the experts on religious law who make up a sort of Islamic clergy. For instance Mohammad 'Abdoh's *fatwas* of around 1900, authorising the faithful to eat food prepared by non-Muslims, very belatedly legalized a practice which had become perfectly common everywhere except within certain very small, highly religious groups. The religious precept forbidding such practices, which goes back to the Middle Ages, had by then already long since fallen into disuse.

A dislike of change amongst the least privileged, especially amongst the poor peasants, has often been noted and blamed on Islam. But a closer look at the specific examples given often shows that such resistance has been mainly based on the fact that the proposed innovations had very little to do with the real needs of the people to whom it was offered as a model; indeed in some cases it was actually to their disadvantage. G. Destanne de Bernis' work on the modern houses rejected by the Tunisian peasants is a case in point. It was realized that these houses were in many ways ill-suited to the peasants' life and work; when the peasants were offered houses more in keeping with their needs, they adopted them enthusiastically. The same applies to a number of agricultural innovations, which were essentially progressive but imposed the sort of risks which the peasants' poverty made it difficult to accept. When the additional expenses involved in such innovations were clearly shown to be worthwhile, the new measures were willingly accepted.

Of course, this is not to deny that the Muslim world went through a long period of misoneism during which innovation encountered considerable resistance. But it is clearly misleading to explain this phenomenon in terms of religion which was only a secondary factor. Many other causes were at play but the main factor was the dynamic of social structures. Here especially, perhaps, reference to religion was used to sanctify the traditional way of life as a whole. Dozens of customs introduced long before the advent of Islam, such as the veil for women, or quite independently of the religion, were later consecrated as being linked to Islam. Faced with any infringement of these customs conservatives protested shrilly and denounced the impiety of the innovators. Just about anything could acquire, through a quite contingent link with Muslims, the status of a Muslim practice. To take an example which should not be contentious in Algiers, the use of *qat*, an intoxicating plant introduced into Ethiopia by Muslims from the Yemen, is considered by the indigenous Christians as a specifically Muslim practice, to the extent that after a victory over Muslims, the Christian kings would have *qat* plants uprooted.

Hostility towards much-hated innovators, especially foreign ones, also often appeared in the guise of religious misoneism. I remember the case of a Muslim cemetery in Beirut during the French Mandate; the Beirut Muslims invoked religion in their fierce opposition to any redevelopment of the land. Once independence had been achieved, however, the cemetery was soon disposed of and the plot used to build a cinema or some other such building. There have been countless cases of the sort.

Resistance to innovation has naturally been most intense when such innovation has conflicted with established interests. Religious arguments have been marshalled all the more vehemently in such cases, whether appropriate or not. One only has to look at the resistance put up by many Syrian *ulemas* to the nationalizations decreed by the Ba'ath party, or at the religious arguments used by the conservative religious ideologist Mawdoudi, against the nationalization of lands in Pakistan. It is quite obvious that the motives behind such campaigns are religious in name alone.

Does the Cultural Tradition Allow for a Radical Transformation of the Economic Structures?

It is the cultural tradition's normative form, the Muslim religion itself, which is in question here. Does Islam allow for a free choice between the two models of industrialization, the capitalist model and the socialist model? Does it prescribe one or other of these paths, or does it favour a third model? In other words, does it allow for a radical transformation of the economic structures should the need arise?

To give an adequate answer to these questions one must make a clear distinction between several levels within the Muslim religion. Firstly, there is the holy 'corpus' which is the foundation of the official ideology, the Koran, supposedly the word of God as transmitted by the Prophet Mohammad. Even if other normative sources have been incorporated into it, it remains the only absolutely unassailable fount of truth for all Muslims. One could imagine an Islam which rejected all other sources; but rejection of the Koran would imply rejection of the Muslim religion itself.

The Koran is essentially a religious text which also contains political directives and precepts of social reform. But it contains very few purely economic injunctions. In fact the only significant injunctions are the ban on *riba*, the prescription in favour of legal charity and, to stretch a point, the legislation on inheritance. The prohibition on *riba* is obscurely phrased; the old tradition identified *riba* quite simply with lending at interest, but in fact it apparently refers only to a particularly pernicious type of money-lending. Perhaps it referred to the doubling of the debt should a debtor not repay his creditor on time, as may be implied by a particular Arabic term. Or perhaps it referred to compound interest, which Justinian had banned just a few decades before in the neighbouring Byzantine Empire. There was also the *zakat*, a heavy tax imposed to meet the operating expenses of the Muslim community and to provide for the poor. Contemporary Muslim ideologues have often argued that these prescriptions, in association with the legislation on inheritance, which ordains a sharing-out of goods acquired in each generation, make up a divinely inspired economic system which is incomparably better than any possible alternative. It is supposedly far superior to both capitalism and socialism, in that it creates a society of free property-owners whilst preventing any excessive accumulation of wealth. Such a viewpoint is difficult to accept, unless one shares the Muslim faith. The prohibition on interest cannot apply to a modern free enterprise economic system, and the Koranic texts are rather favourable to the freedom of private enterprises. In a socialist system, lending at interest may be practised by the state, but not by private individuals, or at least not without very heavy restrictions, without changing the essence of the system. If one restricts oneself to forbidding exorbitant rates of interest and compound interest, one must not expect that this will prevent, or has ever prevented, the formation of large fortunes. The rate of income tax in Britain, for instance, is much higher than that of the *zakat*. But no Muslim ideologue seems to consider that British society is organized according to the will of Allah. As for the laws on inheritance, in theory they should indeed ensure a fragmentation of great fortunes with every passing generation; in practice, however, because Muslims have tended to live as extended families, holding their goods more or less in common, such fragmentation has often been avoided. But in any case, the experience of other equally 'redistributive' legislations has shown that such prescriptions can do little to prevent the founding of great fortunes. In the present period it is difficult to see how such legislation could stand against the formation of companies, trusts and cartels holding huge assets.

In fact, it is clear that the Koran in no way set out to modify the economic rules operating in the society in which it surfaced. Naturally enough, it recognized the right to private ownership of property, without making any distinction between the ownership of the means of production and that of other goods. This was only normal. At the time there was absolutely no point in regulating the private ownership of means of production, such as windmills, for example. The real power then lay in the ownership of a different kind of wealth, such as extensive land or slave holdings, or huge monetary fortunes. In any case the Koran does little to restrict the ownership of any of these types of wealth.

One must make a distinction between the Koran and the various divergent and contradictory interpretations of it made by many conflicting authorities during the Middle Ages. What one could call Sunni orthodoxy is only that trend of thought which circumstances, and its relative suitability to those circumstances, brought to the fore. These trends of thought manifested themselves as doctrines, dogmas and systems whose authority was bolstered by normative acts and words attributed to the Prophet. Indeed historical research has cast some doubt on these attributions. Thus one is not dealing with 'Islam', a single and coherent doctrine, but with several ideologies, several Islams.

Few of these subsequent ideological systems envisaged precise economic or socio-economic revolutions. Those which did were, as a rule, defeated, as happened to parallel revolutionary systems in societies of the same type as traditional Muslim society. This regularity of defeat makes it more than likely that it was the prevailing social conditions which prevented the victory of these trends of thought. Many of them expressed a revolt against the prevailing order, which was judged to be unsatisfactory, exploitative, oppressive. But such denunciations were not backed up with a programme of structural changes. People had no idea how to modify the existing structure.

There was a constant trend towards what Christian theologians call a 'return to the source'. Here, as elsewhere, evil was explained in terms of neglect or inadequate application of the original precepts. It was assumed that a return to the rules of primitive Islam, itself conceptualised in a particular way, and to the rigorous application of those rules, would ensure a radical change, the beginning of a new era, the establishment of the happy and harmonious society prescribed by God. Revolutions were made on the basis of such a programme, and were sometimes even victorious, as in 750 with the Abbasid 'revolution'. But pretty soon people realized that the new society contained as many iniquities as the old. The history of Islam is not that of a paradise lost. It is the history of a permanent revolution, a constantly betrayed and constantly resumed revolution.

The Muslims had good reason for their untiring comparison between Islam as it was and Islam as it should have been, between the iniquity of existing society and the norm it had itself proposed and proclaimed. The divergence between the principles and the reality was, it is true, far older than they realized, but it was nonetheless also true that primitive Islam had never contented itself merely with calling on the faithful to serve God and to save their souls. It had had the more far-reaching ambition of being the basis for a harmonious and just community. But unfortunately, it never went beyond preaching this harmony and justice, presented as the aspiration of Man and the will of God, and to be realized by purifying one's heart, praising the Lord and curbing one's bad instincts. More than many other religions, including Christianity, it had also laid down certain rules for social life, called for the abolition of certain harmful practices and proposed certain institutions. But the history of the Muslim Middle Ages proves quite clearly that that was not enough.

Muslim ideologues, just like those of many other faiths, tend to sing the same tune over and over again: 'If only people applied the commandments . . .!' If only the holy canons were obeyed, they argue, evil, social evil at least, would vanish from the face of the earth. In this they are certainly correct, and the same would be true if the precepts of Christianity, Judaism, Buddhism, Platonism or Kantianism were strictly applied. But this is precisely the problem which they fail to grasp. Why have they not been applied? The history of Islam demonstrates once again one of the most well-established laws of history, albeit apparently one of the least understood: reference to religious, moral and philosophical principles is necessary, but it is never enough in itself.

The tendency for new iniquities, new exploitations, new oppressions to emerge after old ones have been eliminated is eternal and has proved far stronger than all the religious, moral or philosophical barriers one can erect against it. There is only one solution to the problem. The answer does not lie in the endless repetition of precepts and principles which thousands of sermons and lessons have not succeeded in making socially effective. It is to give the victims of oppression the means to resist it and to create and defend their own institutions which guarantee that ability.

There is within Islam a third level, which must be carefully distinguished from the other two, comprising the way in which the various ideologies have been lived, the practices to which they have been linked, practices which certainly influenced them if they did not inspire them. The various systems into which Mediaeval Islam resolved itself were each lived in a different way, transformed from within even where they remained identical in terms of external references and texts. What is at issue here cannot be reduced to a mere contrast between the doctrines and texts of the 'heretical' tendencies on the one hand, the Muslim 'orthodoxy' recognized by the majority of Muslims on the other. In a conformist setting, here as elsewhere, it is often the case that the re-interpretation of one phrase of a holy text is enough to bring about an existential change and the adoption of a critical or revolutionary attitude, which may remain an individual attitude or may spread to others. By contrast, it often happens that, as time goes by, a revolutionary or innovatory breakthrough comes to be interpreted in a conservative, conformist and quietist sense. There are many examples of such a process, which could indeed be called a general law for ideologies. The evolution of the Ishmaeli 'sect' is particularly striking. In the Middle Ages, the Ishmaelis preached revolutionary subversion of the established order. Today, its leaders are the

Aga Khans, millionaire potentates whose main concern is to enjoy the *dolce vita* in the company of film stars and celebrities, as the scandal sheets never tire of telling us.

In conclusion, the holy texts make no explicit pronouncements. The cultural tradition in general, be it in its more explicit formulations, its proclamations, its doctrinal texts or in the attitudes evoked by the former, presents a wide variety of aspects and allows one to justify the most mutually contradictory theses.

One can therefore conclude that it would be wrong to interpret the Islamic tradition as conservative. It has another side to it. And it is possible to select, from amongst the variety it offers us, that current which through the centuries constantly protests against injustice and iniquity, and constantly returns to the initial inspiration which fired Mohammad when he first asserted his vision, when, in the name of justice and the will of God, he raised the banner of protest against the rich and powerful of his own city, and against the conformism of his own period. One must also bear in mind that, in general, this tradition can itself be the vital source for a call to struggle for justice. But even now it can also still be interpreted in a conservative sense, in the sense of moral conformism. It has been so interpreted in the past, and will be in the future. Although the tradition may be necessary to the orientation of a revolutionary action, *vis-a-vis* the old structures, it is not sufficient for a precise orientation.

Cultural Tradition and Ideological Mobilization

When one looks closely at contemporary experiences of economic construction, one is struck by how important it is that there should exist a mobilizatory ideology which arouses in the masses a commitment to the often arduous and taxing tasks which are demanded of them. This is particularly true in the context of an economy oriented towards socialism, where individual interest is not enough of a driving force and plays little part in the immediate and personal satisfactions to be derived from the results of the tasks at hand. And to the extent that a country is still not developed, to the extent that it faces unfavourable natural conditions, so will the first stages of economic construction be all the more austere, so will it be all the more necessary to concentrate on building up an infrastructure without immediate benefit for the individual, so will one have to rely all the more on a spirit of self-sacrifice, which can prevail only if all are persuaded of the greatness and supreme value of the ultimate goal.

Does the cultural tradition in the Muslim countries pre-empt the choice of such a mobilizatory ideology? Once again, let us turn to history for an answer.

In cases where new tasks require new ideologies, there are two possibilities. Either the old ideologies are reinterpreted or new ideologies are brought in to replace or, at least, to supplement them. Examples of both cases can be found in the Muslim world's history. To begin with, the Muslim religion has undergone constant re-interpretation. From an economic point of view, this is particularly noticeable when one examines the economic development of the Muslim world and the rise of the commercial bourgeoisie during the Middle Ages. The religious texts were then full of exaltations of the merchant's role and importance, highlighting the values particular to that social class. One could cite many other examples. Once again, there has not been one Islam but twenty, a hundred Islams, each different in many respects.

Re-interpretation took place within orthodoxy itself. It also brought about the creation of new 'sects' opposed to the orthodox faith, introducing new elements and forging new syntheses. But each nonetheless claimed to be the only true Islam or the only legitimate outcome of Islam. These re-interpretations were themselves situated in a religious framework. They were conceived of as flowing from new conceptions of God, His relations with men and His intentions for them. They fitted into a new theology which sometimes gave rise to new rites. And within such new perspectives the tables were turned on the orthodox, who were denounced in the classical terms as enemies of God, *a'da'Allah*.

But Muslim history has also often witnessed new ideologies invoked instead of or alongside the old. In the Middle Ages for instance, Hellenistic thought was one of these complementary or supplementary ideologies. Muslim thinkers were entranced by this grandiose attempt to interpret the world by means of reason alone, sometimes going so far as to prefer it to Islam itself. For example, the great 10th-century doctor and philosopher, Razi, proclaimed that Socrates exemplified a higher order of humanity than the Prophet. Hellenistic thought also permeated several extensive strata of mediaeval Muslim society, which, despite current opinion, was as much the continuation of the Eastern Hellenistic society as it was that of the pastoral or commercial tribes of the Arabian peninsula.

Amongst the Ishmaelis, the effort to interpret the world even resulted in an attempt to change it. This great ideological party kept up a Muslim appearance for the sake of the broad mass of its followers, but the esoteric doctrine embraced by its elite was predominantly non-Muslim in origin. It was, in fact, mainly an offshoot of Hellenistic thought. Generally speaking, Hellenistic rationalism strongly influenced the whole of Islam's approach to theological problems. The various new formulations were nonetheless a continuation of the initial impetus of the Muslim religion, marked by the all-pervading influence of the same sacred texts, the same rites, the same general orientation towards piety.

Although, as we have just seen, some individuals did practically abandon Islam in favour of a philosophical orientation, the great majority combined the two sources of intellectual and spiritual life. Their existential attitude was rooted in the style of Mohammedan piety, modified to some extent by later influences. Their understanding of the great philosophical and theological problems stemmed mainly from Greek rationalism. In the purely intellectual disciplines they quite simply continued and extended Hellenistic thought. Amongst the common people, of course, it was the Muslim pietist inspiration which was dominant.

155

Nationalism is another of these complementary or supplementary ideologies. Appearing in the 19th Century and affirming itself in the 20th, nationalism has juxtaposed itself to Islam and has sometimes even replaced it. For many Muslims, following in the footsteps of European nationalism, the good of the national community has become the highest goal, displacing the service of God and the saving of one's soul. When an individual reaches this extreme stage, he effectively abandons religious values proper. It is easy to understand why men of religion were often hostile to such a current, especially during the first phase of nationalism's penetration. The attitude of many nationalists, who never ceased to praise Islam, was in practice all the more destructive of it. Often enough, they reduced Islam to a flag, a mobilizatory symbol, an identity factor, a useful national tradition; they saw in it something not dissimilar to that which the atheist Maurras saw in French Catholicism.

Some considered Islam to be a useful myth, recognizing, as Voltaire did, that religion was a necessary social institution. As early as the 19th Century, this was the view held by the spiritual father of all the contemporary nationalist movements in the Muslim world, Jamal ad-din al-Afghani. Such an attitude can be very widespread, without those who adopt it necessarily being aware of the fact that they are doing so. It was with a certain sense of shock that the Canadian Christian theologian, W.C. Smith, realized, as he put it, that many are the individuals, political leaders or ordinary people, from Indonesia to Morocco, who believe in Islam and do not believe in Allah, or at least whose belief in Islam comes before their belief in Allah. The properly religious attitude, of course, consists in believing in Allah above everything else.

It should be pointed out that no specifically Muslim nationalism has emerged. It is quite true that the feeling of national community in Muslim countries defined itself in different terms from those appropriate to, say, Italy; there was a variety of levels, a different content and an apparently different aspect to it. But these differences are, in fact, circumstantial and superficial. The essence of nationalism is the same here as elsewhere. The glorification of the ethno-national group becomes the supreme value. The same consequences follow, and in the last analysis so do the tensions between national values in the widest sense and religious values proper; these tensions are similar to those which manifested themselves in Europe, for instance between essential, universalist Catholicism and the various national Catholicisms, which have long been more national and clericalist than truly religious, on some levels at least.

A sifting-out process has begun to operate before our very eyes, especially since independence has been gained almost everywhere. As long as national independence was the major pre-occupation of all the Muslim peoples, as long as nationalism was a call to resist domination by non-Muslim peoples, as long as it boiled down to a struggle against foreign oppression and exploitation, the religiously oriented could not fail to agree with the essential points of the nationalist programme. And this common orientation was naturally reinforced in that Islam has always placed a certain emphasis on the well-being of the community here on earth, and in that the Muslim tradition, despite some contradictions, is essentially opposed to any exclusive orientation towards the next world. But as soon as the nationalists begin to tackle the problems of internal policy, and as soon as conflict with other Muslim states becomes at least a possibility, the religious element can assert its own independence. It then becomes far easier to stress, for instance, that the faith has as its paramount concerns other values than those of the nationalist ideology, and that God cannot be expected to bless indiscriminately every project of every Muslim national group just because they are Muslims. Nationalism can only be embraced up to a certain point and under certain specific conditions by a univeralist religion such as Islam.

Analogous observations could be made concerning socialism. It too is an ideology built round a project distinguishable from purely religious pre-occupations. Again, some individuals have given themselves over to it exclusively, to the point where they have abandoned Islam, whilst others, if not the same individuals, have sought to demonstrate its concordance with Islam and to use Islam to reinforce it. Many attempts have been made to present socialism in religious form. There is, of course, a certain distortion implicit in such an attempt. True, one can show that there is nothing in the Muslim religion, considered in its dominant aspect, which opposes the socialist project of abolishing the privileges associated with wealth. For socialism only opposes the private ownership of the means of production, which makes it possible to acquire such privileges; it does not oppose private property in itself, which the Koran apparently approves of since it contains regulations governing inheritance. The Koran also lays down the basis for limitations of property, as does the Tradition.

There was nothing in the Muslim religion which opposed the nationalist project of autonomy for an ethno-national group. The religion can, however, go even further along the road to socialism than along the road to nationalism. For as long as the socialist project remains quite true to itself, as long as it remains faithful to its goal, the religion can at most condemn the forms its realization takes and the ideology it has developed, but never its ultimate aims. The nationalist project, on the other hand, can remain true to itself whilst moving towards the oppression and exploitation of other national communities. In which case, ideally, religious thought cannot but condemn it. Nonetheless, this does not prove that the Muslim religion already contains the outline of the modern ideal of an earthly sóciety without privileges.

What is true is that the aims of the socialist project can be linked to a humane tradition which Islam, amongst others, has shared. There is thus, after all, some value in that formula dear to the Muslim ideologues criticized above: if only the precepts had been applied . . . On the one hand, one has to admit that historical Islam, like all other religions, did not encompass any specific plan for the eradication of certain categories of privilege, exploitation and oppression, despite the few steps it took in this direction. On the other hand, all great religions and philosophies include a denunciation of iniquity, even if the accompanying specifics are not in accord with the modern ideal. Islam, too, includes such a denunciation. The religious values of Islam, like those of Christianity, can therefore supply an impetus for the struggle against iniquity on the precise lines laid down by the socialist project. We have witnessed a still limited number of Christians participating in the struggle on this basis; and a man like Palmiro Togliatti recognized that some people could be motivated by religious faith in struggling for justice alongside those who found inspiration in a more secular ideology. Such analogies come naturally to mind, for Muslim culture is not the isolated world which some imagine it to be. Like other cultures, and like Arab, Persian or Turkish culture, those more specific to the peoples who have embraced Islam, it incorporates universal values.

In conclusion, radical re-interpretations of Islam, geared to making it into a mobilizatory ideology suited to modern projects, are likely to run into difficulties, because they do not take the specificity of the religious phenomenon into account. It is no easy task, in the present period, to create a new religious 'sect' complete with a new theology in order to draw people into national or social struggle. One can hardly denounce as 'enemies of Allah' pious and devout men who happen to disagree with this or that national task or set of social measures. Nor can one denounce pious conservatives or devout foreign Muslims in the name of a movement whose very leadership will necessarily include men whose religious faith is visibly less ardent, if not completely absent. And where is one to find a new prophet, a *mahdi* sent by God to preach the socialist gospel? All this is surely pure utopianism.

But the rejection of conservative traditions is possible. They are after all only a transitory structure superimposed on the essential background of the Muslim religion. With the passing of the centuries, of which they are themselves a product, they have constantly been transformed. All those which contradict the nationalist project have either been implicitly cast aside or explicitly resisted, all the more successfully to the extent that nationalism, thanks to its particular attractions, has fired the people's imagination. The same thing could happen with the socialist project.

There is thus in principle nothing to prevent the Muslim world from adopting a socialist ideology to mobilize the masses, with the aim of modernizing the economy in a manner hostile to the perpetuation or development of privileges associated with wealth. History offers us many examples of such ideological alliances. Whilst some non-religious individuals may find in the socialist ideology a guide and reason for life sufficient unto itself, it must be realized that many others, having different existential needs, will keep or even rediscover their religious faith. Some will even find in this faith, in the values transmitted by the Muslim religion and in a return to the initial impetus which gave rise to it, the reasons to struggle for a more equitable society.

Modernization and Cultural Originality

The last question I would like to raise here has recently given rise to much discussion. It can be formulated as follows. Will the evolution towards new structures allow the Muslim world to return to a certain cultural originality in continuity with the tradition of the past, in other words, to keep its identity?

A lot of nonsense has been written or spoken on this subject. Such ramblings appeal to very powerful, and indeed legitimate and justified feelings, namely the conception of oneself as personal, original, irreducible to any other; and the will to be so. But all too often this is presented in a way which involves a quite false and idealist conception of civilization. A culture is treated as a reasoning being, a more or less specific, intangible whole, built up over the centuries around the same particular idea, the same values, the same sentiments. In short, there is supposedly a 'soul' of Muslim civilization which has remained fundamentally unaltered over the ages. Furthermore, ever since the thrust of nationalist ideas has made itself felt, the idea of this 'soul' co-exists with that of a Persian, Arab or Turkish soul, each of which is also supposed to be specific, irreducible, intangible and constant. It may not be easy to reconcile these concepts in theory, but their effective echoes are enough to ensure that they are accepted side by side.

Do such ideas have any real value, however? I doubt it. The Muslim world has constantly taken new forms, it has constantly accepted foreign inputs, whilst, at the same time, influencing other cultures. It has constantly created new cultural forms and forever modified itself. And, I insist on the point, it is at the times when the Muslim World has been most receptive, most open to the outside world, that it has been most prestigious, most imitated, most taken up as a model by others, and most powerful. There is thus nothing to fear from the outside world, or from change.

For example, let us take Muslim art, one of the most obvious, most accessible and most specific aspects of classical Muslim culture. During the Ommayyad period, one saw the creation and formation of this art, drawing on disparate elements to form a synthesis which itself never stopped evolving and bringing in new elements. It was only tenuously linked with primitive Islam. We know roughly what the poor 'Mosque' or Medina was like, a meeting place for the faithful of the primitive Muslim community as well as the dwelling of its leader, the Prophet; in its courtyard, where expeditions were launched and the sick were cared for, stood his wives' huts and a bench for otherwise homeless paupers.[2] There were no soaring arches or minarets. This humble setting looked nothing like the typical monuments of Muslim architecture, the Mosque of Cordoba, the Alhambra, the Blue Mosque in Istanbul, the Taj Mahal!

The Greek contribution to mediaeval Muslim civilization was considerable, especially in the sciences and all the intellectual disciplines. This was integrated into the admirable synthesis which was Muslim thought in the Middle Ages, to join a vast range of foreign borrowings from Hindu, Chinese and many other sources. The great thinkers of Islam were never reticent about using these foreign elements; the great scholar, Biruni is well-known for his translations from the Sanskrit, Arab historians used Persian, Hindu and European sources, and the great Persian historian, Rashid ad-din, used Latin texts.

One could go on indefinitely. Many customs which seem specifically Muslim today were originally foreign, even though they were sanctified by Islam. Thus the veil for women is, as we have seen, rooted in the practices of the ancient East and mentioned in Assyro-Babylonian laws three thousand years before Islam. The Hammams are merely Greek or Roman baths under another name. It was this synthesis which was so admired and imitated during the Middle Ages, and which enjoyed incomparable prestige. The Muslim civilization was the supreme civilization which people everywhere, and especially in Europe, imitated out of snobbism or fascination.

Today one can foresee new syntheses. Some things will change, for sure, and many have already changed; customs will be abandoned as so many have been in the past. Others more relevant to the modern world and with the universal forms of technical civilization will appear. There is no reason to fear such transformations. Fear in the face of innovation is a sign of old age, of stagnation and of weakness. Boldly turning to the future is the sign of vigorous life.

Conclusion

So, if I may bring to bear upon your problems the opinion of a foreigner — a foreigner who knows your history and the social and cultural structures of your countries well, but a foreigner nonetheless, however sympathetic to your aspirations — I would like to make an appeal.

Firstly, I appeal for lucidity. Myths may be useful for certain mobilizations, but they end up by mystifying, blinding and misleading the very people who manipulate them. To retreat into myths, especially the use of the past to elucidate today's problems, is another sign of weakness. If forceful ideas are needed to guide action, let them be as close to reality as possible.

Secondly, I appeal for open-mindedness. I have already said that societies which turn in on themselves and on their particular problems are dying, static societies. Living, progressive, dynamic societies are not afraid to borrow in order to get down to the task of forging a new synthesis. Indeed the same is true for individuals. The most appealing and most promising trait of the studious Algerian youths I have met is their thirst for knowledge, their desire to drink at every fountain and to assimilate every input.

Finally, and especially, I appeal for an open-mindedness towards a universal vision of the existing problems, the only kind of vision which is genuinely revolutionary.

I hope I will be forgiven for insisting on the point. There are three ways of devoting oneself: to God, to the group and to Man. To devote oneself to God is to have a faith which it is not given to everybody to share, and which in any case does not, in general, exclude the other types of devotion. To devote oneself to the group to which one belongs is necessary, and when that group is humiliated or oppressed, it becomes a primordial human duty. But the group should not be deified, placed above everything else. That would be what classical Muslim theology calls *shirk*, associationism, the act of assimilating some other person with God. The group is not everything. An exclusive aspiration to the greater glory of the group, taken as a supreme value, would lead to an anarchic world of hate-filled nations in perpetual struggle one against the other.

Beyond the group, ethnic or national, there are universal values which stand above it: liberty, equality and fraternity, for all men. Integral and exclusive nationalism logically leads to a barbaric attitude towards all humanity outside the group. Its motto, 'my country right or wrong', translated into German, stood over the gate of the camp at Buchenwald. And in Algeria, one could ask how, if the nation is the supreme value, can one justify the actions of those Frenchmen who defended the cause of Algerian independence. Were they then traitors? If, on the contrary, the value one places above all others, the vision one holds before one's eyes, is a universal value, namely the struggle against all iniquity, this implies a perpetual renewal, for the forms iniquity takes are perpetually renewed, and pose problems which are always new, unexpected and unprecedented.

The Kingdom of God is not of this world, there is no end to history, the struggles will not cease. He who struggles for justice, the militant, the radical revolutionary, he who tackles the root of iniquities, as Marx puts it, will never have the right to settle back into the blissful self-satisfaction of the righteous man through whom Heaven has descended to Earth. I am no prophet and do not like the prophetic style. But if one can draw a lesson from past experience and from rational analysis, it is that the future before us is a future of struggle, a future which demands courageous souls, and thus a future worthy of Man.

There is no reason to believe that such struggles will spare the Muslim world. Man is neither beast nor god, said Aristotle, whom the Muslim Middle Ages knew as *al mo'allim al-awwal*, the first master; he is the *zoon politikon*, whose life is civil society, and whose life is thus protest, struggle and conflict. The man whose life in Muslim society is neither the monkey nor the robot pictured by the colonialists; nor is he the angel in direct communication with the heavens imagined by the naive, by the apologists and the mystics. He has enjoyed no fantastic privilege nor has he been the victim of some terrible curse. History shows him to have engaged in the struggles and tasks which are common to all humanity. He shares the same kind of aspirations, reactions, conceptions and illusions, the same opposite tendencies, the same efforts to defend himself, to free himself and to enslave others, to conserve and to go forwards, which are the common lot of all mankind. There is no *Homo Islamicus*. The history of the Muslim world is specific, it has its own style and colour, it is an incomparable part of human diversity. But it is not exceptional. Men everywhere have faced similar problems, to be resolved by analogous means. There is no reason to believe that this will not always be so.

To face the forthcoming struggles, one must be armed. One must learn to distance oneself from the myths, to assimilate the lessons of human experience, to reject complacency and self-satisfaction which are causes of stagnation; one must always seek to surpass oneself and the existing situation, in the effort to accomplish the great human tasks.

References

1. I am pleased to be able to invoke another appeal for closer scrutiny of these so-called 'national', 'ethnic' and 'religious', socialisms, namely that of a Muslim sociologist, my Yemeni friend, Mohammed Said El Attar, in his *Le Sous-Development Economique et Social du Yemen, Perspectives de la Revolution Yemenite*, Editions du Tiers Monde, (Algiers, 1964), p. 388.
2. This description has been taken as an insult to the dignity of Islam. I cannot see why. Or must one assume that 12th Century Mecca was full of concrete buildings in order not to be accused of being disrespectful towards Islam?

9. The Political Structure of Egypt Under Nasser

Like all authoritarian countries with no legally institutionalized opposition, Egypt since 1952 calls for a particular approach, if one is to understand its internal policies. One must pay particular attention to what can be learnt about the ruling group's ideas, about the struggles which have taken place within this group and about the challenges it has faced from social forces external to it. Finally, one must make a careful study of the steps this group has taken to ensure that the country it rules has a political structure in keeping with the group's ideology. The characteristic background to internal policy in pluralist societies, namely the competition and conflict between various pressure groups, is not totally absent in authoritarian countries, but it takes on a very particular aspect.[1] Although the basic ideology of the rulers plays a primordial role, one should always bear in mind that it is the interactions between this ideology and the requirements of the internal and external objective situation of the country under consideration which shape political developments.[2]

The Ruling Group's Political Ideas

The various members of the Free Officers' movement came together on the basis of a shared way of looking at things, even though there were various shades of opinion within this overall consensus. Their relative unity, both while they were preparing to seize power and for a while afterwards, can only be explained in terms of a common dominant orientation towards the implicit and explicit goals of their actions. This common dominant orientation can be reduced to two main projects, namely national independence and modernization. And even then the latter was conceived of, not as an end in itself, but as an indispensable aspect of the nation's independence. As Nasser himself put it so clearly in his *Philosophy of the Revolution*, the key issue was 'political and economic liberty' (*horriyya*).[3] Significantly enough, the official French translation rendered '*horriyya*' as 'independence'. This seems quite appropriate when one considers that Nasser had written previously that what was at stake was 'the realisation of the Egyptian people's longstanding desire to have the final say over its own destiny, its hope that power should eventually pass to its own sons'.[4] Modernization was seen as a means to increase the nation's decision-making autonomy. And as for the project of democratizing economic and social life, it figured in the Free Officers' programme mainly as a corollary of their other two main aims: a strong and independent nation would naturally find it incumbent upon itself to abolish privilege and injustice.

In fact, all social and political ills were seen as essentially the result of either foreign influence or individual immorality. It was recognized that the old political regime in Egypt was characterized (*taba*) by injustice (*toghyan*), oppression (*zolm*) and generalized destitution (*kharab*).[5] But all this was attributed to the effects of the foreign domination exercised by the Mamelukes.

The most Marxist-influenced passage in Nasser's *Philosophy of the Revolution* brings the point home. One could sum up his argument as follows: 'Each people must undertake two revolutions': a political revolution, defined as freeing oneself from foreign domination, and a social revolution, consisting of a struggle between classes, in order to ensure that 'equity will prevail between all the children of the same nation'. Whilst the first type of revolution demands unity between all the elements of the nation, the second 'overthrows (established) values and undermines traditional ways of thinking (*al-'aqa'id*); compatriots struggle against each other as individuals or as classes; discord, suspicion hatred . . . and selfishness reign'.[6]

The Egyptians, whose misfortune it is to have to carry out these two revolutions simultaneously, will therefore witness not only the growth in their midst of unity, mutual love, total devotion to the desired objective, as part of the political revolution and the struggle for national independence; they must also expect an upsurge of divisiveness, hatred and egocentrism, an upsurge which, says Nasser, will occur 'despite ourselves', as part of the social revolution.

All this clearly indicates that we are dealing with a nationalist conception of history. Although Nasser has to admit the necessity of an internal social struggle, he sees it only as an unfortunate requirement of destiny, which exposes the nation to an upsurge of its own worst instincts. National unity equals the Good, divisiveness equals Evil. This conception of things is the exact opposite of the Marxist one, in which internal struggle is seen as healthy, as the fertile ground on which the noblest qualities can flourish. Marxism treats external struggles, even when directed at liberation, as a deplorable source of divisiveness between the workers, who should unite (Workers of the World Unite!), a divisiveness which fosters a prehistoric group selfishness and drags humanity backwards. There is only one context within which Marxist ideology can accept the nationalist vision of social unity, and that context is socialist society. But for the time being — and things may soon change — Marxism sees socialism as a transcendence of national antagonisms, as a force whose vocation is to bring about a reconciliation and even a fusion between nations.[7]

In the nationalist vision the fundamental ideal is the strong, united and autonomous nation. Social struggles may be justified as means to achieve this goal, but they are in themselves unpleasant, in that they momentarily undermine this unity. The Marxist ideal of a nation free of all internal oppression and made up of free and equal individuals is rejected or misunderstood. Hence the internal political project of democratization remains secondary, as indeed it does in the Marxist conception. Marxists see social oppression as harmful because it alienates individuals, thereby standing in the way of progress by causing needless conflict, and because it is unfair to the exploited masses. Nationalists see social oppression as harmful inasmuch as it weakens the nation and strengthens the hand of foreign oppressors. Democracy is not treated as an issue in itself by either group. The Marxists expect it to emerge more or less automatically from the elimination of internal oppression; the nationalists see it as stemming naturally from the real independence of the nation.

One can therefore suggest that the Free Officers did seek, amongst other goals, to establish the reign of democracy, conceived of rather vaguely as the ability of the Egyptian people to choose their own political options freely, without being influenced by outside pressures or by the power of those selfish internal economic pressure groups who refused to serve the national interest, namely feudalists, monopoly capitalists and others. But this was not translated into a precise programme geared to set up particular political institutions. When Anwar es-Sadat asserts that the original aim of the Free Officers was forcibly to establish a democratically-based republican government,[8] one should realize that this refers mainly to the need to get rid of the Monarchy, a structure which facilitated indirect foreign domination. He himself adds that later, when Hasan al-Banna proposed a fusion between the Free Officers and the Muslim Brotherhood, he replied that the Free Officers had no wish to affiliate themselves with any political party and did not intend to 'explicitly define the future political infrastructure'.[9] They assumed, implicitly and naively, that the vast majority of the Egyptian nation could not fail to rally round the vision of the national interest formulated by the Free Officers' group, especially since the latter was devoid of any selfish motivation.

The Free Officers thus expected that once the pressures which had distorted the nation's life were removed, the people's will would find a way of expressing itself through some reliable system, for example through classical parliamentary institutions. Nasser's writings convey very accurately the tremendous disappointment he and his fellows experienced when they realized that the Egyptian masses were not spontaneously, joyfully and demonstratively expressing their support for the military *coup d'etat*. This lack of response was put down to a delayed popular understanding of what had taken place. The Free Officers therefore continued their efforts to carry out their fundamental projects without changing the existing political structure any more than was absolutely necessary. It was the pressure of events, not the original ideology, which eventually made changes in this structure unavoidable.

The Political Struggle For a Progressive Nationalist Orientation

Dual Power (August–September 1952)

In reality, of course, as far as the group's key figures were concerned at any rate, there was never any question of giving way to any tendencies the Egyptian nation might express through elections, even apparently free elections. Their argument went something like this: On the one hand, every Egyptian knows full well that in a country whose population is largely illiterate, and where the economic and cultural domination exercised by a small minority is particularly striking, all sorts of pressures can be brought to bear on the most 'regular' of 'free elections'. On the other hand, even if all these pressures could be eliminated — which would certainly be very difficult — the fact would remain that the 'legal country' is not the 'real country'. The people do not understand their own best interests. Their consciousness is distorted by centuries of foreign domination and by ignorance. Only the revolutionaries have grasped where the nation's real interests lie, and they have no right to let the people stray from the correct course.

It is quite normal for revolutionaries to hold the attitude described above, whether they are nationalist or social revolutionaries.[10] One may justifiably object that such a view carries considerable dangers, notably because it privileges the vision of an ideological group. But one cannot deny that it has some objective justification.

From July 1952 to March 1954, the political situation remained ambiguous. Power was exercised by the Council of the Revolution, in other words by the old Executive Committee of the Free Officers' Association, a structure which had been organized in 1949 on the basis of long-standing contacts between various groups of friends. This Committee, with its co-opted members, enjoyed the backing of a powerful force, namely the Army. In fact it was essentially a network of officers, who had apparently established their control over the country's armed forces, and who were eventually able to mobilize behind them almost every military unit, or at least every essential unit. This was the real source from which the Free Officers derived their authority.

But they were anxious to legitimize this authority. They wanted it accepted by the people. Egypt's new leadership was made up of officers whose very names were unfamiliar to the public at large; by contrast, the country was full of famous politicians, some of whom had long enjoyed considerable popularity; there were organized parties which claimed to represent important sections of the population, and which had indeed polled hundreds of thousands of votes at the elections, even as late as January 1950. It was against this background that the Free Officers' group were nonetheless claiming to be truly representative of the people. Unlike the Bolsheviks in 1917, the Fascists in Italy and the N.S.D.A.P. in Germany, they could not present themselves as the leadership of an already established party. Nor could they pretend to draw their authority from the charisma of some illustrious and popular figure, like Bonaparte, Petain or de Gaulle, whose great services to the nation could not be denied. And they did not wish to flout all appearances and install themselves in power by virtue of force alone, like certain South American juntas. Their ideal remained representative democracy.

A first attempt to resolve this dilemma had been made even before the seizure of power. After some hesitation, the presidency of the movement was offered to a figurehead, General Mohammad Neguib, who already had a certain reputation and around whom it seemed easier to build an instant myth. Furthermore, the Committee believed him to be sufficiently honest and unambitious, unlike many other possible candidates, to be trusted not to turn on those who had raised him to prominence.

But this was not enough. The Committee was convinced that the people would back it if harmful pressures could be kept at bay. Its self-appointed task was thus a negative one: to eliminate these pressures. One part of the problem had been resolved, in that the Army had made sure that most of the material forces which could support such pressures had been effectively stymied. It continued to fend off all dangers of this sort. But what the Army could not do was to eliminate the structures which were organizing these pressures; nor could it create other structures through which the *real* wishes of the people could finally find expression. That would have to be a job for the specialists in politics, who would also have to be entrusted with the day-to-day running of the country. Mohammad Neguib, in a letter to the members of the Provisional Regency Council dated 7th September 1952, wrote that: 'Right from the start my colleagues and I were agreed that we would hand over power to the politicians.'[11]

And indeed the Army was quick to call in a veteran politician, Ali Maher, to preside over a Cabinet which took office immediately after the *coup*, on 24th July 1952, even before Farouk had abdicated. 'We are military men, and we will have nothing to do with politics', declared Neguib on 27th July. And on 1st August it was proclaimed that: 'All political matters, and everything concerning the machinery of government is in the hands of the Government, which will settle these affairs constitutionally.'[12] However, the Army, 'representing the might of the people', to use the words of the ultimatum addressed to the king on 26th July,[13] reserved one task for itself; the task of making sure that the broad lines along which the revolution should develop stayed fresh in the minds of both the people and the Government, who were thus assumed liable to forget them. These broad lines formed 'a code and a programme'[14] based on specific principles.[15]

At the beginning, there were thus two main seats of power. On the one hand, there was the Army, a mysterious force with Mohammad Neguib as its only spokesman. The general public was given no indication as to the process whereby the decisions Neguib transmitted were being reached. What it amounted to was that the Army had the power to set the overall course, which it conveyed both by direct messages to the people and the parties, and by demands addressed to the Government, some of which were published. All this makes it quite clear that the Army was operating as an autonomous force. On the other hand, there was the Government, which, in principle, exercised executive power, and legislative power since Farouk had dissolved Parliament in May, but could do so only within the limits set by the 'Army's' directives. This strange situation obviously became unendurable in the long run.

There is no reason to doubt the sincerity of the members of the Military Committee. They were quite ready to fade into the background the moment they were convinced that a normal institutional process had been set in motion whereby the nation was advancing steadily towards the goals which had been set for it and which it should set itself.It was at this stage that they decided to organize new elections which they planned to call six months later.

But gradually a painful realization began to dawn on the Free Officers. They discovered that the general orientation of Egyptian politics, an orientation they deemed harmful, stemmed not only from the king's role as a vehicle for British imperialist influence, but also from the interplay of a great variety of pressure groups. With fine contempt, Nasser recounts his contacts with the many individuals who offered themselves as saviours. With Farouk out of the way, the parties thought they saw an opportunity to make a bid for power; they attempted to woo the Army, and at first those who could claim considerable popular backing, such as the Wafd and the Muslim Brotherhood, had the nerve to show a certain haughtiness towards the military as they presented their case. Other less structured but probably more powerful forces, the privileged social classes and strata, also made their demands and objections known. All these pressure groups found outlets for expression, notably within the Government. Ali Maher himself became a spokesman for some of them, as did Rashad Mohanna, a particularly ambitious officer and member of the Provisional Regency Council, despite the fact that this latter body was supposed to play only a symbolic role as a sort of collective head of state. In fact, the pressure groups made use of every remaining political institution, while the still uncensored press discussed, criticized and expounded on the various stances at great length.

How was it that, in its efforts against the pressure groups, the Military Committee proved incapable of channelling the tremendous but disorganized force of the people? Nasser later spoke of how disappointed he was that the vast masses did not flock to support and encourage the Armed Forces movement. But how could the people, most of whom were certainly sympathetic to that movement, express themselves other than through the existing structures, the most significant of which were the parties? Every one of these parties, each channelling the aspirations of various social strata and often deforming them in the process, had proclaimed its wholehearted support for the Armed Forces movement. Where else could the people turn?

In contrast, the Army, by appealing for calm[16] and by banning demonstrations, had closed off the possibility of any spontaneous movement emerging and perhaps initiating some kind of re-structuring. The Free Officers believed that an atmosphere of social calm was essential to the process of re-organization, as was made tragically clear, from 12th to 14th August, by the Kafr ed-Dawar workers' demonstrations and the ensuing execution of two of their leaders. The Cabinet hastily decided in principle to use the classical means to ensure the required social peace, namely conciliation commissions and profit-sharing. But the Egyptian proletariat was relatively small. The problem was not urgent.

The first political crisis was triggered off by issues of foreign policy and the agrarian reform project. On 7th September 1952, Neguib himself took over from Ali Maher. Bit by bit, the Army's intervention was becoming institutionalized. The symbolic spokesman of the authorities behind the scenes had become the president of the official government. The civilian Ministers were from then on directly under the orders of the Military Committee, their role reduced to that of errand boys. These changes brought it home to the various pressure groups, and especially to the political parties, that the Military Committee had resolved to assume effective power in the country. Until then, this had still not been absolutely clear.

The Trial of Strength (September 1952–March 1954)

A straightforward struggle for power could now begin. On one side, there was the Military Committee and its networks, which could call on the entire force of the Army. On the other, there was every structure in Egyptian society, every pressure group at every level, struggling desperately to hang on to the opportunities offered by pluralist society. For some, these opportunities meant the ability to bring direct or almost direct influence to bear upon the authorities, through Parliament or through various sectors of the administration. For others, notably for the Communists and the Muslim Brotherhood, what mattered was the opportunity to use pluralism in their efforts towards eventually seizing supreme power themselves. They too wanted to realize the aspirations of the 'real' country, aspirations which the oppressed masses, or the community of the faithful, ought to have, and which the Military Committee was expressing inadequately or not at all. In fact both the Communists and the Muslim Brotherhood could recognize that some at least of the young officers had the right sort of intentions, the only problem being that they lacked the benefit of correct theory, as outlined by the proper specialists in Marxism-Leninism or in the lore of the Koranic state.

One of the big puzzles of the period is whether or not the leadership of the Free Officers had, at the time, already decided to take power so completely. The nature of their intentions is still debatable. Personally, I do not think that there is enough evidence to the contrary to justify rejecting the official thesis, according to which the group was gradually forced to adopt this position, even though it had originally hoped that it could eventually hand over power to representative parliamentary institutions. The fact that the Junta took authoritarian measures so quickly after coming to power has misled many people into believing that it actually started out with the deliberate intent of setting up an authoritarian regime. The democratic pronouncements made by Nasser and the Officers have consequently been treated as hypocrisy.

However, it seems to me that the flow of events can indeed be explained as follows: The purpose of the first authoritarian measures was to remove external pressures which were thought to restrict the free will of the people; the party apparatuses were particularly singled out as anti-democratic forces. As Calah Salim put it, in his May 1953 interview with the liberal journalist, Ahmad Aboul-fath, 'before we could allow a return to constitutional life we had to extirpate every corrupt element in the nation.'[17] Under such conditions the dynamic of power inevitably led the Junta to adopt increasingly authoritarian and meddlesome measures. And these very measures gradually made them aware that the opposition was far stronger than they had thought. It became apparent that they would definitely have to extend the period of preparation for that blessed era when all the pressures would be eliminated and all the effects of past pressures eradicated, thereby finally enabling the people to express the true depths of their legitimate aspirations.

Before long, the Free Officers' group began to misconstrue any opposition to its power as a deliberate effort to gainsay the evolution it envisaged. But this should not be taken to imply that they had consciously decided to establish a lasting system in which their own will would be the only law. The evolution the regime underwent was not essentially different from that experienced by every group which has taken power when fired by the conviction that it is expressing the essential, but not necessarily clearly understood, aspirations of the masses: the French Jacobins and the Russian Bolsheviks are typical examples. What supposedly happened was that bit by bit the Junta came to understand that the projects which were its very reason for existence (independence and modernization) had no chance of being carried out by a parliamentary regime based on party activity. It then resorted to purging the parties of those of their members who seemed most opposed to the projects in question, and finally promoted a rival organization which expressed the military group's viewpoint. Eventually, however, all these measures proved inadequate. One must also remember that those who formed the basis of the leadership group's power, namely the officers, were not immune to a certain conscious or unconscious appetite for power, or to a certain greed for various material advantages. These factors undeniably did play a considerable role in pushing the regime towards authoritarianism.

The only means of struggle available to those whom I shall refer to as the pluralists, for convenience's sake, seem to have been the following. Firstly, whilst giving in under pressure to the military authorities' demands for a purge within their ranks, the groups made an effort to re-organize themselves and to strengthen themselves internally. In some cases at least, it seems quite probable that some factions within the various parties were very glad to see what they considered to be a lot of politically harmful dead wood cleared out. But there must also have been more serious efforts towards internal reinforcement. Some groups, particularly the Muslim Brotherhood, may have tried to arm themselves. Naturally enough, the press was used as much as possible to express a veiled opposition. Later, as the situation got worse for the political groups and parties, they formed a United Front, despite being opposed to each other in so many ways. The temporarily shared goal of a return to parliamentarism became a common ground on which Wafdists, the

Muslim Brotherhood, the Communists and others could all meet.

But it may well be that the pluralist opposition's most effective method of struggle was a sustained lobbying, which incidentally is well in keeping with Egyptian political tradition. Each group did its utmost to gain support within the Army through various social and family connections. Nor can one exclude the possibility of the odd attempt at straightforward corruption, though in any case it is difficult to draw the dividing line between blatant corruption and the more traditional and subtle means of persuasion so characteristic of this sort of relationship. Obviously any one of the Free Officers who had ever presented himself, however fleetingly or superficially, as a sympathizer of one of the various groups was jumped on as a potential source of support. Considerable efforts were made to break up the unity of the military group. Neguib, in particular, was assiduously courted and proved especially receptive; but neither he himself nor the political groups who sought him out realized quite how isolated he was amongst the Free Officers.

At the same time several groups were offering the military the backing of their cadres and their ideology, in an effort to restructure Egyptian public opinion. The Communist M.D.L.N.[18] (HADETO in Arabic) had realized the potential of this idea right from the start. But they could not pursue it after the Kafd ed-Dawar hangings which aroused the indignation of the other Communist groups, and reinforced the hostility of certain foreign Communist Parties, who felt confirmed in their judgement that the Officers' group was nothing but a U.S. inspired fascist organization. The Wafd and the Muslim Brotherhood were more serious contenders for the role, and were further- more quite confident that before long they would turn the tables on these inexperienced young officers, who would become mere political agents, most of whom would in any case be sent back to barracks as soon as their 'historic task' had been accomplished. The fierce struggles and the constant outside pressure which characterized this period helped to clarify and polarize matters within the Free Officers' group itself. Its right and left wings were forced to step forward and take clear stances. Political demarcation lines were drawn, and the core of a centrist majority faithful to Gamal Abdel Nasser and to the movement's original ideological foundations began to emerge. Since the rule of the political parties still seemed incompatible with the movement's original projects, this centrist majority rejected it, along with the ideological tutelage of Muslim fundamentalism and Communist dogmatism, and, of course, of the organizations whose creeds these were. Some of the officers, for instance Khaled Mohyi ed-din and Yussuf Siddiq, both members of the Junta or at least very closely linked to it, allowed themselves to be influenced not so much by outside pressures as by their own liberal Marxist ideology.

Those who have been convinced by the particularly American notion of a fundamental opposition between Marxist regimes and democracy may be surprised to learn that supporters of Marxism were at the time ardent champions of parliamentarianism and a return to constitutional life — a fact not without a certain historical importance. Nor was this stance conditioned by any Machiavellianism or separate organizational ambitions. I can say this from my own experience, since I myself was in Cairo, in close contact with the Marxist groups and generally committed to the same ideas, during the dramatic final phases of this period. Had the Marxists taken power, they would probably have been forced into a broadly similar approach to the problem of power as that undergone by the Free Officers. However, the fact remains that at the time, like all Communists outside of the Communist states, the Egyptian Marxists were committed to democracy, and to the role of parties in the expression of the people's will; the whole problem of taking power, in a country where the majority would not respond to the appeal of Marxist solutions, was avoided. The solution envisaged was that a minority, which expressed the unconscious, essential and potential will of the majority, should be entrusted with power. But, of course, only Marxist-Leninist doctrine was deemed capable of truly expressing this. Since the core group within the Junta was not equipped with this scientific doctrine, its influence over the people could only be both dictatorial and reactionary.

Faced with this polymorphous opposition, the military group was forced to use every means at its disposal. It had already achieved one essential: control over military force. But it was well aware that its power could be undermined in several ways. The group decided to assume closer political control over the country; gradually it came to find that uncontrolled power was more and more to its liking, and it began to give in to the appetites mentioned previously. The Officers increasingly infiltrated the ministries, and controlled the administration more and more directly. Police bodies were set up or developed. Their powers and the means at their disposal increased regularly. The Junta's propaganda became more and more systematic and insistent. The instructions given to the newspapers became more and more imperative. Censorship, which had been lifted in July, was re-established and entrusted to the military. The opposition press was gagged. The political parties were disarmed by a purge extending into the administration, the Army and every possible grouping. Finally, they were simply dissolved by decree on 16th January 1953; the only political grouping to survive was the Muslim Brotherhood, which was considered to be an organization rather than a party. The foundation of the Liberation Group (*hay'at at-tahrir*) on 23rd January 1953 equipped the Junta with a body through which it could broadcast its slogans and eventually rally the support of the population at large. Real, potential or even imaginary dissidents were arrested and imprisoned in ever-increasing numbers. Special tribunals were set up, which officiated with considerable severity and cursory respect for judicial considerations.

The Junta's power became institutionalized. The Provisional Constitution of 10th February 1953 conferred supreme political power on the plenum of the Guiding Council of the Revolution, whose existence was thus finally given official recognition, and upon the Council of Ministers, the latter to be nominated by the former and to exercise legislative and executive power under its control. But the Junta continued to endorse the promise of a return to constitutional life; and despite a growing scepticism, this helped to calm the opposition's impatience. A constitutional committee was charged with drawing up a new Constitution. The country was designated a Republic, but not, after some hesitation, a parliamentary republic. The authorities were, however, taking definite decisions about the future. The Republic was proclaimed on 18th June 1953, despite Neguib's opposition. A socio-economic manifesto published in July by the Liberation Group 'recommended' a regime which would differ from fascist and communist systems as much as from capitalism and 'modern socialism'.[19]

The only seemingly powerful lever available to the opposition was General Neguib himself, a man who was, in theory, the leader of the Government; who was definitely committed to a return to constitutional life; who was increasingly worried about the authoritarian leanings of the team which, as far as the public were concerned, he was supposed to be leading; and who deeply resented the way he was constantly being snubbed during the secret deliberations of the Guiding Council of the Revolution. One of his only assets was the great popularity his humanity, his cheerfulness and his affability had earned him. He had set out to cultivate it systematically.

Gamal Abdel Nasser was well aware of the danger, and no doubt fairly upset by this rival's popularity. At this point one could almost say that a personal element crept in amongst the factors of political history. The creator of a movement which had triumphed by his own endeavours was quite entitled to feel aggrieved that the grateful crowd should shower all its praises on a man who had really been nothing but a tool. And on top of it all, this man was giving himself liberal airs which cost him nothing. In January 1954, Nasser dissolved the Muslim Brotherhood, the only remaining organized political force. The complex trial of strength which followed during February and March brought every card in the political deck into play. On 25th February, Neguib was thrown out, only to be reinstated by Khaled Mohyi ed-din's 'cavalry' (tank) corps, backed by the other 'pluralist' elements in the Army and by street demonstrations manipulated partly by the Communists but mainly by the Muslim Brotherhood. The imminent convocation of a Constituent Assembly was proclaimed and it was announced that when this took place the Council of the Revolution would be dissolved, press censorship and martial law would be lifted, all political prisoners would be released, and the political parties would be allowed to re-form. July 24th was put forward as a date when 'the Revolution would be considered over'.[20]

Gamal Abdel Nasser and the centrist core of the Council of the Revolution took only a few short weeks to regain the ground they had lost. All they really needed to do was to arouse the Army's fears about what would happen to its own privileges, and to re-unite it, which was crucial, by isolating the deliberately 'pluralist' elements within it, such as Khaled Mohyi ed-din. Pluralist opinion was given a certain amount of rope, but at the same time dissension was fanned in its midst. The more aggressive members of the Muslim Brotherhood were imprisoned and great stress was laid on Neguib's dubious compromises with the old politicians and on the imminent return of the most discredited of these.

A press campaign, in the best Marxist utilitarian style, was mounted to show the difference between the 'formal liberties' demanded by the pluralists and the much more real freedom which the Revolution would ensure. Can one really say that the workers who paraded in Army lorries and chanted 'Down with Liberty!' were convinced of the validity of this argument? Anyway, what is indisputable is that, apart from the Army, the only support actively sought out by the centrist core was that of the common people, the masses, to whom parliamentary pluralism was nothing more than the name of a regime which had in the past presided over their misery and subordination. Carefully orchestrated demonstrations from 25th to 29th March made it possible for the regime to go back on its promises of a return to parliamentarianism and liberalism. Significantly the communiqué which announced this abrogation based itself on the country's manifest desire 'to see the Revolution carry through the task it has begun and achieve its aims, the most important of which are the evacuation of foreign troops and the introduction of social justice amongst the various classes of the population, notably amongst the workers and peasants.'[21] The regime was thus putting forward two projects: the project of attaining true national independence, and the project of modernizing the country, the latter being presented in the guise most attractive to the masses, namely the abolition of ancient privileges. It was implied, and understood, that the corollary of all this would be a rise in the standard of living of the masses. And, of course, the internal political project of democratization was deliberately sacrificed.

'Rational' Power

If I have dwelt at some length on the events of 1952—54, it is because internal political struggles were obviously taking place during this period. To use Leonard Binder's classification,[22] there was a struggle between those who upheld, even if only provisionally, a 'constitutional' system and those who upheld a 'rational' system. In March 1954, the latter were clearly the victors. In principle, from then on, internal political struggle came to an end, on the surface at least. The authorities no longer needed to gain the support of this or that group; all they had to do was to defend themselves and administer the country.

The Political Goals

Every decision had to come from the central authority. How this authority reached those decisions, whether general or specific, can only be explained in terms of its internal policy, but these decisions affected foreign policy and the economy as much as they influenced home affairs. As in the 'constitutional' system, the main internal issue was which social group's demands should be given priority. But in a 'constitutional' system, all subsequent decisions are taken as a way of coming to terms with the projects of the social group which has been given priority. In Egypt, on the other hand, the basic underlying problem was how best to implement the overall decisions taken by the top decision-making body. This body had its own projects, which we have already mentioned: independence and modernization. Its conceptions of the precise form these projects should take, and of the methods they would involve, were not static; the way they changed was essentially conditioned by economic factors and aspects of foreign policy which are beyond the scope of our discussion here.

On the whole, however, one can say that almost every internal policy mechanism was geared to realizing these projects. Internal policy had three instrumental aims: Firstly, to ensure that the decisions which had been taken were carried out; in other words to administrate. Secondly, the creation and use of the structural means necessary in order to generate the greatest possible mass support for Government projects, so that the decisions taken would be carried out efficiently; in other words, to create a cadre structure and to educate the people. Thirdly, to combat anybody within the country who opposed or might oppose the projects in question. Everybody who wanted to overthrow the ruling group was rightly or wrongly, sincerely or hypocritically, cast as an enemy of the said projects.

The Decision-Making Mechanism

Very little is known about how the supreme decision-making body reached its decisions. It does seem to have been a very simple process, as in all regimes of this sort. The supreme body consisted of the select group of officers, Gamal Abdel Nasser's comrades, who were still members of the Free Officers' Association once it had been purged of all the elements whose allegiance to the group's overall ideology and to Nasser himself had been undermined by outside interests. This group has been analyzed in a work by P.J. Vatikiotis,[23] and vividly 'profiled' by J. and S. Lacouture.[24] According to what one of its members, Abd al-Latif Baghdadi, told Don Peretz in 1956, the group consisted of six men; apart from Nasser and himself, there was also Abd al-hakim Amer, Zakaria Mohyi ed-din, Kamal ed-din Hussein and Hussein Shafi.[25] Nasser dominated the group and imposed his decisions. But he always took his comrades' opinions into account. Occasionally he rejected someone's advice, but only when he had the backing of most of the other members, or at least of the ones who really mattered. At each step he had to assess whether he could afford to take a course of action counter to one recommended by this or that member of the group; he always had to gauge whether such a decision might push the member in question into adopting a stance of systematic opposition, and whether such opposition could eventually become dangerous.

Executive and Legislative Institutions

Two centuries of liberal political ideology have so thoroughly persuaded world opinion of the superiority of the 'constitutional system' that no 'rational system' can present itself in undiluted form. Every 'rational' government must create at least some semblance of a constitutional mechanism. It must adjust this mechanism so that it does not interfere with the real decision-making process. And this constitutional mechanism can, of course, be allowed some substance so that it can serve as a useful means to sound out the real aspirations of the country's citizens and even provide an outlet for the desire of those citizens who wish to make their opinions known to the authorities and thereby have some influence upon them, however minimal.

After the leadership group's victory in March 1954, a new Council of Ministers was established on 17th April 1954, with Nasser as its President. It replaced the 'Congress' which had conjoined the Guiding Council of the Revolution and the Council of Ministers under the provisions of the 10th February 1953 Provisional Constitution. Members of the Guiding Council of the Revolution now took ministerial decisions directly instead of acting through the intermediary of a subordinate Council of Ministers. They now made up the sole executive and legislative body; there was also a National Consultative Council, but this was given no decision-making power whatsoever and was restricted to a purely advisory function. Undisguised 'rational' power was the order of the day; there was no institutional mechanism to check decisions taken from above, not even the semblance of one, and no attempt was made to hide the fact that all decisions were being taken from above.

This could not go on indefinitely, of course. One way or another, the people would have to be given an opportunity to speak out. One should always bear in mind that, according to the military group's ideology, once the institutional and external pressures had been lifted, the people could not fail to approve and support its policies, which had been framed in terms of the national interest.

As it happened, the Anglo-Egyptian Treaty, which ensured national independence, had been signed on 19th October 1954, and the last organized political force, the Muslim Brotherhood, had been dissolved on 28th October. On 14th November, Neguib had quit his symbolic post as President of the Republic. A return to constitutional life, which was still conceived of as the ideal to be attained, had been promised. Furthermore, on the international level, it seemed opportune to present as democratic a face as possible, not only to the United States, which was still being courted at the time, but also to the socialist and neutralist worlds with whom closer links were being established. Thus in April 1955 Nasser attended the Bandung Conference; on 26th September he announced the Czech arms deal. It seemed that although there were several different systems of democracy in the world, and although the proponents of each of these systems ridiculed the mechanism whereby the others supposedly conferred power upon the people as a sham, it was nonetheless apparently essential to have at least established some mechanism of the sort. Everybody was accusing Egypt of being a military dictatorship, which was very damaging in terms of international public opinion.

After some hesitation, the Junta set aside any projects still tinged with pluralism. It did not deem the Egyptian people quite mature enough yet not to be diverted from the expression of their 'real' aspirations by the cunning tricks of the political parties, who would not hesitate to play upon the various social strata's concrete aspirations, however inadequate these might be in terms of the 'real' national interest. The mechanism used to set public opinion back on the correct course and to keep it from being misled by politicians was the one-party state, which had already proved its worth elsewhere. The Constitution presented to the people on 16th January 1955 and confirmed by plebiscite on 23rd June, enshrined the sovereignty of the people and the Republic's democratic character, and proclaimed a series of inalienable rights, including the right to vote and to criticize the government. Free elections were to be held for a National Assembly, a purely consultative body, which would also approve the Government's laws and financial measures. Thus the Assembly could come into conflict with the Government, which itself was nominated by a President, elected by the National Assembly and confirmed by the people; but the President could dissolve the Assembly. Any possibilities of opposition which this presidential system might have contained were cancelled out by the screening mechanism whereby candidates for 'the party', a convenient term for the three successive formations which played this role, were chosen. The National Union established by Article 192 of the Constitution, and prefigured by a Provisional Committee comprising the most eminent members of the Junta, was empowered to eliminate any undesirable candidates. Competition between candidates was thus kept within acceptable limits and one could rest assured that the parliamentarians, whose brief was to discuss ways and means, would not go beyond it and oppose the Revolutionary leadership's fundamental projects.

It was nonetheless recognized that this regime was only transitory. One might even expect that a new law would be passed re-legitimizing party political activity. But at the same time everything was being done to show that a constitutional era had already begun. The Central Revolutionary Command was dissolved immediately after the plebiscite. The subsequent constitutional evolution was essentially a matter of adapting the 1956 Constitution's principles of government to changing circumstances. The 5th March 1958 Provisional Constitution, drawn up after the union with Syria, merely extended the Egyptian regime to the two 'provinces'. Following the inauguration of a new social policy, signalled by the May 1962 Charter, a Constitutional Proclamation was issued, on 27th September, but this merely 'completed' previous arrangements. The Executive was re-organized along more 'collegial' lines, with a twelve member Presidency Council and an Executive Council made up of twenty-four Ministers. In some ways this was a return to the 1953 situation: a policy-making body was handing down its decisions to an administrative Executive Council. It seems likely that this system was adopted for purely technical reasons, with the idea of freeing the real leaders from the burden of secondary tasks.

By contrast, the 23rd March 1964 Constitutional Proclamation, which put an end to this division of the Executive, probably because the system had proved too unwieldy in practice, also contained clearly socialist proclamations and a clause which gave some satisfaction to those who desired a constitutional regime, in that it empowered the Assembly to cast a vote of no confidence in the Government or in a Minister. But, in fact, this presented no threat to the regime, since the President could dissolve the Assembly whenever he chose.

It seems clear that the mechanism whereby decisions were made and carried out effectively restricted the possibilities for political struggle to those at the very top of the pyramid. Every precaution was taken to ensure that possible divisions could neither be systematized nor result in any re-evaluation of the leadership's projects, let alone the composition of the leadership itself. The details of how decisions were carried out, and the whole local level of state administration need not concern us here, since this essay is essentially a survey of political choices.

Education and the Creation of a Cadre Structure

The Egyptian leaders were, as we have seen, quite convinced that by its very nature the true will of the people could not fail to be favourable to their projects. And since they had eliminated the institutional obstacles to the people's understanding of their own best interests, the main remaining problem was how to overcome prejudices and reshape ideas; the people's still-dormant aspirations needed to be helped along towards true awakening and undistorted expression. The Egyptian leaders had, as we have noted, already shown themselves willing to use coercion when necessary. But what Stuart Schram said of Mao Tse-tung is also true of them: they never stopped trying to persuade people to believe in what the leaders thought they ought to believe in; they were always hoping that people would not have to be forced into doing what they ought to want to do.[26]

The usual propaganda methods were employed: the press, radio and cinema were all strictly controlled. Censorship prevented the expression of any 'inadequate' ideas. Other bodies more or less directly suggested which was the correct way of thinking.

But such means, however powerful, are only fragmentary and can reach only particular aspects of an individual's personality. Another method was therefore used, which had already been tried out elsewhere, which reached out to the whole man, which mobilized him and regimented him in every sense of the word and turned him not just into a firm believer in the truths handed down from above, but also into a militant, an ardent campaigner wholeheartedly dedicated to achieving those goals which the leadership deemed desirable.

This method was the formation of a party. The Junta had already considered the idea in January 1953, obviously with the aim of replacing those parties which had just been dissolved (cf. above). True, the General Secretary of the new *Rassemblement de la Liberation* did assert that his organization was not a party but a 'means for organizing popular forces so as to reconstruct society on a new and healthy basis'.[27] But all he was really doing was rejecting any assimilation with the old style pluralist type parties. The new *Rassemblement* was definitely a party, the sort of party which one finds in 'rational states', and Nasser himself defined it as such. There was also the National Union, provided for by Article 192 of the 1956 Constitution and officially formed on 28th May 1957. This was a more structured body, with local rank and file cells, a pyramidal hierarchy of organizations, and an

Executive Committee appointed by the President. The Syrian secession in 1961, and the wave of re-evaluation and self-criticism which followed, resulted in the setting up of a new organization, the Arab Socialist Union, born on 7th December 1962 in the wake of the National Congress of Popular Forces and the National Charter. These various reformations, these repeated attempts to get off to a fresh start were not, as some people have claimed, a reflection of some permanent and structural inability of the Egyptian people and their regime to set up stable structures. It would be more accurate to say that they were the expression of a constant effort to come closer to the ideal totalitarian one-party state. Historical examples encouraged the rulers to turn to this structure in the expectation that, in terms of the mechanisms of power, it would have certain advantages, particularly from the point of view of a nation seeking to modernize itself and to ensure its independence. The aim was to create an elite which was independent of and parallel to the country's adminis-tration, but from which the latter could recruit. This elite was to establish a two-way contact: contact between the authorities and the people, in that it would spread the watchwords handed down from above; and contact between the people and the authorities, in that it would make the aspirations of the people known to their leaders. From its position alongside the administration, the elite would keep it under surveillance and above all instill in it the neces-sary dynamism.[28] In short, the party which gave its structure to this elite was meant to supply both the state and the people with cadres, real not formal ones.

There was, however, one obstacle to the authorities' plans, an obstacle which they sought to sidestep and to remove, and which Nasser attempted to define in his famous self-criticism of 16th October 1961, following the Syrian secession. The root of this problem was that those who joined the new party were the same people who used to make up the cadres of the old pluralist parties; or at least they came from the same social strata. Whenever members of lower social strata did join, they found that they were still in an inferior position, even within the new party.

The political and economic measures taken by the regime had already produced a body of cadres. Many of these were members of the old elite, only a minority of whom had had to be marginalized because of attach-ments to social position, ethno-religious loyalties or political choices which could not be reconciled to the new system. And most of the rest were drawn from a social layer which, although it had in the past been deprived of political advantages, was nonetheless relatively privileged in social terms. It was very difficult, and unusual, for those who came from really underprivileged backgrounds to integrate themselves successfully into this newly formed elite. And the latter occupied the dominant positions in the Party. The old Egyptian tradition enjoining the poor and the uncultured to be humble prevented those members of the Party who did come from poor backgrounds from contesting the leadership role played by the old and new elites. The Party could thus not provide the required social renovation.

What little renovation there was, came about quite differently. The tragedy was that the only cadres who could have fulfilled the authorities' expectations were precisely those from under-privileged backgrounds, the ones who, as things turned out, were first excluded from the Party and then, when allowed in, maintained an attitude of due humility. They were the only ones who could have really translated popular aspirations, and in return produced a dynamic administration which could really mobilise the masses for the tasks set by the Government. Some of the Arab Socialist Union's statutes did lay down that workers and peasants were to play an important role within the organization. But statutes were not enough. The regime itself, by providing members of the military bureaucracy with positions of economic, political, social or cultural power, accentuated the rift and reinforced the humility and passivity of the representatives of the masses.

The statutes probably did give the latter some encouragement, however. There did seem to be some degree of upward movement from the under-privileged layers. Possibly, this was increasing, but it was very slow; so slow that self-satisfied and conformist integration into the elite was more likely than any ardent efforts to mobilize the masses by setting an example of devotion, abnegation and self-sacrifice which were so vital in the tragically difficult situation facing the Egyptian economy. It appears that only some profound social and cultural upheaval could have so overthrown the old elites and the old values as to allow for a genuine replenishment of the elites. The Egyptian leaders could not resolve themselves to bring about such an upheaval, a failure which was no doubt largely due to the real nature of their power. They could not just ignore the fact that the real basis for this power was the Army, and not the Party.

For the record, let us add that the Party fulfilled its technical role as a corrective to 'formal' democracy: it selected the candidates for legislative and executive bodies, thereby preventing undesirable elements from being elected. But this role, however indispensable, was hardly difficult. In fact, it was so simple that during June–July 1957 it was carried out not by the National Union, which had in principle already been founded although its statutes were not published until November, but by a Provisional Executive Committee of the National Union, made up of a few members of the Junta. Why such a task should then require a vast country-wide structure is certainly not obvious.

Was political struggle possible within the Party itself? Of course, one cannot exclude the possibility that clans, particular loyalties and divergent trends continued to exist. But the pyramidal structure, the institutional authority concentrated at the top, kept such competition within very strict bounds. In May and June 1962 during the preparations for the Arab Socialist Union, there was a much wider and freer confrontation in the National Congress of Popular Forces. But this was only a temporary affair. As in the Communist Parties, and for similar reasons, organizational and other pre-cautions were taken to ensure that the various tendencies could not solidify into 'fractions' committed to a political struggle against one another, and thereby effectively constituting 'sub-parties', which might then provide the various pressure groups with outlets and spokesmen.

Forms of Competition and Struggle

However much the mass of the people may accept a regime, and however integrated that regime itself may be, it cannot eliminate competition between the various elements of society. It can only impose limits upon such competition and generally speaking ensure that during long periods it does not lead to any direct physical conflict. In non-pluralist societies, the regime can also set itself the more difficult task of preventing the formation of permanent tendencies and the subsequent organization of factions.

Competition and even struggle have certainly not been absent in the 'rational' Egypt of the last twelve years. They have taken place on three different levels: between the authorities and those who still refuse to accept the regime; between various pro-regime tendencies which are not part of the leadership; and between the members of the leadership itself. Those who still refuse to accept the regime have a potentially wide basis of support, but few means of mobilizing it. Even organizing themselves is quite a problem. Some of the old political groups, notably the old political parties, have apparently given up all hope of forming real organizations for the time being. At most, they wait for appropriate occasions, during which they surface briefly, giving those who still regret the passing of the old order an opportunity, however short-lived, to express their discontent. The funeral of Moctafa Nahhas was a typical example. Exiles such as Ahmed Aboul-fath can publish anti-Nasser pamphlets abroad, and may quite probably operate in Egypt under the cover of false identities. But none of this presents any serious danger to the regime. The radio broadcasts of Arab states hostile to Nasserism may well constitute a more serious threat.

As for the Communists, they have formally and solemnly declared that they will form no organizations of their own. The efficiency of the repression, the regime's liberalism towards them as individuals, the fact that they agreed in principle with the goals upheld by the regime during the previous period, and the Soviet Union's support for the Junta, all contributed towards their adoption of such a position. Their intellectuals, or in other words practically the entire core of the old groups, have been allowed to express themselves in their own monthly journal (*at-Tali'a*), in the pages of *Al-Ahram*, and in other papers. Although they have no organization, their wide-ranging inter-personal contacts effectively enable them to constitute an ideological group. Posts (but not key posts) have been found for the most eminent amongst them. The regime is well aware that, although the Communists no longer constitute an opposition, and are, in fact, one of the tendencies which supports the Government, they could nonetheless, under given circumstances, supply an eventual opposition with an ideology and an organization. They are therefore kept under fairly close and none too discreet surveillance, and are from time to time deliberately reminded of the fact by a temporary arrest. It appears that a tiny minority of the Movement, the pro-Chinese perhaps, or the Trotskyists, have maintained or re-adopted a stance based on genuine rejection of the regime. The arrests of April 1966 may well have been aimed at these particular elements, who are in any case quite power-less, disavowed even by their old comrades, and incapable of reaching out to any wider audience. Foreign Communist elements such as the Syrian C.P. probably still view the regime with considerable suspicion and latent hostility; but they have no means of influencing Egypt's internal affairs.

Within Egypt itself, there is probably a potential opposition which is more or less in sympathy with the Syrian Ba'ath. It does not seem to have generated any organization however. The only really serious and dangerous challenge is the Muslim Brotherhood. It has been dismantled and must surely have lost much of its support, but it retains an organization abroad and very probably maintains clandestine, organized, perhaps even armed cells in Egypt itself. And what is much more serious, it quite possibly has a number of supporters in the Army. Do the latter go so far as to form clandestine groups, which could eventually control specific military units? Possibly, but one cannot be certain. In any case, civilian support can from time to time express itself under the cover of the defence of Islamic values and especially the Muslim tradition.

There is no way of drawing a clear distinction between the regime's real opponents, whose enmity towards it is unequivocal but who are reduced to camouflaging their protests, and committed Muslims, who may well accept the regime whilst hoping to influence the authorities towards a particular approach. Everyone realizes that under favourable circumstances some of the latter could well give their backing to the former. The regime is aware of the danger, and must surely be on its guard, but that is all that one can say for the moment. Under regimes of this sort, dissidents usually resort to building up underground organizations and secret arms depots, eventually embarking upon a military programme of training and clandestine propaganda. None of the opposition groups in Egypt seems to have been willing or able to go very far in this direction. The real threat facing the regime is that such groups might conceivably come to enjoy the support of sufficiently numerous and coherent elements within the military, thereby acquiring friends in high places and, who knows, perhaps even at the very top. We do not have enough information available to decide whether or not such a process is taking place.

By contrast, amongst the regime's original and even eventual partisans, the divergent tendencies, each more or less expressing the interests and aspirations of the various pressure groups, as well as divergent ideological orientations, are clearly discernible. They can be found at every level, be it amongst the more or less politicized masses or in the ranks of the administration itself. The National Congress of Popular Forces gave the various tendencies an opportunity to express themselves. And as long as they moderate their terms they can even confront each other in the National Assembly, in the Arab Socialist Union, in the press and over the radio. Each tendency does everything it can to capture key positions in the administration and elsewhere, especially in the press. Some of them have complete or partial control over various journals and magazines. But all this conflict between tendencies can only become serious if it hardens into a genuine struggle; the authorities have no intention of allowing such a development.

Is there a power struggle at the top? Each high-level member of the Junta certainly has his own particular orientation, and Egyptian political observers believe that these are fairly clearly definable. Differences of opinion about the course to be adopted have certainly arisen on various occasions. But every member of the leadership has always rallied round once the decision has been taken. These men are clearly bound by a definite loyalty to Gamal Abdel Nasser, who until now has always shown them the way out of apparently inextricable difficulties by cleaving to their original common orientation, maintaining them in power in the process.

No doubt major international upheavals and catastrophies would accentuate the differences between them and stimulate competition for individual power, each member of the leadership mobilizing in his favour all the support he has established and that which the option he stands for may attract at the time. But I do not think the enemies of the regime can place much hope in such a turn of events, at least in the foreseeable future. True, it was the Fascist Grand Council which overthrew Mussolini. But first a significant part of the country had to be occupied by enemy troops, with no favourable outcome in view.

The means available to the authorities in their efforts against actual or eventual dissidents are the traditional ones. One can morally disarm the opposition by successes abroad — Suez still counts as something of a triumph, but on the other hand there is the failure of the union with Syria and the present stalemate in Yemen — or on the economic level at home. Most underprivileged sections of society have indeed drawn some benefit from Government measures, although many others have suffered from them. But Egypt's objective economic difficulties make any great progress in this direction highly unlikely. It is far easier to rely on propaganda and counter-propaganda; of course there is always the possibility that over-use may blunt the efficacy of the latter, resulting in widespread cynicism.

There remains police repression. The authorities have shown themselves to be past masters at organizing the police, or rather the various police and intelligence services, with their ultra-modern equipment. The efficacy of their coercive power has been clearly demonstrated, notably in the struggle against the Communists and the Muslim Brotherhood. This efficacy is only partly diminished by the brutality, stupidity and lack of culture which characterizes most senior police officers. And, as usual, there is always the possibility that the police and the intelligence services end up by becoming an autonomous force, and that some hierarch may eventually be able to avail himself of them as a weapon. They have certainly already been infiltrated by right-wing elements, but one can only speculate as to whether this infiltration is sufficiently large-scale and organized to constitute a real threat.

The Army remains the regime's main source of strength, since for the moment the Party does not represent a really significant force. Consequently, it is from the Army that the most serious eventual threats to the regime may come, and for this reason the regime has done everything in its power to keep the Army behind it. It has had to grant important privileges to the military caste, a concession which, as we have seen, has in some ways been a definite handicap in the attempt to mobilize the masses. And the military themselves are by no means immune to the ideological and other pressures which surround them. Doubtless there are different tendencies competing for their support, and individually they may well align themselves behind various key figures. The important thing for the regime is to prevent organized centres of resistance forming within the Army. One can only hope for its sake that it has succeeded.

Conclusion

According to folk wisdom, 'A happy people has no history'. A happy people . . . or do we mean one whose form of political organization precludes pluralism? The absence of any legal opposition in a society makes for a regular way of life, and as long as there are no catastrophes, this may well be taken for happiness. Such societies seem to have hardly any internal political history worth mentioning. Palace revolutions are carried out discreetly and are in any case carefully presented as merely a matter of personalities.

Since 1954 at least, Egyptian society is one of the societies in which unity, and not dissent, has been the dominant theme. Relatively speaking, the authorities, and especially the central core and its leader, have enjoyed a very high level of stability ever since 1952. And when one comes down to it, the troubles of the first two years arose because the real authorities were having to cope with spokes set in their wheels by the figurehead government they had originally felt it necessary to set up.

But this does not mean that there is no recent Egyptian history, or at least no internal history to speak of. It hardly matters whether one calls it political history or not. The fact remains that a profound re-structuring, which has sometimes been referred to as national construction, has taken place. Industrialization, more widespread education, the breaking of the power of old classes and old ethno-religious groups, and the rise of new sections of society, sometimes under the cover of state control and far-reaching socialization, have all been features of this modernization. The great socio-economic options, agrarian reform, nationalization, and the general ideological orientation, all necessarily implied political choices, as the young officers who wanted nothing to do with politics soon found out. There were choices which took power away from certain classes and gave more to others; choices which stimulated demands and opposition; choices which decided in favour of certain methods at the expense of others. As we have seen, the group's original intentions were not framed in terms of any clear internal policies. The Free Officers wanted independence and modernization, and one must admit that they remained stubbornly faithful to their chosen goals. But while pursuing their vision they soon found themselves facing political and socio-political problems: how to govern, and with whom? With whom, in other words, with which sections of society and with which pre-existing groups? And there were two levels to the question. Where were the new state's cadres to come from? And who would provide its mass base?

The tragedy was that the whole question of where the cadres would come from had a foregone conclusion. The Army had originally supplied the cadres for the Revolution; it continued to be the only source of trustworthy cadres. It soon became clear that the regime could rely neither on the politically inert lower classes nor on the already politicized classes who were, with good reason, proving far too susceptible to the attractions of the old party apparatuses, such as the Wafd, the Muslim Brotherhood and the Communists. But as time went by, it transpired that the Army was in fact keen to keep its privileges and greedy for more, that it was cut off from the working people and incapable of the sacrifice required if the masses were to be mobilized. The Army, by showing itself unwilling to work and suffer with the masses and on their level, confirmed its inability to inject them with the required dynamism.

The lesson Nasser chose to draw from the secession of Syria was a new understanding of the great strength of the apparatuses which had managed to break what he thought of as the Syrian people's aspirations to unity. If this is the lesson he chose to draw, it was because in some obscure sense it had already been suggested to him by some other experience. We may disagree with his interpretation and prefer another; but we can also recognize that what he was really thinking of was Egypt, and that in this sense he was right. New cadres had to be found, and the only way to break the old apparatuses was to sink deep roots amongst the common people. The Communists, who had put themselves at the regime's disposal, were nonetheless still a potentially autonomous force which might not keep to the course set for it. In any case they did not have many more of the type of cadre required than the Army did. And as to the method they would employ to recruit new cadres, the authorities did not even have to wait to hear it clearly formulated to know that it was likely to have worrying overtones. Hence the creation of the Arab Socialist Union, with its statutory requirement that workers and peasants should make up half of the membership of its basic bodies. As we have seen, however, the Army's monopoly was a constant barrier to this attempt to form new popular cadres right from the start.

The methods of government seem to have gone through a long process of adjustment by trial and error. The regime had a much clearer idea of what it did not want than of what it did. It very soon became apparent that parliamentarism favoured the 'bourgeois' organizations and would eventually lead to the abandonment of the proper course. On the other hand, there could be no question of a form of democracy based on local 'Soviets'; the masses were far too crude, barbaric and brutal, given to uncontrolled fads, influenced by the old elite and generally likely to opt for economic orientations offering immediate returns but seriously handicapping the attempt to ensure independence and modernization. Such masses could only be granted any decision-making autonomy after all the right precautions had been taken, and even then very gradually.

In the end the regime decided that it would have to hold on to power since it was the only trustworthy leadership available: meanwhile it could carefully pave the way for the admittedly necessary replenishment of the elite. The outcome was a particularly lame compromise. The Socialist Union not only sifted the candidates for parliament, it also controlled and shaped more local bodies according to the Junta's overall instructions. Later, perhaps, a little more democracy could be allowed to creep in.

These were the choices which the grand ideological formulations expressed. It should be obvious by now that the way Europeans, and more especially Americans, formulate the problem (Is Egypt going Communist?) is quite false and reflects their obsessional anxieties and their manichean conception of the world far more than any clear-headed analysis of the facts.

Why does the Egyptian regime proclaim that it stands for 'scientific' socialism, thereby implicitly rejecting Muslim religious socialism? Because it wants to maintain the drive towards modernization. Because it fears the influence of the Azharists, the ulemas and the Muslim Brotherhood, the forces which use conservatism in their effort to maintain their hold over the masses, and which have made no secret of their hatred for the military group. Because it opposes the attempts to reinstate the *shari'a*, which would inevitably lead to a reactionary orientation.

On the other hand, why does the regime insist that it stands for an Arab deist socialism which rejects class struggle? One can easily understand that the idea of Soviet-style socialism, and the implied complete and definite alignment with the Soviet Union in all matters of foreign policy, makes the Egyptian leaders apprehensive. But why do they not choose some independent Marxist socialism à la Castro or à la Tito? Because they are frightened of unleashing a profound mass upheaval and a revolution in values. Once Caliban is unchained, who knows how far he will go? Thorough-going social and ideological struggle is a terrifying prospect for the regime. We have already seen how much stress the Free Officers' ideology placed on national unity. And above all, the Army would probably refuse to back such an upheaval. The road between all these pitfalls is hard and narrow, and it is no easy matter to forge an ideology appropriate for the projects of the transition period. But it is the only road open to the present leadership if it wants to remain true to itself, which on the whole it has succeeded in doing.

What emerges is the dynamic of power in this sort of state. Neither all-embracing voluntarism nor implacable determinism are completely dominant. The projects these young men conceived were the outcome of the situation in which they found themselves in. They were the only ones with the necessary instrument at their disposal to carry out these projects. They had to summon the will to go on with the enterprise and to choose between all the pathways that opened before them. At each crossroads they found they had to adapt their intentions to the demands of the situation. They were neither demiurges plucking a world out of nothingness, nor puppets dancing on strings pulled by some blind God of History; they were men who acted as relatively free agents and who were able to accept the inevitable in their attempts to shape a recalcitrant clay.

References

1. For an excellent picture of how this dynamic operates in the European 'people's democracies', see Ghita Ionescu, *L'Avenir Politique de l'Europe de l'Est*, SEDEIS, (Paris, 1967), (*Futuribles, 6*).
2. A very interesting analysis of this type of interaction appears in Barrington Moore Jr.'s, *Soviet Politics – The Dilemma of Power; The Role of Ideas in Social Change*, Harvard University Press, (Cambridge, Mass., 1950).
3. Gamal Abdel Nasser, *Falsafat ath-tharwa*, Dar al-ma'arif, (Cairo, n.d.), p. 49.
4. *Ibid.*, p. 10.
5. *Ibid.*, p. 43.
6. *Ibid.*, p. 25 ff.
7. Karl Kautsky, *Die Befreuing der Nationen*, Dietz, (Stuttgart, 1917), p. 32 ff; Stalin, 'Letter to Comrade A. Kholopov', *Bolshevik* no. 14, 1950.
8. Anwar es-Sadat, *Revolt on the Nile*.
9. *Ibid.* Hasan al-Banna was the founder and leader of the Muslim Brotherhood.
10. Cf. for example, H. Marcuse, *Soviet Marxism: A Critical Analysis*, Columbia University Press, (New York, 1958), Chapter 1. Also my 'Bolsheviks and Colonized Muslims' in this volume.
11. *Cahiers de l'Orient Contemporain*, 26, (Paris, 1952), p. 168. Future references to this journal, which contains translations and summaries from the Middle Eastern Press, will appear under the heading C.O.C.
12. *C.O.C.*, 26, p. 160 ff.
13. *Ibid.*, p. 157.
14. *Ibid.*, p. 156 ff.
15. *Ibid.*, p. 169.
16. *Ibid.*, p. 159.
17. C.O.C., 27, (1953), p. 51 ff.
18. Democratic Movement for National Liberation.
19. C.O.C., 28, (1953), p. 165 ff.
20. *C.O.C.*, 29 (1954), p. 52.
21. *Ibid.*, p. 55.
22. L. Binder, *Iran, Political Development in a Changing Society*, University of California Press, (Berkeley and Los Angeles, 1962).
23. P.J. Vatikiotis, *The Egyptian Army in Politics, Pattern for New Nations?* Indiana University Press, (Bloomington, 1961), p. 223 ff.
24. J. & S. Lacouture, *L'Egypte en Mouvement*, Le Seuil, (Paris, 1956), p. 182 ff, (2nd edn., p. 180 ff.)

25. Don Peretz, 'Democracy and the Revolution in Egypt' in *The Middle East Journal*, Vol. 13, No. 1, (Winter 1959), pp. 26–40, p. 33 ff.
26. Stuart R. Schram, 'What is Maoism? (A Symposium): The Man and his Doctrines' (*Problems of Communism*, Vol. 15, No. 5, (1966), pp. 1–7.
27. P.J. Vatikiotis, *op.cit.*, p. 83.
28. Cf. M. Duverger, *Les Partis Politiques*, 2nd edn., A. Colin, (Paris, 1954), p. 286 ff.

10. Islam as a Political Factor in Egypt After Nasser

Will Islam be a significant political factor in the Egyptian power struggles to which Nasser's death has given a new impetus? The wide range of current stereotypes about Muslim fanaticism, various vague ideas about the influence of religious systems, spectacular demonstrations of Muslim piety and ample evidence of its deep roots in the masses all combine to make the question one that the West is particularly prone to ask.

Unfortunately, even informed opinion demands simple diagnoses, when in fact explanation of this complex and unfamiliar ideological dynamic requires extremely elaborate exposition which is inappropriate here. The oversimplification inherent in passionate commitments and underlying ideologies does little to clarify the issue. Partisan opinions on the Arab-Israeli conflict also come into it. Some people feel justified in calling the Arab states, as a whole, theocratic, thinking they thereby dismiss the Arab case against Israel by adding yet another item to the list of the Arab states' alleged failings. Such an approach is hardly logical, especially as those Arabs who are most militantly opposed to Israel are often also the most outspoken critics of such failings. Some members of the public at large and even some Arab or pro-Arab specialists tend to see the Muslim masses at least as having one eye permanently fixed on the Koran. The thoughts of Allah are interpreted as informing the every action of the Muslim masses. Many left-wingers, followers of an ultra-schematized Marxism, give in to the opposite tendency and, in their impatience to reduce all political and social struggle to the bare bones of the class struggle, deny any relevance of the religious factor.

Some Preliminary Questions

Various worthwhile studies on the problem are nonetheless beginning to appear.[1] Like every problem of this kind, it requires various preliminary clarifications, which are often quite cheerfully dispensed with.

What is one to make of the various affirmative or negative statements concerning Islam as a political factor? Is the point to find out whether there is a political division on religious lines, as there was during our own wars of religion? Surely not, for there is no question of a power struggle between the preponderant Muslim majority and the Christian Coptic minority which represents perhaps 8—10% of the population, or 15% according to some Copts. Maybe the point is whether the political position of individuals and groups can be reinforced or weakened within society as a whole according to the more or less intensely religious attitudes they adopt? This is certainly relevant, for self-proclaimed irreligion is a definite handicap in the Arab world, just as it usually was in Europe until recently, and still is in the U.S.A., for example. Or are we talking about the influence of religious doctrines and traditions upon the practical policy adopted by the state? Such an influence does exist, but the measures involved are always minor ones, with no bearing on the major political, economic and social decisions.

What one can talk about is a certain use of religious feeling as a political ideology. Religion then becomes instrumental. Furthermore, one must distinguish between two possible forms of this process. One party affecting a religious identity — the Muslim Brotherhood, in this case — attacks the state's efforts towards secularization in the name of religion; it seeks to link such efforts with the state's political, economic and social policies, in order to mobilize the masses' deep attachment to ancestral religion and sacred tradition against these policies — which are the real target of such a party. On the other hand, religious themes are integrated, practically if not theoretically, into the programmes and actions of other parties, both in power and out, in order to mobilize the masses behind their programmes.

Egypt's Options

Given the above, it is clear that the Egyptian state or the groups which seek to dominate it have a variety of choices to make.

Militant atheism and an atheist state ideology is one possibility. It could, but by no means necessarily would be the choice of a Maoist-type party, if such a party came to power. But this is distinctly unlikely, to say the least.

Then there is the choice of radical secularism on the French model: a complete separation of religious bodies from the state, with religion reduced to a private opinion. Both Ataturk and Bourguiba opted for such a course, although the latter did so only temporarily and rather timidly. Such a choice appeals to many members of the ruling class who personally find it very attractive. But currently, they judge it to be too dangerous in terms of the maintenance of their own power, given the masses' indubitable attachment to Islam. The present ruling classes would be tempted to adopt such a course only if the fundamentalist Muslim party succeeded in narrowly linking religion to its own struggle for power. It would then be necessary for those in power to use all available weapons against this party. Only if practically all contact with people influenced by religion were lost would it be necessary to launch an attack on the religious institutions.

The Muslim Brotherhood has opted for a fundamentalist state programme, aiming in principle to restore, or rather to set up, the mediaeval ideal of Islam as a lay theocracy without a real clergy and to apply the religious law as a whole to every aspect of political and social organization. Even in mediaeval times, of course, such an ideal was far from being translated into reality. This programme might attract considerable mass support, under certain conditions at least, since in principle the ideal has a highly egalitarian tone to it. Even more important is the historical association, during the last few centuries, between Islam and the sometimes silent, sometimes violent opposition to the penetration of Western ideas and patterns of behaviour, themselves linked to Western imperialist expansion.

Needless to say, even if the Muslim Brotherhood came to power, such a programme would have no chance of being put into practice. Only Saudi Arabia has had any success with policies of this kind, thanks to its population's archaic way of life and to the strength of its coercive apparatus. Pakistan set itself the same aims, but has been forced to make extensive compromises. It is quite impossible today to govern a state, even an underdeveloped one, by the *shari'a* (religious law) alone. Of course this does not mean that its authority cannot be invoked when adopting or rejecting various courses. Measures could even be taken purely and simply to prove the authenticity of the state's attachment to Islam. A typical example is the Koranic penalty for theft, amputation of the hands, which has been restored in Saudi Arabia. Such measures would naturally weigh very heavily on some people. Women, especially, would have to give up many modern aspirations.

Nobody knows the extent of the Muslim Brotherhood's influence today. The party has been driven underground, its appeal fluctuates considerably, but it probably has many cells within the state and army apparatus. Many of its sympathizers are still hesitant, but a serious political or economic crisis could mobilize them. The blame for the crisis would then be attributed in terms of the leaders' lack of religious faith, and their links with atheistic communists. The ruling classes could either draw some advantage from such a turn of events, or simply bow before it, to defend themselves against developments which might threaten their privileges.

The Nasserist Attitude

For the moment, the most likely outcome is the continued predominance of the Nasserist attitude, that is to say the state's respectful religiosity. Islam remains the state religion. The rulers ostentatiously observe the religious rituals, with varying degrees of sincerity. The *shari'a* is treated with great respect, but integrated into an originally secular code of laws. The process is facilitated by accommodating interpretations. Social pressures and opportunism effectively discourage any blatant atheism, but in Egypt the law against it is not invoked, as it is in other Muslim countries. The legal code, secularized as a whole, only just allows faint vestiges of the ancient religious structures to persist, juxtaposed with special tribunals whose jurisdiction extends only to marriage and divorce.

This is not to say that these ancient structures which until recently held full sway have not left stubborn traces. Those hostile to the Arabs have often referred to the persecution of the Copts, whilst strenuously denying that there was the slightest difference in the two communities' social situation. Both claims are based on exaggeration. In fact, the Christians and Jews were privileged communities during the period of European hegemony. Because of their closer relationship with Europe, they were amongst the first to introduce Western customs and to facilitate penetration by the European economies. They therefore seem less reliable Egyptian or Arab patriots than the average Muslim, and this even without the fact that the Jews are constantly compromised by Israeli Zionism's *urbi et orbi* proclamations of solidarity. There are traces of a rampant, subtle and inconsistent discrimination against the Copts, who were often engaged in the sort of private trading which suffered during the nationalizations. Such traces are fading away, however, although the discrimination against Christians of foreign origin is much more acute, to the point of pushing them towards emigration.[2]

Above all, religious themes are used for tactical ends. There can be no question of letting the Muslim Brothehood and the like have a monopoly on such usage. A self-proclaimed Islamism can also facilitate the regime's foreign policy in the Arab countries, in Africa and in the Muslim world as a whole. The main task, however, remains the re-interpretation in Islamic language of the regime's aims and ideals; modernization, patriotism, socialism, even secularization, and a certain humanism. The Koran is presented as guaranteeing such ideals, as calling upon the faithful to realize them, and indeed as the first to proclaim them. As Morroe Berger says, 'The military regime, whilst not opposing religion as such, has attempted to make the masses see beyond religion, or to see religion differently — to see it as the regime would like to use it, as the bearer of nationalism, socialism and a one party state "popular democracy".'[3]

The religious 'class' is therefore protected, so that it can propagate the regime's ideology in religious form amongst the illiterate and semi-illiterate masses, so that it can form 'missionaries of socialism amongst the people'. The aim and result of the thoroughgoing reorganization of Al-Azhar, Cairo's great university, was to call the Sheikhs to order, to ensure the government's hold over this whole social stratum.[4] The protection of the latter is conditioned on its strict subordination, which in Islam is facilitated by the absence of any autonomous religious hierarchy such as the Catholic one.

It seems to me that one can conclude that the factors which will and do affect the direction of Egyptian policy are not religious ones. Neither dogma, nor faith, nor even denominational loyalty determine the fundamental options. This is not to deny the depth of the people's attachment to a religion which alone has given meaning to their lives, and which is still their basic social ethic. It is not to cast aspersions on the genuine religious faith of individuals. It is not to deny the sentimental resonance of everything Islamic. It is indubitably difficult and perhaps even impossible to confront this sentimentality head on. But the fact remains that Muslim themes are essentially used as partial ideological camouflage for options drawn from elsewhere.

References

1. For instance, M. Berger's *Islam in Egypt Today: Social and Political Aspects of Popular Religion*, C.U.P., (London,1976).
2. See Gaston Zananiri, *L'Eglise et L'Islam*, Syes, (Paris, 1969). This Egyptian Dominican's observations do justice to the subtleties involved.
3. M. Berger, *op.cit.*, p. 60 ff.
4. See Daniel Crecelius, 'Al Ahzar in the Revolution' in *Middle East Journal*, (Washington, 1966), Vol. 20, No. 1, pp. 31–49.

.

11. On the Contemporary Culture of the Muslim World

Intellectual Life in the Arab Countries

The Conditions, Contexts and General Tendencies of Intellectual Life

One cannot talk of the intellectual life of the Arab countries without some reference to the past. The Arab world is still at a turning point, or rather the corner it has just turned is still only a few steps behind it. A decisive transformation has taken place during the last few decades, there has been a radical metamorphosis. Traces of the old situation are still very obvious, not only in souls, hearts and minds but also in institutions, habits and the prevailing morality. One moment these traces are seen as the appealing imagery of the past, the next as a burden. They are omnipresent, and evoke both nostalgia and revolt. The new man has been born, but as he walks towards the future he cannot but turn back for a last regretful or irritated glance at that which is going to disappear behind him.

The Arab society of more than a century ago, a society which loses so many of its finer aspects when lumped into the huge category of 'traditional' societies, was not without its intellectuals. These were of two kinds. First, there were those whom one could call the religious ideologues, whose role was effectively that of a clergy, although strictly speaking Islam does not recognize such a body. These *ulemas*, as they are called, were wise in the lore of religion, often dependent on the powerful, and were often close to the people in their way of life, becoming their spokesmen when serious circumstances demanded it. Then there were those who gravitated towards the princely courts: the courtier poets, the poet laureates, the civil servants, the copywriters for the finely-worded proclamations and decrees, the blatant or subtle propagandists and the court jesters. Of course, none of these were in any way independent of the established authority. To these two categories one must add that of the part-time intellectuals, the distinguished amateurs, the aristocrats, the senior functionaries, the soveriegns themselves, who were not averse to an occasional flirtation with the Muse and whose reflections sometimes gave rise to serious works. All these made a significant contribution to the elaboration of traditional Arab culture. With the beginnings of modernization, from the 19th Century onwards, the scene gradually changed. For the moment I will set aside the directly colonized regions, such as the three Maghreb countries, which the French have an unfortunate tendency to consider as typical of the Arab world, whilst in fact such countries are an area in themselves, with their own specific characteristics, marked in some respects by quite exceptional traits. We shall consider these areas later. But it was in the Arab East that the first stages of a profound, albeit slow transformation emerged. It was the beginning of a mutation of structures.

New classes appeared: bureaucrats, the military, employees. These had featured in the traditional society, of course, but they had been totally integrated into the surrounding society, participating in a culture in which they were submerged, with no voice of their own. By contrast, the new members of the tertiary sector, as it is called today, were directly connected with a foreign culture and society, namely Europe. At the beginning they were even recruited from foreigners and from those of the indigenous population who were separated from the masses by definite particularities, such as the minority religious communities, the Christians and the Jews. These minorities had links with their co-religionists in Europe and were less attached to the global values of the society to which the Muslims adhered. The Europeans considered them as potential separatists — rightly in some ways, wrongly in others, which resulted in many tragedies. In the Army, the old foreign aristocracies at first maintained their monopoly over military functions. But as time went by, these new classes were increasingly recruited from the indigenous population and from the majority, that is to say from the mass of Sunni Muslims in general.

Technological power, military force, the dynamic of institutions, everything rubbed in the facts of Europe's superiority. The entire East was haunted by a single problem: what was the secret of the awesome superiority by which Europe forced the giants of the past to bow before her? Every aspect of life was examined as the possible basis of this superiority: the type of government, the religion, unknown racial factors, scientific activity, sexual morals, all were suspect. But one thing was quite clear: the East had no choice but to learn from Europe. The indigenous population began to attend the European schools established in the East, then local schools were set up on the same model. At first these attracted the children of parents with means, the aristocrats and the new merchants, who most appreciated the advantages of modern education. As society gradually adapted to European values, the local elite found it increasingly necessary to adapt also, in order to meet the demands of the new society, to challenge and confront the strange foreign world which was imposing itself upon them.

One of the tragic aspects of this contact was the fact that the local elites did not choose, as the subject of their children's studies, that branch of learning through which Europe's superiority had made itself so pervasive and irresistible: technology. The explanation for this failure does not lie in any innate lack of abilities, as the most imbecile racism would have us believe. Even the cultural tradition of contempt for manual labour was only secondarily responsible. A far more valid explanation can be found in the concrete situation. The wealthy elite wanted its children to be able to cope with the new dominant culture, but had no reason to wish them to give up their life of leisure. At most, their children might eventually enter some prestigious service such as the diplomatic. The new merchants could hope that their sons would succeed them and show even greater competence in running the family business. Others prepared their offspring for the modern professions. Such training presumed overall access to the world of modern values, and usually led to well-known, well-established ways of earning a living, even if not always exceptionally lucrative ones. Compared to the miserable and precarious existence led by the bulk of the population, such security was eminently desirable. Thus vast armies of civil servants, teachers, lawyers and doctors were formed. But technology remained foreign. The modern factories and vast civil engineering projects were still mainly foreign, usually staffed by imported foreign technicians. The market for technically trained indigenous labour was extremely small and unsettled. Engineering was not a safe career.

Of course, there was always the Army. The Army needed men in great numbers. Soon the aristocratic castes and the foreign cadres could not supply enough officers to meet its requirements. Indigenous elements had to be brought in. In this case the cultural tradition must have contributed considerably to diverting the sons of the elite away from this dangerous and despised occupation. They had been used to leaving such tasks to others for centuries. It was children from less elevated classes who chose this path, a path which was easier to tread if one was young and poor. And even if the military had only a subordinate position at the time, one could always hope for some turn of events in one's favour. For many sons of well-to-do peasants or petty bourgeois, the army was an efficient means to social advancement.

We have noted that all these types of training involved some apprenticeship in the foreign culture. As a result the new elites formed by the schools were cut off both from the groups who continued to lead the traditional life, such as the peasants and artisans, and from new groups, such as the proletarians and sub-proletarians, whose poverty prevented them from participating in the new culture.

This situation explains many of the complex and contradictory aspirations held by the intellectuals. They wanted a closer understanding of modern culture, that is to say European culture, but at first they could only apprehend it vaguely, from the outside and without grasping all its nuances. On the other hand, those amongst them who had the closest links with the indigenous masses from which they had emerged, were resentful and felt humiliated by the idea of having to make the assimilation of a foreign culture their primary aim. Hence there developed — and not only amongst the intellectuals — a desire for political autonomy, which I cannot go into here, and hand in hand with this there arose a desire for cultural autonomy. Ashamed of their cosmopolitanism, and sometimes even of their privilege as compared to the disinherited masses, many intellectuals began to criticize the foreign culture, often quite fiercely. They sought to put themselves on the same level, to demonstrate an originality rooted in the national traditions. But ironically they often knew very little about these traditions, and sometimes unconsciously introduced European ideas, values and notions under the cloak of traditionalism! True, Europe had often originally borrowed such ideas, in part at least, from Eastern culture, but that's another story.

Social evolution and political revolutions allowed new social strata to attain a certain cultural level, especially during the last decade. These strata remained unaffected by the foreign culture, and soon expressed their resentment of the privileges granted to that foreign culture most bitterly. The fact that these new strata were no longer aware of the foreign origin of many of their own received notions and values, which had developed in an already profoundly changed situation, only accentuated the issue. Having received a more cursory education, they were also less able to appreciate the nuances and finer qualities of European culture. It was thus in terms of an open appeal to national values, albeit mythical ones, that they justified both themselves and their struggle against those intellectuals they judged too favourable to cultural adaptation.

In short, the main tragedy of the Arab intellectuals of the time, which is in fact the tragedy of all Third World intellectuals, was that they were torn between, on the one hand, the demands of modern life which pushed them to adopt the Euro-American model, on the other, nationalist sentiment which was itself essentially the result of these same demands.

Time suffices merely to stress one of several crucial points here: one must understand that in the new situation the intellectuals had become a power in themselves. In the traditional society, the centre of power was the court and perhaps, secondarily, the mosque. The professional intellectuals were essentially subjects. They could indulge in gratuitous speculation but could only intervene in public affairs under orders, to illustrate or propagate the decisions of the mighty. Hence a recurrent theme of disenchantment dominated their personal works. They sang of the vanity of the world, exalted pious resignation, and concentrated their attention on those fugitive beauties of the universe which relieve the pain of existence; fleeing from a pitiless reality they found succour in the song of the nightingale, the strains of a lute, the furtive grace of a look, the gentleness of moonlight. Love, music, wine and mystical contemplation were so many blessed opiates.

By contrast, in the modern period, the centres of public life are and have long been the coffee house and the newspaper office. These were the centres of power, and for all that the influence of action from these centres was often only felt in the long term, it was nonetheless real. It was from such centres that themes which had nothing of contemplation or resignation were elaborated: mobilizatory themes which could rouse the masses, themes such as the nation, liberty, equality and progress. The new intellectuals were committed intellectuals, or at least the living, moving majority of them were. They re-focussed their attention on a reality which they sought to describe in all its sordid details, since they now sought change, not consolation. Slowly, new genres were born, the novel and the theatre, which gradually rejected the old attitude, and, in keeping with their vocation, increasingly espoused reality.

One must realize, however, that vestiges of the previous approach are still to be found amongst many intellectuals, especially amongst those who see mainly the partial and rather unattractive effects of action, the illusions it implies and engenders. Perhaps now that independence has been achieved, such vestiges will combine with new attitudes based on an attempt to remedy the oversimplifications which inevitably accompany a militant orientation.

The new regimes which have triumphed more or less everywhere all seem to favour the aspirations of the middle strata; at least they appear to be less Europeanized, closer to the people, aiming in principle at an egalitarian society, and above all committed to a project of economic modernization. This triumph has provoked a split amongst the intellectuals. On the one hand, some army officers as often as not, have gained access to the corridors of power and sometimes to its centre. They have become a part of the country's political leadership and back the new ruling classes. They must therefore make sacrifices to the demands of getting things done and, of course, personal advantage is not necessarily always the least of their considerations. Then there are the silent opponents of the regime, both at home and abroad, who more or less understand the historical necessity of the attitude taken by their brothers of yesterday, but who are still too sensitive to the intellectual and moral sacrifices that revolutionary action seems to imply to imitate them.

Unfortunately there is insufficient time to deal at any length with the Maghreb here. As a result of the colonial situation, it underwent a rather different evolution. The new classes emerged much more slowly; the foreign, French culture was so overwhelmingly dominant that the tendency to assimilation was much stronger; furthermore, it was reinforced by the fact that it was the only superior culture that the proletarian elements had ever known. The past was clearly far too distant for any return to it to be seriously considered.

I know that I have not even touched on many crucial problems. In conclusion I will stress only the salient features which seem to me to be the most important. Modern technological society has established a firm foothold in the Arab world, not only with its machines but also with its values, its ideas, its ways of thinking. An irreversible step has been taken. Every layer of society has to a greater or lesser extent been affected by a wave of innovation. All have witnessed the transformation of a mentality, even if that transformation has sometimes been disguised in traditional garb. Everywhere there are dynamic elements which seek to push the whole society into even more far-reaching transformations, even greater adaptations to the new conditions. This real revolution is in the context of intellectual life within which every intellectual must now situate himself. Such a movement may be slowed down by social conditions and political vicissitudes. But there is no inherent, essential brake to this march forward of a whole people. And as the new culture, which is still often adopted in its standard international form, takes root and links up with the cultural inheritance of the past, it will tend to take a more and more particular and original form.

The Political Ideologies and their Elaboration

One cannot talk meaningfully about the intellectual life of the Arab countries without recognizing that the problem of political ideologies is a central topic. The circumstances of their recent history have led, and still do lead, these ideologies to play an overwhelming role. They find their way into everything, they spill over into every aspect of life. Even those individuals who refuse to adhere to them are negatively conditioned by their power; the very violence of such rejections is merely a reflection of that power.

The ideologies in question can be reduced to two main ones: nationalism and socialism. These two correspond to the two projects stemming from the Arab people's basic aspirations during the present period: respectively, the achievement of independence, or of autonomous decision-making, to be more precise, and the modernization of the economy, leading as quickly as possible to a rise in the still abominably low standard of living.

Two clarifications are needed here. Many people may be inclined to believe that the first of these goals, independence, is no longer so relevant, as it has already been attained. They conclude that its corresponding ideology, nationalism, must be losing its appeal. However this view is only partially correct. It is true that political independence has been achieved almost everywhere. But, firstly, there is the fact that the Arab peoples feel that there are two Arab countries which remain under a foreign yoke: Israel and Southern Arabia, the latter of which is still administered directly or indirectly by Britain [as of 1965, the time of writing]. Whatever its legitimacy, this is the Arab viewpoint. As far as their collective consciousness is concerned, two countries remain unredeemed.

Secondly, there is a widespread feeling that this so widely acquired independence is precarious and threatened in every case. Rightly or wrongly, many Arabs believe that the industrial powers of the Northern Hemisphere, whether they be old colonial powers or not, have only one desire, namely to reconquer the hegemony which so recently slipped from their grasp. These arguments are backed by examples from the not-so-distant past, such as the Suez expedition. In many cases the belief is that such a re-conquest will take a non-violent but nonetheless quite efficacious form, reliant more on economic pressure based on technological superiority than on mere force of arms. Tactics of this sort are nowadays referred to as neo-colonialism. Some may find such fears unfounded. But the fact remains that the fears exist and are widespread enough to count as an important factor.

Many readers will wonder why I do not include the religious ideology, Islam. This is no oversight. I do not deny that religious feeling remains a potent force amongst many Muslims, nor that many others are strongly attracted to the traditions which have been sanctified by religion. But I do not think Islam is an autonomous *political* ideology at present. The Muslim faithful are often enough apolitical, whether their faith encourages them in such an attitude or not. True, both individuals and organizations can use the faith to justify a variety of political options. But the options in question can in no way be explained in terms of the religious dogma. They remain aspects of those essentially secular ideologies, nationalism and socialism, and simply provide these secular ideologies with a religious garb and a religious justification.

The primordial drives I have mentioned, the aspirations towards national autonomy and a higher standard of living, are very simple. But the elaboration of these ideas is much more complex. More or less coherently, the ideologues have cobbled together theories based on these aspirations — such is, after all, their historical task — using material from abroad, the world of Europe and America. The very structures of the ideologies, their basic orientations, are drawn from that world, from nationalism as forged by the revolutionary democrats of the 19th Century, complete with its often rather suspect offshoots, and from socialism in its Marxist or 'utopian' form.

This importation from the West of the very doctrines in whose name Western domination was rejected has given rise to many ironies. Some have attempted to denigrate it. Certain particularly well-informed specialists have gone to the length of pointing out that one of the first books setting out the tenets of Arab nationalism is recognizably recast from a work by an Italian, Alfieri. Other discoveries of this kind have been made, but for all their usefulness to the history of thought, they are hardly relevant to the authenticity of the aspirations and demands.

The drive towards the goals mentioned above is universal. It is therefore also indigenous. Its existence in the Arab countries has been apparent for centuries, but it has been held back by force. Europe's contribution was to put an end to resignation, by offering a dynamic model which apparently led to liberty and progress, and by introducing the elements of a dynamic economy which circumstances had previously prevented from developing in the East. Since it was Europe which introduced the stimulating and attractive values and approaches of modern life, it was only natural that the Arabs should turn to Europe for the forms of ideology best adapted to those values and approaches.

Incidentally, it should be mentioned that the socialist ideology, in its elaborated form, must also be considered as an import from the European world, despite the current fallacious terminology which postulates an opposition between East and West. However, one must stress that until now this ideology has often been adopted in Arab countries, and in the Third World as a whole on the basis of pre-occupations very different from those which gave it its attraction in Europe. It was brought in as a model of development capable of leading to national independence through modernization of the economy, rather than as a formula for the egalitarian redistribution of the national income. This was only natural, given that during the recent period, the demand for national independence was clearly predominant. But things are probably changing now. In many circles, amongst the Algerian proletariat and sub-proletariat, for instance, socialism's egalitarian meaning is already at the top of the agenda.

Ideologies were imported without any noticeable reluctance to make use of foreign sources, as long as the latter helped to express genuine indigenous aspirations and enjoyed the prestige of modernity. But such was the power of the feelings expressed that there was no need to make use of complex elaborations and refined theorizations. These ideologies, of which only the broad lines were retained, were simple and crude instruments, but quite adequate for the necessary preliminary steps in the great endeavours which were being embarked upon. It was only gradually that a certain need for elaboration became manifest, and that the strength of the ethno-national tendency forced the ideologies to assume a more local veneer, just as in religious circles attempts were made to embellish them with vague references to tradition and its religious values. These attempts at indigenization were not genuine, however. Although the internal drives were, as I have said, authentically indigenous, the theorization was imported from Europe and given a superficial coat of local tradition.

Nonetheless, the indigenization of the ideologies is necessary and will be carried out. But it will be a slow process in which local forces, local needs and deep-seated national tendencies will all have a part to play. Since the fundamental aspirations remain unchanged, the tendency will be, I believe, towards the elaboration of more precise theorizations which are better adapted to the local situations. But this is as yet still in its early stages.

As I said, for the moment, socialism and nationalism are still in many cases closely linked. Many intellectuals in the Arab countries, who have put their hopes in the ideals expressed by both ideologies, think that this linkage will continue, and are led to see socialism as an intrinsic, permanent and necessary feature of their own particular nationalism. I can see no grounds for such a necessity, however. Once the national aspiration has been satisfied, I see no guarantee that these countries will avoid the usual course of evolution. The nationalist ideology, which has previously been revolutionary, will become, and has already become so in places, a doctrine of self-satisfaction opposed to the dissatisfied and those who still seek to achieve the other aspiration. Acceptance of inequality and privilege will be preached in the name of national unity. The two themes will increasingly become separate.

With special reference to Arab political ideologies, amongst other things, much has been made of the especially powerful role of symbolism amongst the Arabs. The suggestion is that the Arabs are far more aware of symbols than of realities. I cannot agree with such a notion. During periods of revolutionary struggle or foreign campaigns, worthwhile developments are often slow, precarious and erratic, but a symbol makes them immediately tangible. In the midst of a struggle, explanations can appear cumbersome, long-winded, difficult to follow. It is so much easier to use a symbol which encapsulates all the values for which one is fighting or against which one is fighting. The use of banners, the glorification of the sign of the cross by Christians, the thousands of martyrs forced to symbolically renounce their faith by spitting on a bit of wood or a scrap of cloth, all bear witness to the necessity of such a shorthand. Those who think that Arabs have a particular obsession with symbols should re-read the sections on the flag in the military manuals of any European army.

Of course the Arabs are attached to certain symbols. But this trait is not peculiar to them, and in any case is not equally prevalent in every field. They will not part with Arabic script which has its good points but also many disadvantages. It symbolizes all their past and all their historical originality. But neither the British nor the French would willingly give up their ways of spelling, which are amongst the most awkward and irrational in the world. On the other hand, most Arab countries have adopted European dress, the symbol of modernism, rather as the French peasant has given up his smock. What really needs to be stressed is that the autonomy of the symbolic is only relative. A people may provisionally, even enthusiastically, accept a symbolic satisfaction of its aspirations. But by itself such a satisfaction cannot last for very long.

In politics, it has been said that during the de-colonization period it was the most emotionally loaded and inspiring symbols which drew the masses. Such a thesis can only be accepted if one immediately limits its scope, and even then . . . It cannot hold without the rider that the symbols in question must always be of a certain specific type, and cannot be chosen at random. If it is to draw the masses, the symbol presented to them must always correspond in some way to their aspirations, observations to the contrary notwithstanding. This has been clearly demonstrated in certain colonies where attempts at a psychological winning over of the masses by the use of certain symbols have failed. The masses just did not recognize their own aspirations behind such symbols, even though these had been chosen according to special traditions.

The symbol is nonetheless a useful tool, and often all the more dangerous because of it. It is as creators and elaborators of ideologies, and as manipulators of symbols that intellectuals are sought out by rulers. An ideology is by definition mobilizatory or conformist, and intellectuals are asked to mobilize or to appease. In either case they have to prove their efficiency. Therefore when committed, be it to an ideal or to a means of earning a living, they can be sorely tempted to go straight for the simplest and most efficacious solution, papering over any cracks and side-stepping any obstacles thanks to the particular flexibility of symbolism. Those with the most demanding consciences may, as is usual, object. But far more importantly, the energetic protests of the facts themselves will eventually make themselves felt. For no symbol can for long betray and defy the real world with impunity.

The political ideologies are thus right in the throes of elaboration. Faced with the necessity to confront situations in which the proclamation of elementary demands is no longer sufficient, they are gradually broaching more complex themes, and are acquiring deeper meanings. In the process they are being differentiated. Although the European contribution on the broader issues is still taken into account, increasingly it is specific local problems which must be tackled. Consequently the process whereby thought is becoming sharper, more detailed and subtle in its analyses is also leading to its acquiring a genuinely national character; no longer do we have the old trotting out of European notions in traditional national garb but a real grasping of local problems in all their complexity and originality.

In conclusion I would like to stress that this appreciation of national originality can in no way be assimilated to a return to the past. There is no such thing as an Arab local culture which has retained its fundamental essence over centuries and millenia. In these countries as in others, it is the existence, not the essence, of civilization which counts. Far more than is generally recognized, this civilization has been outward-facing throughout its history and has constantly transformed and renewed itself. There is no reason to believe that the same will not happen today. In politics as in other fields, Arab culture faces the future with a character which is both all its own and new.

12. A Marxist Policy for the Arab Countries

The Tasks Facing Contemporary Arab Societies

The tasks facing contemporary Arab societies are the tasks of specific under-developed societies. It is quite obvious that although the ultimate goals are the same as those of the developed societies and of all human societies, they present themselves under very different conditions from those prevailing in the developed societies. The tasks involved are to some extent the tasks specific to all underdeveloped societies, but they are also, for instance, quite different to those on the agenda in countries where the national problem appears to have been settled, as in Iran and Turkey, for all that the latter are part of the Muslim world. The essential tasks of the Arab societies consist in ensuring independence and a rising standard of living, under clearly defined conditions.

On this level, and given these limits, every Marxist and indeed everybody who holds to a humanist orientation can support them. This support need not stem from any particular affection for Arabs *qua* Arabs. Such an affection, when it is not the manifestation of specific forms of vested interest, some-times results from a particular romantic psychological makeup, from what one could call the Lawrence syndrome. Such Arabophilia is a subjective orientation which is not influenced by rational argument. It often leads to uncritical support for everything the Arabs do or say. This is quite different from humanist or more specifically Marxist support for the legitimate tasks the Arab societies assign themselves, which implies a corresponding commit-ment to oppose anything illegitimate in an Arab project and any Arab project which is itself illegitimate, for instance any project of domination, oppression or exploitation. Romantic Arabophiles or Arabs blinded by patriotism might answer that the Arabs are by their very nature incapable of forming such projects. But that would be to put forward a racist vision of history which is quite unacceptable to those who have chosen the above mentioned orientations.

Independence
To ensure independence is to commit the Arab countries to autonomous and autochthonous development in keeping with the needs of Arab society guided by national expectations. This goal obviously implies a struggle against

everything which might restrict the liberty and the autonomy of the Arab nations, or nation, as one prefers. Since the Arab nations are now nearly all independent, the main danger they face comes from other human societies or ethnic groups either seeking to restrict this freedom through some political or economic mechanism, or even involuntarily coming to do so. In some cases these other societies are dangerous to Arab independence because they are impelled to go beyond the legitimate goals recognized by a universalist ethic; in other words these societies are not content merely to ensure their own independence and a rising standard of living. Such societies or nations can obviously not be expected to cut off trade relations with the outside world; no one is suggesting that they should. But their will to power, their quest for well-being or some other mechanism impels them to implement these trade relations in a manner which is detrimental to others, a manner which limits and interferes with the freedom of others; in a word, a manner which subordinates others. These are the nations which are usually described as having imperialist tendencies.

Imperialism is not some mythological one-headed monster feeding on the blood and brains of men; it is not the legendary Dahhak which angrily preys on every attempt at progress and freedom throughout the world. There are several imperialisms, and every society is potentially imperialist. No society has ever hesitated to look after its own interests whenever an opportunity to pursue its own well-being at the expense of others presented itself.

However, all this should not blind one to the fact that the most dangerous imperialism today is capitalist imperialism. It is still debatable whether the very structure of present-day capitalist society does or does not force it to be imperialist. The problem is not as simple as it may seem to those who are unaware of all the factors. In particular, I would stress that there is no irrefutable Marxist 'science' which demonstrates beyond all reasonable doubt that present-day capitalism must inevitably realize its imperialist tendencies, whether as envisaged by Lenin or by others; such a thesis can never be proven in the way a law of physics can be.

The facts are that a capitalist economic imperialism does exist today, and that the capitalist nations have at least temporarily renounced political imperialism, the direct political domination of other countries. When the capitalist states seek to dominate other nations, they do so by means of the pressure and influence they can exert over the leaders of the nation itself. But, generally speaking, the main factor is an economic imperialism; deliberately or otherwise, the developed capitalist societies take advantage of their economic superiority to limit the underdeveloped countries' power of autonomous decision-making in economic matters, and use this same mechanism to restrict the political autonomy of these states. The mechanism of capitalist imperialism is all the more efficacious in that it originally manifests itself in purely economic factors and thus can imperceptibly impose a course to be followed without all the consequences of that course being apparent. To take a crude example, the decision to build a textile factory rather than a tractor factory can stem from considerations of immediate profitability and thus appear as a free choice of investment, be it public or private. But the consequences of this choice, and of hundreds of analogous choices can weigh so heavily on the state's freedom of decision as to amount to effective coercion.

At the moment attention focuses mostly on American imperialism, for the simple reason that the United States is the most economically developed country in the world, and correspondingly the world's most politically and militarily powerful state. But the same mechanism can and does further the interests of each and every capitalist nation. There is clearly already a European imperialism, or European imperialisms, as well as a Japanese imperialism, for example. They merely vary in the degree of danger they hold for Third World countries.

From the moment a developed capitalist economy establishes its superiority and its ability to subordinate underdeveloped economies simply through the normal mechanisms of economic liberalism, through the laws of the market, and from the moment the capitalist state can use this effective economic domination to institute a political domination, even a partial one, it is quite clear that the struggle against this imperialism demands at the very least a strict control of the liberal economy; that is to say, it demands a minimum of economic planning.

The socialist imperialisms must also be taken into account. True, classical Marxism assumes that a socialist state cannot be imperialist. It is faithful to Marx himself on this point, if not on others. But no proof is given to back up this thesis, which is practically a postulate. The arguments advanced, rightly or wrongly, to demonstrate the existence of a mechanism which impels the capitalist economy, in some or all of its phases, to economic or political imperialism, in no way prove that similar pressures are not exerted upon other, non-capitalist economies. The whole history of humanity, and the ethnographic study of populations who still live at the socio-economic stage in which our pre-historic ancestors lived, tend to prove the contrary. In spite of his tendency to idealize the socialist state, even Lenin himself admitted, in passing, that the peoples who had carried out a socialist revolution would still be exposed to a tendency to exploit their superiority for political ends. Recently, Mao Tse-tung came to the same conclusion. One can, of course, avoid the issue by labelling the economic regime in the Soviet Union pseudo-socialist. One can blame everything on the Stalinist orientation, or on some other contingent factor. But whether one is talking about a state economy directed by a monolithic party, or about a free association of producers, there is still nothing which proves that such formations are incapable of exerting pressures on other nations. Such an assumption can only rest on some irrational belief, such as Rousseau's, that Man is naturally 'good', that he is fundamentally altruistic, and that his deviations into selfishness are due only to the social systems under which he lives. Of course, one can always invoke socialism as it should be, as opposed to the socialism which has been instituted. Whether one believes in the eventual realization of the former or not, the fact remains that we can only base our arguments on what exists or on what has existed.

We shall therefore refer here to socialist imperialisms; even though the juxtaposition of these two terms may seem a blasphemy to some. At the moment these socialist imperialisms are mainly potential; that is, if one excludes the problem of the national minorities subordinated within the frameworks of the Soviet and Chinese states, a problem which is important but which does not really fall within the scope of our discussion here. The Soviet Union and China certainly do seek to exercise their influence wherever they can, and they use their economic, demographic and military strength to do so. It has also been noted that in some cases the Soviet Union has drawn an excessive return from the 'aid' it proffered, not to mention the straightforward Soviet spoliation and economic pillage of the people's democracies in Eastern Europe following the Second World War, which can, after all, be seen as a mistake, the product of past deviations.

Apart from the above cases, however, it appears that, on the whole, the socialist powers have not used economic aid and trade relations to impose the sort of imperceptible and tenacious dependency that the developed capitalist economies have imposed on the countries with which they have this sort of dealing.

The important point is that, because the socialist countries' economies are subject to complete political control, any economic intervention in another country's affairs is both controllable and visible. It is controllable in the sense that the political authorities in these countries can determine the extent of such intervention in terms of the consequences they expect from it. It is visible in the sense that any effects brought about by such economic intervention can easily be attributed to a specific cause and a specific origin. Thus, when Stalin sought to impose a treaty concerning oil concessions on Iran in 1945, the immediate response was a wave of nationalist hostility, as it was quite clear that the subordination of the Iranian state was an integral aspect of such a treaty. But once the Iranian Parliament had refused to ratify the treaty, the Americans immediately granted Iran very significant 'aid', and American investment poured into Iranian industry and the subordination which resulted from *these* measures only made itself felt slowly and indiscernably. It could always be put down to the dynamic of the world market.

The socialist powers took careful note of this and other similar experiences. From then on they tried to gauge their interventions so as not to arouse nationalistic reactions. The key difference between socialist and capitalist 'aid' is perhaps that the leaders of underdeveloped countries can always evaluate to what extent the need to call in socialist 'aid' has resulted in subordination. At any time they can put an end to such subordination by means of specific sudden political measures, by calling in the counterbalancing 'aid' of the capitalist countries and by striking the right balance between the two.

Essentially, it is not at present in the interests of the socialist powers to restrict the economic independence of the underdeveloped countries; and unlike the capitalist countries, the socialist political authorities always have the means to control any tendency which would amount to such a restriction. Under present conditions it is, on the contrary, in the interests of the socialist powers to free the underdeveloped countries from capitalist patronage as much as possible, and on the whole, the latters' leaders have a sound empirical grasp of this situation. Those who genuinely seek the economic independence of their countries therefore naturally prefer socialist 'aid'. They seek out alliances with the Soviet Union and with China, but they do so only with the greatest caution. One can only approve of such an approach.

Since we are dealing specifically with the Arab countries, we must consider the one imperialism which especially threatens them, namely Israeli imperialism. The issue is complex and delicate, and requires a very subtle approach, which is a great deal to ask of the men and communities directly engaged in the struggle. Any objective treatment of the question is likely to attract violent accusation from all sides, and many of these will be inspired by feelings which are in themselves quite laudable. Since I have been so rash as to step into this minefield, I shall venture a little further.

As I have shown elsewhere, one can legitimately consider the massive implantation of a Jewish population in Palestine, and the creation of a Jewish state there, as a colonial phenomenon, a somewhat belated aspect of Europe's imperialist territorial expansion. A new Hebrew-speaking ethnic group gradually developed out of what had been an association of like-thinking men, the Zionist Jews. Thanks to British protection, their strength increased and they used this to subjugate a part of the indigenous population of Palestine and to expel the others.

It is difficult to imagine how else the Zionist project, which set out to create a Jewish state on Arab territory, could have been realized. True, this implantation did have its own specific characteristics. Furthermore, and this is most important, the Jewish population, from amongst whom the Zionists were recruited, had good reasons for seeing the creation of a Jewish state as the best solution to the ills that assailed them. But the fact remains that they got what they wanted by forcibly imposing their will upon another human group. And that is the definition of an imperialist venture, even when there is no question of such a venture being the result of some Machiavellian decision made by a mythical monster called Imperialism, even when it is not part of the overall plan established by some mysterious General Staff in order to enslave the freedom-loving peoples and suck their blood.

There would be no need to carry the analysis any further had the new state and the new population been accepted by their neighbours. Australia was established in a rather similar way and today only a minority of Australian aborigines contest the outcome, and even they do not put Australia's very existence into question. In the neighbouring island of Tasmania, nobody questions the Tasmanian state's right to exist, for the simple reason that the indigenous population who might have done so have all been exterminated. The same is not true of the state of Israel, as we well know. Hence, besides the imperialist measures which led to the setting up of the state, there is the problem of that state's own eventual imperialist tendencies.

The subject demands a more serious analysis than can be found in moralistic declarations, in propaganda or in the flourishing mythology of the subject which supplies the simple-minded with simple explanations. On the economic level, the state of Israel enjoys an undeniable superiority over its neighbours. The massive inflow of capital and the considerable number of producers and organizers endowed with the Industrial Age's most advanced attitudes guarantee this superiority. As I mentioned above, this means that the country's economic expansion can proceed apace, to the detriment of its economically less developed neighbours, thereby conceivably reducing the autonomy of their economic decisions. To some extent this potential for economic expansion was already being realized during the British Mandate. The Jewish *Yishuv* (settlement) in Palestine had no difficulty in distributing its products in Lebanon, Syria and Transjordan. The creation of the state of Israel and the breaking off of all links between this state and its neighbours almost put an end to this process. However, it did continue more or less clandestinely, thanks to the Arab traders concerned.

After the June 1967 War, measures were taken to facilitate the flow of merchandise across the new borders conquered by the state of Israel, and the practice revived. Were peace to be established between Israel and its neighbours, Israel's economic expansion would certainly be greatly facilitated. To defend themselves against this economic onslaught, the Arab states would have to adopt significantly protectionist measures. But until their economies had reached the same level of development as the Israeli state's, they could never be sure that the threat of economic domination had definitely been removed. Indeed it is quite certain that any protectionist measures would immediately run up against the stiff resistance of commercial pressure groups within the Arab states themselves.

Contrary to the view generally held by vulgar Marxists, which is also accepted by non-Marxist nationalists who have an ideological vested interest in the question, it is not the case that a potential for economic expansion necessarily leads to political expansion. From a strictly economic point of view, Israel could perfectly well thrive and prosper without extending its territory, just as Norway and Switzerland have done. Israel's territorial expansion has resulted from political factors, not economic ones. Expansionist projects have only existed from time to time, in certain sectors and amongst certain groups in Israel. Like any political projects they were liable to be pursued, limited, extended or abandoned according to the prevailing circumstances.

What is at issue is not expansion in the abstract, but expansion in terms of the limits given. For instance, both the chief executive, David Ben Gurion, and his group at first more or less accepted the limits set by the United Nations 1947 partition plan; then, thanks to the War, sought to expand beyond these limits. But, in general, what they have constantly sought is to impose recognition of the new state upon its Arab neighbours. The key factor is that the strategy they chose in order to achieve this aim has been a strategy which implied primarily the use of military force.

Our object here is not to discuss whether this strategy was the only possible one, nor to pass moral judgements on this choice or even on its goals. In any case, it is quite clear that, until now, the result has not been full recognition of the state of Israel by the Arab states but rather an Israeli territorial expansion stemming directly from the dynamic to which this strategy committed those who adopted it. In this sense, Israel has effectively taken imperialist measures. This became all the more apparent when, four years after the June 1967 War, the Israeli Government plainly refused to evacuate the conquered territories in exchange for recognition by the Arab states.

Of course, one could argue that this expansion is the result of the refusal by the Arab states, and even by the Arab masses, to recognize the newly-formed state. But this refusal itself stems from the imperialist character of the way this state was formed. When Arab or pro-Arab polemicists refer to the Israeli state's expansionist nature, they have its eventual future as well as its past in mind.

Here again one must avoid myths if one wants a clear understanding of the problem. To say that the state of Israel enlarged itself because it had an expansionist nature brings us down to the level of the doctors caricatured by Molière. If the Arab states continue to make it a condition for recognizing Israel that the latter should evacuate more territory than it is willing to, and if Israel persists in its refusal to give up the territories as part of the peace negotiations, then obviously war will continue to be a dominant aspect of the situation, latently at least. Under these conditions the Israeli Government is constantly exposed to the temptation of acquiring other territories, and the vicissitudes of future conflicts may even push it to do so. Everything will depend on the strategic calculations of the Israeli leaders, who will have to assess the advantages and disadvantages of new annexations.

Yet another situation can and must be envisaged. Let us assume that a peace is established between a more or less enlarged Israel and those neighbouring Arab states which have so far actually entered the conflict. It is highly unlikely that such an outcome would put an end to the demands of the Palestinians. True, it might well lessen the virulence of these demands, and make it impossible for them to be expressed in military confrontation. One should always remember that it is very difficult for the Palestinians on their own to launch a military offensive against Israel, for the simple reason that they can only do so from bases situated in neighbouring countries, and that if peace really were established, Israel could evidently demand that no such bases be provided. Of course the movement could operate from internal bases, situated within the territories occupied by Israel. But in the context of the hypothetical situation sketched above, Israel would have at its disposal an unanswerable weapon with which to put down any genuinely dangerous insurrection: it could quite simply expel all or most of its Arab inhabitants.

Pro-Arab and leftist opinion often holds yet another view of Israeli imperialism, although this approach is not always taken to its logical conclusion. It is essentially based on a representation of Imperialism, with a capital 'I', both as a blind impersonal force and as a being endowed with an implacable and malevolent will of its own. Is there some real basis for this representation, just as behind the myth of the multi-coloured shawl worn by Iris, messenger of the Gods, there is the actual phenomenon of the rainbow? What does emerge, when those who use this conceptualization consent to provide some further details, is that they consider the state of Israel to be a bastion of the world apparatus through which American forces are deployed. But an obvious incoherence manifests itself in their very use of this concept of 'Imperialism' as opposed to more precise terms such as the American Government, the capitalist economy, the American economy or the Atlantic Alliance.

Admittedly, Israel is undeniably linked to the U.S.A. in a variety of ways. We all know that Israel's economic survival is largely dependent on gifts from American Jews and that the U.S.A. has contributed very considerably to building up Israel's military arsenal, as well as providing general assistance on the diplomatic level. It is also very likely that the American and Israeli General Staffs are closely linked. But this does not mean that the Israeli state has no will of its own, or that it blindly follows every directive from Washington. We are talking about a genuine alliance. Even though Israel is minute compared to the U.S.A. and directly dependent upon it, it still has certain very efficient means of pressure at its disposal. Therefore, should the need arise, it could depart from strict adherence to the American line. But the U.S.A. obviously has every interest in keeping Israel dependent. Under present circumstances it has in the Israelis a coherent national group, surrounded by a hostile world, who can be relied upon to remain well-disposed towards their patron.

Now one should not forget that the U.S.A. also enjoys the friendship of influential classes in several Arab states, whose interests are no less linked to those of the U.S.A. It thus has various substitute alliances available, although in this respect it is handicapped by domestic public opinion, which would not countenance Israel being totally abandoned.

It is thus reasonable to conclude that the Arab countries are threatened by Israeli economic imperialism in peacetime and by Israeli political imperialism in wartime. They could avoid the latter by making peace on Israel's terms, by accepting the effects of past political imperialism. Failing this, the continuing state of war both exposes them to the danger of greater Israeli expansion in the future, and forces them to expend considerable resources on defence, which reduces their development possibilities, and thus limits their economic autonomy. Should there be a peace, whether on the present Israeli terms or on future possibly more moderate and acceptable ones, the Arab countries would find it much easier to resist Israeli economic imperialism. Simple protectionist measures might suffice.

A truly comprehensive survey of every conceivable outcome must include the possibility of a total Arab victory over Israel. There would then be no threat whatsoever. But this seems extremely improbable, for the foreseeable future at least and not worth further consideration here.

The threat of Israeli political imperialism would also be lifted if the internal structures of Israel produced a government genuinely and lastingly committed to a peaceful strategy which set out to achieve Israel's primary goal, recognition by the neighbouring states by diplomatic and peaceful means. A hopeful sign of this would be the opening of negotiations on the basis of withdrawal from the territories occupied in June 1967 and recognition of Israel; this would involve the Israeli side agreeing to overlook various subtle points in the formulations imposed upon the Arab states by Arab ideology and public opinion. Such a development is difficult to conceive without a profound modification of Israeli ideology and its corresponding political structures. But were there to be an international political initiative which shared such a new line, it might just give sufficient momentum towards the effective transformation of Israeli ideology, even if it was backed by pressure from the great powers. This is what is meant by the rather vague catchall phrase 'de-Zionisation of Israel', a phrase for which I shall try to provide more accurate substitutes later.

But we must not forget the problem of Arab unity, since many Arab ideologues consider it a necessary precondition to total independence, although outside observers do not in fact find this idea particularly convincing. If one examines the question with the greatest possible objectivity, it becomes apparent that many factors unite the Arab peoples, but that there are also many differentiating factors. In principle, therefore, it is difficult to see why unity is so absolutely crucial, since similar unifying and differentiating factors can be found in Spanish Latin America and even in the Anglo-Saxon countries. However, it is quite true that the Arabs have many projects in common and that one of the main handicaps to the realization of these projects is precisely the fact that the Arab world is split up into several states following necessarily different and often conflicting policies. Furthermore, within each state itself there are a variety of competing groups and many other factors which all lead to even greater differentiation. Indeed, this was probably the main cause of the Arabs' inability to pursue a coherent military policy towards Israel or indeed any coherent policy at all, even in peacetime. Networks of interests and aspirations particular to each state had developed which would not necessarily have welcomed the creation of a large unified Arab state.

Ideally one could envisage a rather loosely linked confederation or highly decentralized federation, which would reconcile unity and diversity. But it is not at all sure that this is a likely enough solution to be considered seriously. In any case it is not an outside observer's job to decide on this or that option. The options must be chosen as part of the strategic evolved by the Arab political leaders. An outsider can only hope that a programme of unity will not be put forward merely as a camouflage, to justify other options, by leaders who do not even believe in the watchword of unity themselves. If one wishes the Arabs well, one can also hope that this watchword will not become a dogma which paralyzes political thought. The cult of unity can easily become a cheap blackmail weapon, in that one can denounce one's opponents for their lack of unitarian positions and ideas. This can be extremely harmful. Anyway unity is not the only possibility.

Development

The Arab countries, like all other underdeveloped countries, set themselves the task of development primarily as a means to ensure independence, but also as an end in itself. Underdevelopment engenders not only dependence but also the familiar horrors of mass poverty, famine, epidemics and illiteracy.

Every country in the world today has a choice between two models of development: the capitalist model and the socialist model, which have given rise to a few variants and to seemingly intermediate forms. Once again, if we are to approach the matter rationally, we must not begin with an *a priori* judgement that one option represents good and the other evil, or that one is the choice of the past and the other of the future. No one knows what the future may hold, and those who claim to do so either seek to mystify or are themselves mystified. Furthermore, it is crucial that we should have a clear understanding of the key problems which this choice of model implies. The choice fundamentally defines the mode of redistribution of the social product, and the agents to whom investment decisions are entrusted. I repeat: although these two issues are more or less determined by the basic choice, many variants and intermediate forms can nevertheless arise.

On the other hand, it should be clearly understood that, once the fundamental choice has been made decisively, it entails a whole dynamic which can only be escaped with difficulty. To camouflage the real nature of the options with new words, like solidarism, or adjectives, as in Islamic or Arab socialism, is also detrimental to a lucid appreciation of these problems. The only purpose of such verbal tricks is to mask ideological mystifications. One should always look behind the words and ask the real questions: how is the social product redistributed? Who takes the investment decisions?

To take up only the second point, it seems clear that investment decisions, and thus economic choices, can only be made by the state, or by autonomous non-productive individuals ('capitalists'), or by associations of productive workers. Mixed forms are possible, however. The essential thing is to see what the real options are; when attempts are made to hide these behind a barrage of misleading verbiage, the impartial observer should always be wary of mystification.

Under present conditions, as has already been said repeatedly, the Arab countries cannot opt for pure economic liberalism. In theory, liberalism grants any individual member of society the power to make economic decisions affecting investment, free of all state intervention; in practice, however, as long experience has shown, such power is concentrated in the hands of the owners of important resources, who have themselves either never been involved in direct production or who have ended their involvement as quickly as possible. The Arab countries, like all underdeveloped countries, need planned state intervention. There are many reasons for this. Given that few resources are available, a country committed to growth cannot afford the wastage which seems to be a necessary by-product of lack of planning. The infrastructure of the economy must be built up, and since work on this is usually not too profitable, albeit indispensable, it cannot be left to capitalists, even indigenous ones. And above all, as we have mentioned, economic liberalism in practice entails subordinates to foreign capitalists.

The Soviet or Chinese states can use their superiority to obtain political or even economic advantages at the expense of the countries which they 'aid'. But generally speaking they have no major interest in preventing modernization. In principle, of course, neither does the American state or other capitalists. But as a class they do have such an interest. Obviously this is not out of simple 'nastiness'. It is because the mechanisms of the liberal economy normally impel them to keep for themselves a monopoly of the most modern and profitable types of production, and therefore to push the underdeveloped countries into the production of raw materials or consumer products, which increases the latters' dependence. Even when the Western capitalists themselves have a certain interest in Third World modernization, they conceive of it and carry it out in a manner which ensures the continuation of this dependence. Even should they wish to, the capitalist states have few means available to restrain these tendencies of their capitalists. And in practice the capitalist states are far more inclined to support these tendencies, being well aware that this economic domination gives them the possibility of exerting significant political pressure, and because the said capitalists have at their disposal very powerful 'lobbies' to influence government decisions.

However, it is true that a powerful capitalist class with important resources at its disposal can occasionally draw a country along the path to modernization without sacrificing independence. The classic example is that of Japan under the Meijis. However, the conditions which made the Japanese success possible, namely the world conditions which prevailed when the enterprise began and the geographic and sociological conditions peculiar to Japan, probably have very few equivalents today. It would require a very careful study of countries such as the Ivory Coast, Morocco or India to ascertain whether existing conditions are such that genuinely independent development is still possible. On first sight it seems unlikely.

In short, genuinely independent development cannot usually be achieved without strict control of the economy, and without some overall body taking a hand not only in production and redistribution but also in the whole area of work methods.

The Organization of Effort

The considerable effort necessary for modernization without loss of independence can thus only be achieved under the aegis of the state, which entails the sort of mass general mobilization which only an ideology can effect.

It is not difficult to list the ideal qualities for a state committed to modernization without loss of independence. Such states should be strong, independent, dedicated to their task, lucid and mobilizatory. This is the ideal which one can only hope to approach. It is worth reminding ideologues, which our era has spawned in their thousands, that reality always contains impurities, that there is nothing to ensure that a state set up to accomplish the task in question will necessarily be able to carry it out and to remain faithful to its original options, even if it starts out with an impeccable ideological programme. Even if the state is genuinely national and adheres to socialist principles, it can still not be guaranteed to fulfill its mission.

The state must be strong, if it is to produce an effective plan for modernization, and it needs to be able to withstand internal pressures in order to preserve its independence. In the Middle East these pressures stem mainly from the religious communities, which practically form states within the state, Lebanon being a classic example. The 'states within the state' produce a situation comparable to that which the feudal regime created in Mediaeval Western Europe. Every national enterprise is liable to be undermined by the sectarian interests of some group or other. The various pressure groups submit each project to envious scrutiny, in case it confers some special advantage on some other group; and they do not hesitate to put spokes in the wheels of any project which they deem particularly favourable to a rival group, even if this project also benefits the national community as a whole.

A strong state can obviously not tolerate the existence of such groups. But it would be wrong to think that a mere decree is enough to abolish them. As long as a group continues to exist sociologically, as long as its roots in the life of the community hold good, one cannot simply suppress its means of expression without taking a course which ends in tyranny and ultimately revolt. If communities continue to exist sociologically as entities backed by networks of shared interests and aspirations which are not reducible to a common faith, cult or ideology, then to suppress any organizations which express these interests and aspirations usually amounts to establishing a tyranny exercised by the majority community over all the others. The barrenness which frequently results from such an enterprise afflicts both the disheartened minority and the self-satisfied majority, which is corrupted by its own power. Under such circumstances there is liable to be a considerable 'brain-drain' towards the developed countries.

Such dangers should be taken into account while carrying out the necessary destruction of internal feudal structures. They can only be avoided by ensuring that at each stage all the existing groups are allowed to retain the means to express and defend their legitimate interests. If this is done state by stage, pluralist secularization should be perfectly possible.

The state should be independent of outside influences. Presumably it is much easier to bring this about when one has rejected the sort of liberal economy which, especially in underdeveloped countries, automatically creates powerful pressure groups linked to foreign interests. In an independent state with a non-liberal economy, the country's leaders usually have a natural tendency to defend their decision-making autonomy against outside forces. However, there is always the possibility that specific groups will rise to defend the interests of a bureaucratic sector, or simply to struggle against another clan; such groups may well seek to further their cause by any means available, and may even not hesitate to bring in outside pressures to back up the pressure they themselves exert. And, of course, there is another factor, which we have not yet mentioned but which should never be overlooked: blatant bribery.

But the greatest difficulty lies with the structural measures which are so necessary if the state is to be genuinely committed to the task of achieving modernization without loss of independence. Of course, if one shares Rousseau's belief that Man is fundamentally good and unselfish, if one accepts the implicit assumption of the ideologues who claim that the adoption of a just and progressive programme automatically turns those who adopt it into devoted and just men, then the problem disappears. However, to those of us who do not take such a rosy view of things, it seems clear that the best way of ensuring that the leaders of the state remain devoted to their task is simply for the interests of the leaders to coincide more or less with the interests of the nation. Things must be structured so that these two interests do not diverge, or at least not excessively so, at a certain point.

In truth, there is no such thing as totally representative government. No leadership structure is purely and simply the undistorted reflection of the interests and aspirations of the masses it represents. Every translation presupposes a minimum of treason. The more schematic and dogmatic forms of Marxism, prevalent in the Arab world as elsewhere, offer a simple answer to the problem. They claim that, if the leadership has a genuinely proletarian class character, totally and undistortedly representative government will ensue. Should a government be all too obviously non-representative, the Marxists have a simple explanation: the leadership is non-proletarian. This simplistic dogmatism, which does not deign to concern itself with the study of facts, is clearly purely scholastic, as is brought out in particular by the fact that this analysis accepts a distinction between a group's class character and the class origin of its leaders.

In many cases, especially in the Third World, supposedly proletarian groups are in fact made up of small or big *bourgeois*. What happens in practice is that the person making the judgement decrees that a group express the aspirations and interests of the proletariat, without the latter having any say in the matter simply because that group happens to adhere to his preferred interpretation of Marxism-Leninism, or belongs to the particular international communist organization he supports. Such assertions may contain an element of truth, in that the ideology and sometimes the structure of the organizations in question carry a considerable weight of their own, but they do not account for everything.

The notion of an ideology or group's 'class character' is actually far more complex than Marxist ideologues suspect. It can never be more than a partial and relative characterization. Nothing ever guarantees that the interests and aspirations of the masses will be translated in an undistorted way. In any case, devotion to the cause is not a function of class origins. Many 'proletarians' have betrayed their own class's interests and aspirations. Communist leaders, Stalinist or otherwise, have usually come from petty bourgeois backgrounds. The history of Europe is full of monarchs who served the aspirations and interests of the bourgeoisie, despite being very closely linked to the aristocratic class to which they belonged. Peter the Great's decimation of the Boyars is a typical example.

The organization, in practice the party from which the leadership is recruited, should do its utmost to bring in structural measures which will protect its members from the temptation of seeking fortune and power through the characteristic enterprises of a liberal economy. If the leadership is given the opportunity to invest in private 'free enterprise', for instance, all the disadvantages of the liberal economy re-emerge, and may well be aggravated by the fact that, if the state continues with some degree of economic planning, the individuals in question find themselves at the very centre of power, in an even more influential position than the 'lobbies' in the capitalist states. The more opportunities of this sort are available, the more the leadership must be lured away from these temptations by advantages peculiar to high office, such as the enjoyment of prestige.

One should obviously also ensure that rival groups cannot emerge on the basis of sectarian power, distributed amongst various fractions according to some dynamic other than that which characterises states having a liberal economy. A typical example of such a dynamic is the setting up of more or less autonomous territories or regions. One should not forget that it was the growth of such regional powers which destroyed the empires of the past. Tendencies towards the emergence of this sort of power have already been observed in the first socialist states. Similarly, if rigorous measures are not taken to ensure that the Army is always subordinate to the political authorities, one is likely to find oneself in the sort of situation which prevails in Latin America, and which has also been experimented with in Arab countries under Ba'athist regimes; the armed services become autonomous pressure groups competing for power amongst themselves, to the detriment of the state's overall interest.

It must be clearly understood that neither the ideology nor the social system can provide guarantees against the emergence of rival centres of power each competing to impose their own political interests over and above the general interest of the nation. The same even applies to the different factions grouped around the various strategic, tactical or programmatic options. Such factions almost inevitably seek out the means to strengthen themselves against other factions. They have no choice but to denounce the others as traitors to the national interest. Since each faction believes that it alone has understood and represents the interest of the nation, it cannot but seek to capture all the key posts. Such an endeavour is often originally motivated by the most sincere intentions. But the power which these key posts confer inevitably becomes attractive in itself, and we are back to the classic power struggle and, ultimately, the supremacy of sectional interests over national interests.

These difficulties are not the outcome of 'deviations' from the 'correct' ideological line or orthodoxy as the Greeks called it; they stem from profound contradictions inherent in human society. Ironically, Marxists, who in principle take contradiction to be the heart of all things, are in this case often to be found either denying the existence of the fundamental contradictions or depicting them as benign. The fact is that for lucidity and a minimum of freedom, one needs an ultra-democratic party in which everybody has some control over everybody else. But there is then always the danger of evolution towards a power polycentrism, towards selfish struggles between factions, in short, towards anarchy. Unfortunately, as history has shown all too often, the remedy proposed by Lenin, so-called 'democratic' centralism, which implies central control over all, can easily lead to a despotic monolithism, to the suppression by force of all opposition, to a sterility of thought at the top, in short to unspeakable horrors, to appalling offences against freedom, justice, truth and plain humanity.

Both extreme and moderate forms of the two solutions in question exist, but the dangers we have mentioned are always present. There can be no magical resolution of this terrible dilemma. It must be tackled head on, on the understanding that any solutions will be both complex and temporary.

The state should also aim for lucidity. Primarily, this obviously means that competent bodies must be available to inform the leaders about the internal and external circumstances relevant to their decisions. But it is also crucial that these leaders do not allow themselves to be blinded by their own ideology. This does not mean that I am recommending some cynical renunciation of the goals they have set themselves, or of the ideals and values which originally motivated them to enter into the field of political action. But although an ideology is necessary to mobilization in the type of state which we are dealing with here, every ideology has a tendency to develop its own myths and dogmas. Leaders who start out with a clear grasp of the reality which dogmas express metaphorically, often enough come to take at least some of these metaphors quite literally. This belief in the validity of mythical formulations has been particularly mystifying and harmful whenever the need to conceptualize 'the Enemy' and his decision-making process has arisen. I am referring, of course, to the mythological conception of Imperialism, which I have often had occasion to mention. Now, if there is one thing which is absolutely essential to those who play the game of politics, it is to know one's adversary and the internal mechanisms which condition his reactions, so that one can predict how he will respond. No amount of conscientiously prepared expert reports piling up on Ministers' desks will ever, in themselves, be enough to confer such knowledge. They have to be examined with an eye unjaundiced by ideology. Leaders have so often shown themselves to be incapable of reading the accurate reports with which they were provided! Examples abound: despite the high quality of their experts, the Israeli leaders still cannot understand Arab reactions; Nasser had a completely false conception of the relationship between America and Israel; Stalin had no idea of how Hitler reached his decisions; Hitler was quite wrong about both

Anglo-American and Soviet motivations. And in each case these misapprehensions had disastrous results for the leaders themselves.

The sort of state we are talking about here must be capable of mobilizing the vast masses of the people. Without such extensive mobilization, there can be no development, no struggle for independence.

Ideological stimuli are the most effective way of mobilizing the masses, and can be supplemented, to a greater or lesser extent, according to circumstance, by material stimuli. The most mobilizatory of all ideological stimuli is the presence of an irreconcilable enemy. Mobilization against such an enemy is often almost spontaneous; Vietnam is apparently an example of this kind of response. It is therefore tempting to manufacture a bogeyman, or to exaggerate some real threat. But in order to be successful, this type of 'mystification' needs certain conditions: the myth must be objectively credible and the people it is aimed at must be receptive to it. This receptivity depends on the circumstances faced by the people. Furthermore, the diffusion of the myth can be dangerous, to the extent that it can handicap those who put it about by preventing them from going back on their past declarations; they may, for instance, find it very difficult to establish a necessary peace with an enemy whose evil-mindedness they have portrayed at great length.

Mobilization, ideological indoctrination, the effective supervision and management of essential projects, cannot be carried out without a tight network of devoted minor cadres. The formation of such a network is one of the most difficult tasks facing the Arab countries, and those in similar circumstances today. These cadres' dedication to their task is crucial; naturally it must stem primarily from ideological conviction, but it must also be reinforced (*pace* the examples to the contrary which the Chinese and the Albanians might yet surprise us with) by material advantages, notably by social advancement linked to their cadre status. This dedication cannot be maintained for long if the minor cadres who, as intermediaries, are well placed to do so witness the higher cadres enjoying undue privileges. Sacrifices and advances must be shared out relatively equally between all cadres if faith in the system is to be preserved. This equality is nonetheless often conspicuous only in its absence.

This is why the most preferable leadership is one which has broken off its organic ties with its generally rather well-off background, a leadership which has renounced the advantages it might draw from falling in completely with its class of origin, from giving in to lassitude and partially or totally rejecting the often heavy responsibilities which disinterested devotion to the nation's progress imposes. Such a break with one's origins can sometimes be ensured by membership of a strictly regulated and disciplined party which, as we have already mentioned and shall have occasion to repeat, is not without its own drawbacks.

What is even more problematic is that the minor cadres must not only be devoted to their task, they must also be competent. In the context of a modern economy, they are called upon to direct the education programmes which must equip the masses with attitudes appropriate to an industrial age: attitudes such as punctuality, the value of time, perseverance and discipline. In order to inculcate these values in others, the cadres themselves must be thoroughly steeped in them. The educators must be educated. And their education must be more than bookish theoretical knowledge; they must learn how to put a code of practice into practice. This is no easy matter under the social and cultural conditions prevailing in the Arab world today; all the more reason to get down to it as quickly as possible and with the greatest possible determination.

We have seen that a great deal is required of a state which is called upon to direct the process of modernization without loss of independence. It would be too much to hope that all the guidelines we have sketched here can be followed completely. But the more they are followed, the better are the chances for autocentric development. As I have said before, I hold no brief for the utopian belief that advantages may be obtained without any inconvenience, and that an ideally harmonious structure will emerge to meet all requirements. Such a belief is still widespread, as it always has been. But the fact is that the state required by present circumstances will be exposed to a permanent temptation to evolve towards despotism. The future will show if this temptation is irresistible. The duty of all men who are aware of their duty as men committed to the struggle will be to do everything they can to resist this tendency, but without giving up their role as the independent mobilizatory force so necessary to such a state. I admit that nothing could be more difficult, but it is best to face the problem with open eyes.

The Ideology

Contents

The only ideology which can stimulate the sort of mobilization we have been talking about is a nationalist ideology. And here again there are many problems. In the Soviet Union, during the 1920s and 1930s, one could use the strength of the universalist proletarian ideology to promote autocentric development. But the Soviet Union was more or less completely surrounded by a hostile world, whose structures were very different. The will to build up a strong and independent economy harmonized with the will to ensure the triumph of a new and unprecedented structure. By contrast, the more or less 'socialist' Arab countries are surrounded by countries which also claim to be more or less 'socialist'. It is still true that, if some Arab country opted for a radically new structure, it could then fight to achieve goals implicit in this ideology without having to put any great stress on national values. Certain leftist Palestinian and South Arabian movements are cases in point. But on the whole, given that the struggle for development is so directly a sequel to the struggle for independence, with all the particular sensitivity to nationalist themes that that implies, it seems unlikely that nationalism will be displaced as the main ideological force. This sensitivity to nationalist themes in itself offers so many opportunities for mobilization; capitalist growth is so apparently attractive a model; nationalist arguments against the dependency which capitalist growth brings about are so much the easiest method of countering this attractiveness. Under these circumstances, nationalism, or any ideology which takes the good of the nation as its primary value, is definitely the most probable choice.

However, I would be the last to claim that such an orientation carries no dangers or difficulties. For instance, there is the risk that it will make an alliance with conservative nationalists seem a tempting proposition, even though the latter take no interest in modernization or even oppose it. If such an alliance is established, it becomes difficult to present ideological arguments against these conservatives; hence the tendency to rely on accusations of treason, meretricious accusations which are easy to make but not always well founded and therefore often unconvincing.

In principle, of course, it is quite possible to reconcile nationalism with internationalism and universalism, thereby giving the ideology a certain open-endedness. Efforts in this direction are often referred to as 'nationalitarianism.' But the concept is highly artificial, as is clearly demonstrated by the deviations of those who propose such an orientation whilst in the same breath indulging in boundless chauvinism. The temptation to hold the rights of others in contempt is such an integral part of nationalism that it is difficult to resist, once the values which justify it have been adopted. The more or less inevitable manifestations of chauvinism, oppressive acts towards others, necessarily alienate the support of international mass forces. Apart from any moral considerations, this is in itself harmful to the cause that is being defended, and usually leads to ill-conceived strategies. There are several good examples of this, for instance, the practices of the Ba'ath Party, which started out with the intention of reconciling national and universal values. One could also mention what has been called Palestinianism, namely the subordination of all internal struggles in the Arab countries to the national struggle of the Palestinian people, to the project of an independent Palestinian state whose internal structure is left vague.

There is no complete palliative to all these difficulties and contradictions. All one can do is to support any tendencies which do something to counterbalance orientations towards excessive nationalism and the total primacy of national values. I have often said that, under present circumstances, purely religious ideology cannot stand in as a mobilizatory ideology. Indeed, this is now so widely recognized that I feel no need to insist upon the point. Let us simply say that men who hold to a religious ideology can contribute to the common struggle as long as they believe in the movement's temporal goals.

Modes of Diffusion, Types of Rallying-point

In the context of a social movement, an ideology is nothing until it is broadcast amongst the masses, until it serves as a rallying-point. And this is in no way a passive process, as the above formulation might lead one to believe. On the contrary, there must be a synthesis with the implicit ideology which is already current among the masses. Everything which significantly runs counter to this implicit ideology cannot but be rejected. And what is accepted may well take on a very different form from that intended by those who originally broadcast the ideology.

The latter must therefore pay attention to this implicit ideology of the masses. And the formulations they use to channel it into a call to action will necessarily involve some adaptation and simplification if they are to be efficacious. As a result, lucidity is immediately at risk in two ways. Firstly the ideologues who are spreading the ideology may themselves come to be influenced by their own adaptations and simplifications. And secondly, the new emerging cadres may gradually come to be unaware of any but the most simplified and rigid forms of the ideology. These new cadres will eventually hold positions of greater or lesser importance in the management of the country's affairs. It is in such men, who broadcast the simplified forms of the ideology and who are themselves profoundly marked by such forms, that the masses will most readily recognize themselves. And should the occasion arise, the masses will support these men against any ideologues who happen to be more inclined to a scientific approach and to an awareness of political nuances. The ideologues who favour simplification, who enjoy the support of the masses and who feel closest to them, may even be tempted by the opportunity to indulge in demagogy, to exalt mass tendencies towards fanaticism and thereby to create pressures which will result in their approach becoming completely dominant.

This possibility is particularly dangerous inasmuch as this kind of tactical call to arms, which may not be harmful in itself, usually leads to a political victory for the demagogues, who can then secure positions of power within the organization. This has unfortunately been the most prevalent of all dynamics, in ideological movements of every sort. Can it be avoided? Can a minimum of critical judgement and awareness of nuances be maintained? These qualities are essential if lucidity, which is after all just as much a necessary feature of action as mass devotion, is to be preserved. Here too there is no reason to believe that there is some preordained harmony between the demands of lucidity and the demands of mobilization. All one can do is to press in one particular direction.

The Organization of Stimulation

We have seen that Marxists favour options based on a socialist autonomous and autochthonous mode of production. They have nothing against nationalist-type options which demand that such development takes place without any loss of independence. Marxists merely add the rider that, if there is to be no loss of independence, development must be carried out by a strong and independent state which is dedicated to its tasks and which fosters the growth of a mobilizatory ideology adapted to particular tasks. Obviously this requires as its starting point the formation of a trend in public opinion which presses for the adoption of such options, which forces those in power to come round to this viewpoint and which weighs heavily upon them so as to prevent any form of betrayal. It is clear that as such a trend in public opinion becomes more and more deep-rooted, broadly-based and enlightened, there will be less and less need for coercive forms of organization.

But how can this trend be established? One can merely offer a few very general pointers. The theory of the party as developed by Lenin — which has come to be considered as an inseparable and necessary element of that ideological synthesis called Marxism — is in fact only one particular development which deserves to be examined in its own right. One should remember that Marx and Engels only briefly believed in the usefulness of a party structure — whether rightly or wrongly is beside the point.

If we approach the question more generally, it seems clear that all progress in general education is favourable to the comprehension of this kind of option. Groups specializing in socialist education can play an important role. Of course this does not mean that it is futile to create a party. A political organization on party lines can be very useful and may well be indispensable. But on the other hand, experience has shown just as clearly that this kind of organization carries many disadvantages which are very difficult to cope with. The communist parties offer us a veritable storehouse of experience. We have seen them lose their effectiveness by concentrating too exclusively on the very pursuit of effectiveness. Disciplined organization and the search for links between internal struggles and international struggles are obviously worthwhile, but they can also be two-edged. The dangers are respectively monolithism and the type of rigid attachment to foreign alliances which imposes particular political options on the home front. These dangers have been the downfall of many communist parties, notably in the Arab world. The C.P.s have also suffered from the rigidity of their ideology — another negative aspect of an excessive concern with necessary discipline — which has closed off the possibility of free debate and of the sort of research which cannot be productive unless it is independent.

One may condemn these orientations. But the new socialistic groups are far too ready to believe that these defects of the communist parties were the result of some sort of accident, for instance that they stem from strategic options adopted in Russia during the 1920s and 1930s, or that they are the effects of Stalin's personality, or that they are due to specific aspects of the organizational structure. This is just not so. The study of the ideological movements of the past and the experience of those of today demonstrate quite clearly that the C.P.s merely followed a course whose bearings, at least, can be detected in the orientations of all sorts of groups.

In other words, such defects cannot be avoided by theoretical declarations condemning Stalinism, or by readjusting one's ideology, strategy and tactical programme. At the very most, one can take organizational measures which may make it difficult to hold to this negative course. In this sense such measures are necessary. And one must also make it a point to stress that the conclusions of Marxist sociology are relative, that ideology is not scientific and that the most enlightened enquiries into the appropriateness of various strategies and tactics may well lead to divergent conclusions. But one can provide no guarantees. One can only repeat the advice of the Czech communist, Julius Fucik, who, on the eve of his ordeal, called out to his fellow men: 'Be vigilant.'

Index

Abbasid period, 17–8, 32, 41, 78, 152
Abbass, Farhat, 96
'Abdoh, Mohammad, 10, 24, 149
Afghani, Jamal ad-din, 24, 79, 156
Aid, 115–6, 207
Algeria, 24–5, 29–30, 94–7, 99–102, 115, 117, 161, 200
Algerian Popular Party (PPA), 29
Al Azem, Khaled, 105, 108
Anglo-Egyptian Treaty, 176
Arab Socialist Union, 179–80, 182, 185–6
Atlantic Coalition, 60

Ba'ath Party (Syria), 29, 68, 106, 108–11, 118–9, 217, 221
Baghdad Pact, 64, 83
Baku Congress, 85–6, 121, 135
Bandung Congress, 83, 107
Bekdache, Khaled, 51–2, 61, 63–8, 70, 72–3, 75, 99, 106, 110–1, 123
Bida' (innovations), 6, 147; see also Islam
Bokhara, 125–9, 132
Bourguiba, 190
Bukharin, 87–8, 90, 121–2

Capitalism, 3, 4, 16, 34–5, 87, 111, 116–7, 144, 149, 151, 173, 206–8, 213–4, 221
China, 41, 51, 63, 73, 83, 85, 87, 90–1, 95, 101, 104, 107, 112–3, 116, 140, 146, 181, 207–8, 214, 219

Christianity, 9, 14–5, 22–3, 25–6, 40–2, 44, 47, 53, 144, 153, 158, 192, 195, 201; (Copts) 81, 190, 192; (Nestorians) 111
Colonialism, 2, 3, 11, 23–5, 27, 50, 53, 61, 88, 91, 94–5, 97, 103–4, 107, 112, Ch. 6 passim, 137, 139–40, 161, 192, 198
Cominform, 103
Community, 9–10, 51, 57, 145, 151, 153, 156, 215; (Vereinen/ Anstalt) 38
Communist International, 1, 44, 53, 85–6, 89–91, 112–3, 120, 134, 137; (First International) 57, 139; (Second International) 21; (Third International) 87, 120
Communist Colonial International, 136, 139
Communist parties, 29, 89, 117, 223; (Algerian C.P.) 97–8, 101, 118, 122; (French C.P.) 1, 6, 57, 62, 88–90, 94–6, 101–2, 104–5, 108, 112, 119; (Egyptian C.P.) 61, 69–70, 109–10, Ch. 4 passim; (Indian C.P.) 105; (Iraqui C.P.) 111, 113; (Maghreb C.P.) 104; (Moroccan C.P.) 102, 108, 118; (Muslim C.P.) 134–5; (Palestinian C.P.) 93; (Syro-Lebanese C.P.) viii, 17, 52, Ch. 4 passim, 99–101, 105–6, 108–10, 123–4, 182; (C.P. Soviet Union) 6, 68, 140; (Tunisian C.P.) 108, 118, 134–5

Deloche, Robert, 97, 123
Democratic Movement for National
  Liberation (MDLN), Algeria,
  171
D'Encausse, H. Carrere, 59, 121,
  Ch. 6 *passim*
Dharr, Abou, 15, 50

Egypt, 24, 26–9, 32, 50, 57, 60,
  64, 68–9, 73, 84–6, 88–9,
  93, 102, 108–12, 118, Ch. 9
  passim, 189–91
Etoile Nord Africaine (ENA), 29,
  96–8, 101–2, 117

Farouk, 167–8
Fascism, 27–8, 62–3, 69, 81,
  95–103, 112
Fatah, Al, 32
Front de Liberation Nationale
  (FLN) Algeria, 29–30, 118
France, 61–2, 64, 73, 80–1,
  95–6, 100, 102–4, 110, 129
Free Officers' Movement (Egypt),
  64, 68, 109, 163–5, 168,
  170–2, 175, 184, 186
French Popular Front, 62–3, 95–8

Galiev, Mir Sayit Sultan, Ch. 7
  passim
Garaudy, Roger, 13, 53

hadith (prophecy), 14, 52; *see
  also* Islam
Hage, Moussali, 97
Hashemite dynasty, 80, 82, 110
Holy war, 86

Ideology, 8, 12–3, 19–21, 23–31,
  37, 41, 44, 46, 48, 53, 56, 79–
  82, 117, 126, 143, 154–5, 163,
  186, 189, 199–202, 212, 218–
  23; (bourgeois) 20; (Mannheim's
  theory of) 22, 36–9, 41, 43, 50;
  (Marxist/communist/socialist)
  2–3, 5, 8, 11, 13–17, 20, 22,
  44–5, 52, 54–6, 58, 200, 320;
  (utopian) 14, 19, 37; (religious)
  14–5; (totalitarian) 22, 28, 30
  (*see also* Fascism)

Imperialism, 63, 81–3, 86–9, 91,
  94, 97, 101, 103–8, 111, 115–
  8, 191, 205–8, 210–12
Independence, 2, 3, 81, 85, 103,
  114–5, 156, 200, 204–14,
  220
India, 24, 73, 87, 91, 103, 105,
  146, 149, 159, 214
Industrial development, 3, 142–3,
  213–4
Intellectuals, 20–1, 62, 67, 88,
  134, Ch. 11 *passim*
Interest, *see* Islam
Iran, 64, 204, 207
Iraq (Turkey), 25–6, 32, 48, 50,
  58, 60, 64, 77–87, 89, 93,
  102, 108, 111, 115–6, 118,
  127, 204
Ishmaeli revolutionary movement,
  47, 147, 153, 155
Islam: (faith) 39, 52, 191; (fanaticism) 61, 189; (fatalism or
  tawakkol) 146; (Koran) 15, 18,
  121, 146, 148, 151, 157, 189,
  191–2; (interest) 147–9, 151;
  (monogamy/polygamy) 48;
  (property) 34 (*see* Property);
  (prophecy) 9; (sects) 10, 147,
  158; (Shi'ite) 111; (Sunnite)
  152, 195; (*sura*–free counsel)
  47; (traditional) 9, 127–30,
  147, 153–5, 182; (Wahabism)
  10; (women) 150, 160, 191
Israel, 4, 59, 61, 64, 82, 100, 115,
  199, 208–12, 218
Israeli Semitic Movement (*Uri
  Avneri*), 115
Isti'mar (imperialism/colonialism),
  48, 58, 94; *see also* Colonialism
  and Imperialism

Jadidist movement, 128–30
Jordan, 60, 83
Judaism, 14–5, 23, 26, 35, 40–1,
  44, 77, 81, 153, 192, 195

Kaldoun, Ibn, 9, 10, 15, 125, 132
Kassem, General, 110–1, 115
Kemal, Namik, 25–6, 117–8;
  (Kemalism) 88, 117

Koran, *see* Islam
Kuomintang, 87–8

League of Arab States, 82
Lebanon, 2, 4, 28, 60, 63, 67,
  80–4, 98–9, 102, 113, 209,
  215
Lenin/ism, 21, 29, 40–1, 44, 48,
  52, 54, 58, 67, 69, 94, 98,
  116, 118, 128–30, 137, 141,
  218, 223
Lewis, Bernard, 32, 35, 56
Libya, 83

Maghreb, 47, 81, 83, 94, 102, 105,
  195, 198
Maher, Ali, 167–9
Mannheim, Karl, *see* Ideology
Mao Tse-tung, 4, 26, 44, 136, 140,
  148, 190, 206
Marx, 4, 6–8, 16, 19, 37, 52,
  67, 69; (and Engels) 22, 41, 44,
  57, 84, 114, 120, 223
Morocco, 84, 94, 99, 101–2, 118,
  156, 214
Military, 21, 83, 110, 167–8,
  183–4, 195–6
Muslim Brotherhood, 28, 37, 41,
  49, 58, 165, 168–9, 170–3,
  176, 182–3, 185–6, 190–2

Nasser, Gamal Abdel, 69, 70, 83–4,
  107–11, 115, 117–9, 164–5,
  168–9, 171, 173, 175–6, 179,
  183, 185, 187, 189, 191–3, 218
Nationalism, 10–11, 13, 21, 27–8,
  30, 62, 79, 81–2, 156–9,
  164–74, 184, 201, 220–1;
  (Arab) 2, Ch. 2 *passim*, 12, 19,
  22, 26–7, 61, 111, Ch. 5 *passim*;
  (bourgeois) 81, 83, 91, 101, 111;
  (Marxist) 91; (Muslim religious)
  9, 10, 12, 24–6
Neguib, Mohammed, 69, 167, 169,
  171
New Economic Policy (NEP), 87,
  90, 136

Ottoman Empire, 22–3, 25–7, 41,
  78–80, 147–9

Pakistan, 37, 41, 49, 82, 105,
  150, 191
Palestine, 4, 28, 80, 82, 86–7,
  89, 92–3, 102, 124, 208–10,
  220–1
Pan Arabism, 83, 104, 106, 108, 111
Politburo, 6
Property, 20, 34–5, 152, 157

Sadat, Anwar, 69, 165, 187
Saudi Arabia, 76, 84, 86
Shari'a (religious law), 9, 15, 186,
  191
Sociology, 21–2, 36–7, 40, 56,
  112, 125, 143–4; (groups)
  38; (Marxist) 3, 5–6, 8, 11, 16,
  19–20, 113; (religion) 38
Soviet Union, 16, 29, 31, 34–5,
  39, 47–8, 51–2, 55, 57–8,
  62–5, 67–8, 73, 79, 82–5,
  87–8, 90, 99, 101–6, 109–10,
  112–3, 116–8, 128–31, 134,
  137–9, 181, 186, 207–8,
  214, 219–20, 223
Stalin/ism, 43–4, 62, 66, 71, 77,
  87–90, 92, 95, 102, 106, 108–9,
  112, 186, 190, 207, 211, 218
Sudan, 81, 83–4
Suez, 70, 82, 84, 108, 183, 199
Symbolism, 5, 21, 40, 48, 201–2
Syria, 2, 26–8, 32, 50–1, 60,
  63–4, 67–70, 82–4, 92–3,
  95, 98–9, 102, 105–6, 108–11,
  113, 115, 118, 177, 179, 185,
  209
Syrian People's Party (PPS), 28,
  33, 81

Tag, Abdurrahman, 47, 57
Thorez, Maurice, 53, 90, 95,
  98–9, 100, 102,
  122–3
Tito/ism, 63, 83, 104, 109–11,
  118, 186
Transjordan, 28, 80, 102, 209
Tunisia, 84, 92, 94, 98–9, 101,
  118, 149

Ulemas (religious experts), 149–50,
  194; (Algerian) 24–5

United States, 44, 64, 85, 87,
101, 103–4, 109, 112, 186,
190, 207, 211, 218

Wafd, 91–2, 168, 170–1, 185
Watt, W. Montgomery, 37, 39, 87

Young Turks, 25–6, 79–80
Yugoslavia, 63, 113, 116

Zhdanov/ism, 21, 43, 67, 71, 84,
103–4, 106–8, 123–4
Zionism, 63, 80–1, 89, 93, 102,
119, 192, 208, 212
Zinoviev, 85–7, 121

Bibliographical Information

The articles translated here into English for the first time originally appeared in French as follows:

Chapter 1: *Marxisme et Monde Musulman*, (Paris: Le Seuil, 1972).

Chapter 2: *Cahiers Internationaux de Sociologie*, No. 33, 1962.

Chapter 3: *Proceedings* of a Colloquium on Muslim Sociology, 11–14 September 1961, (Bruxelles: Centre pour l'etude des problèmes du monde musulman contemporain, 1962).

Chapter 4: *Cahiers Internationaux*, No. 93, (Paris: 1958).

Chapter 5: A much shorter version appeared in two parts in *Voies Nouvelles*, Nos. 8, 9 (Paris: 1950).

Chapter 6: As Introduction to Helene Carrere d'Encausse, *Reforme et Revolution chez les Musulmans de l'Empire Russe*, (Paris: Armand Colin, 1966).

Chapter 7: *Les Temps Modernes*, No. 177, (Paris: 1961).

Chapter 8: *Partisans*, Nos. 24, 25, (Paris: 1965–66).

Chapter 9: Contribution to a conference held at the Centre of Middle Eastern Studies in London, September 1966. A different translation appears in P.J. Vatikiotis, (ed.), *Egypt since the Revolution*, (London: Allen and Unwin, 1968).

Chapter 10: *Le Monde*, 4, 5 October 1970.

Chapter 11: Text of two talks broadcast on French radio, October and November 1965.

Chapter 12: *Marxisme et Monde Musulman*, (Paris: Le Seuil, 1972).